The Bulldog Handbook

LINDA WHITWAM

ISBN-13: 978-1497357365

Acknowledgements

My sincere gratitude to all the Bulldog owners, organisations and canine experts who have contributed to this book. Special thanks to Julie Haigh, Sue Hanson and Chicago English Bulldog Rescue, and extra special thanks to Kathy Jacobsen, without whose expert knowledge and experience this book would not have been possible.

Copyright

Table of Contents

Author's Note: For ease of reading, the masculine pronoun "he" represents both male and female Bulldogs.

1. Get to Know the Bulldog

There are more than 200 breeds registered with the Kennel Clubs and all of them are different – but there is something extra special about the Bulldog.

For a start there's the breed's unique appearance. You could line up 100 non-dog lovers, show them a variety of breeds and every one of them would instantly recognize the Bulldog. The huge distinguished, wrinkled head and powerful body are unmistakable.

Bulldogs have a long and fascinating history dating back hundreds of years to when they were bred for their bravery, tenacity and power to bring down a bull.

They have come to symbolize incredible courage and determination, and are the national symbol of Great Britain. The oldest single breed club in the world is The Bulldog Club, set up in England in 1878.

Over the decades the Bulldog has been specifically bred to retain his distinctive physical features. What is amazing, however, is that the violent and aggressive nature has been bred out. You've heard of a wolf in sheep's clothing? Well, the Bulldog is a sheep in wolf's clothing!

His nickname is Bully - or Sourmug - but nothing could be further from the truth. It's true that Bulldogs have retained their stubborn streak, but they are generally the most placid of creatures, happy to snooze the day away next to - and even on top of - their owners. An adult Bulldog may weight 40lb to 55lb, but nobody has told him that he is not a lapdog.

He is known for his gentle nature, loves sleeping, and enjoys snuggling up on the couch or his owner's knee. If you don't want yours to do this, train him not to while he is a pup, it may be too late when he is a fully grown adult.

Today the Bulldog is a companion dog without equal. He simply loves to be with his people – so if you are out at work all day, don't get a Bulldog. Go for a breed which is less dependent on humans for its happiness.

Bullies also have a reputation for being wonderful with babies and children. They seem to have a natural affinity and protective instinct towards youngsters. However, a Bulldog is a big, powerful dog who doesn't always know his own strength, and young Bullies are often boisterous, so always supervise their time spent together until the children are old enough to look after themselves.

That doesn't mean to say that a Bulldog is a coward; he isn't. He is very courageous. Although he won't look to start a fight with other dogs, he will not back down if involved in a confrontation.

Temperament

Your Bulldog's character will depend largely on two things. The first is his temperament, which he inherits and presumably one of the reasons why you have chosen a Bulldog. What many owners do not realize is that as well as being born with those wrinkles and other trademark physical features, your Bully has also inherited his temperament from his parents and ancestors.

Good breeders select their breeding stock based not only on a Bulldog's appearance, but also on what sort of disposition he or she has. And that's another reason to take your time to find a good, responsible breeder.

The second factor is environment – or how you bring him up and treat him. In other words, it's a combination of nature and nurture. The first few months in a dog's life are so important. Once he has left his mother and littermates, he takes his lead from you as he learns to react to the world around him. One essential aspect of nurture is socialization. Even though Bulldogs are generally placid dogs, it is essential to spend time introducing yours to other dogs and humans, as well as loud noises and traffic, from an early age. A Bulldog comfortable in his surroundings without fear or anxieties is less likely to display unwanted behavior.

Through your guidance and good socialization your Bully learns who he can trust, whether to be afraid - which in turn may cause an aggressive or fearful reaction in him - how much he can get away with, and so on.

To say all dogs of the same breed are alike would be akin to saying that all Americans are optimistic and friendly and all Brits are polite and reserved. It is, of course, a huge generalization. There are grumpy, unfriendly Americans or rude in-your-face Brits. However, it is also true to say that being friendly and optimistic are general American traits, as is being polite in Britain.

It's the same with the Bulldog. Each individual dog has his or her unique character, but there are certain traits which are common within the breed. So here are the typical Bulldog traits:

- ❖ Most Bulldogs are gentle and placid by nature, they have laid-back personalities

- ❖ They are very loving, loyal and enjoy spending time with their owners

- ❖ They make unparalleled companion dogs, provided you can give them the time they need

- ❖ They are patient - especially with children - and dependable

- ❖ They can be attention-seeking and demand your attention for their happiness

- ❖ Despite their physical appearance and nickname, Bullies are not aggressive dogs. They are giant lapdogs

- They often have a comical or clownish personality and do funny, illogical things. Some Bullies love to have a mad few minutes and dash round like crazy, grabbing things in their mouths or rolling over on the floor

- If a Bulldog is energetic it is usually in short bursts, as the breed does not have much stamina

- They are happy to live indoors most of the time, which makes them one of the few larger dogs suitable for apartment living

- They do not need a lot of exercise – although a short daily walk should be the minimum

- They are known for being wonderful with babies and children – although, like any dog, they should be supervised until the child is old enough to look after herself

- They do not like being left alone for long periods

- Bulldogs like to chew, especially when young or bored

- They can be stubborn – or at least strong willed - and some can become dominant if not properly trained and socialized. A Bulldog is most content and a delight to be with once he knows his place in the household pecking order - and that should be below you

- They do not respond well to heavy-handed or loud, aggressive training techniques, but do better with a patient but firm approach

- Bulldogs do not bark a lot, although many of them "talk," especially when demanding attention. This can sound quite funny, like a parrot being strangled or the warbling of an exotic bird!

- They don't make good guard dogs, although some make better watch dogs and will bark if somebody comes to the door

- They are not aggressive, but are tenacious and courageous and will not back down if pushed into a confrontation or fight

- Most are greedy and prone to obesity

- They overheat easily

- They have big hearts and will respond to anyone who shows them kindness, rather than being one-man or one-woman dogs

- Some can be possessive – you don't own them, they own you!

- ❖ They are often good with other dogs and cats, especially if introduced at an early age, although some may be less tolerant of small pets such as hamsters, guinea pigs, etc

- ❖ Many Bulldogs suffer from breathing or eye problems, allergies and/or skin problems. They are one of the most expensive breeds when it comes to veterinary bills

- ❖ They have a wonderful, quiet dignity – and a high tolerance to pain, so you need to keep an eye on your Bulldog for any signs of ill health or discomfort

- ❖ They require personal care on an almost daily level

- ❖ They snore, snuffle, burp and fart and often drool!

If we haven't managed to put you off, then read on and learn more about this wonderful, unique breed and how to fulfill your part of the bargain and take good care of them.

By the way, we asked some Bulldoggers (as the owners are known) to sum up their pets in three words, and this is what they said:

- ➢ Stubborn, funny, loving
- ➢ Loving, lovable, expensive
- ➢ The friendly giant
- ➢ Worth the effort

Julie Haigh from Yorkshire, England, added: "They have a giant personality to match their frame and they are the most lovable, sociable, friendly dogs I have ever known."

Julie and her husband were originally looking for a breed with a gentle temperament which would be good around their young son. They had narrowed it down to the Labrador Retriever and the Bulldog – and chose the Bulldog as the breed does not need as much exercise as a Labrador. Since then the family has never looked back - they got bitten by the Bulldog bug and are now on their third!

Is a Bulldog the Right Dog for Me?

Many owners forge a bond so deep with their Bulldog that they wouldn't consider any other breed. Bulldogs are not a long-lived breed. If you are lucky, your may have a decade with your Bully, and if you're really lucky, 12 years. But sadly many do not make it into double figures.

However, taking on a Bulldog is still a big commitment. Before you take the step, make sure it's the right breed for you. Answering the following questions will help you to make up your mind:

1. Are you looking for a dog to take on daily long walks or go jogging with?

2. Do you want to spend a lot of time outdoors with your dog?

3. Do you want a dog you can take to agility classes and competitions?

4. Do you want to spend hours playing with your dog?

5. Are you looking for a guard dog?

6. Do you want to breed from your dog?

7. Do you live in an extremely hot or cold climate?

8. Are you out at work all day?

9. Do you have a swimming pool?

10. Are you very house-proud or easily embarrassed?

11. Are you a first-time dog owner?

If the answer is YES to any of these questions, then the Bulldog is not for you – and here's why:

1. Although the "couch potato" reputation is a little unfair as some Bulldogs are quite active, the breed is regarded as having low to medium energy levels. They are usually content with short walks. They overheat easily and the shapes of their heads and bodies do not naturally lend them to agility classes, jogging, swimming or other strenuous activity.

2. The Bulldog is a canine which spends most of its time indoors. This is why, unusually for a large dog, it is suited to apartment life as long as there is regular access to the outdoors. Although Bulldogs are often playful and may start out running around very energetically, they soon run out of steam. The breed does not have the physical stamina for active sports.

3. Some Bulldogs can compete in activity classes, but they are not known for it. They lack stamina and can also be a bit stubborn to train. You may have a dog which loves to jump through hoops and over fences – if that's the case, great. But if your Bully doesn't want to do it, you'll have a difficult task to persuade him otherwise.

4. Many Bulldogs are playful, some breeders say that the Bulldog is a perpetual child; he never grows up. He may love playing with you and his toys, but it will be in short bursts of high energy activity and he soon tires.

5. Their appearance alone might scare away any would-be intruders, but that's where it ends. Over the decades, much of the original aggression has been eliminated from the breed. They are generally docile, don't bark much and, although very observant, they are far more likely to watch any burglars walk off with your prize possessions out of a corner of their sleepy eye than try to deter them.

6. Of all the breeds ever created, the Bulldog is probably the most difficult and complex – not to mention expensive - when it comes to producing puppies, which is a practice best left to the experts.

7. People living in extreme climates can have Bulldogs, but it requires a lot effort on their part to ensure that the dog does not become overheated, a condition which the breed is

prone to. In hot weather they should be in an air conditioned room. Neither can Bulldogs tolerate extremely cold conditions.

8. Above all, the Bulldog is a companion dog. One left on his or her own will be unhappy at the separation and may resort to destructive behaviour. If you are out at work all day, maybe you'd be better delaying getting a dog until you have more time for one.

9. Due to their conformation (body shape) and respiratory system, most Bulldogs cannot swim, although they often don't realise that. If you have a pool, it would have to be fenced off for the safety of the dog. Some owners buy lifejackets for their Bulldogs.

10. The vast majority of Bullies - God bless 'em - pass wind and snore! They are also messy eaters and drinkers, leaving trails across the floor - and they shed hair all year round - but not a lot. If you are extremely house-proud, prim and proper, a less gassy canine with elegant table manners would be a better choice.

11. The Bulldog has special needs. Many have health issues as well as an intolerance to temperature fluctuations and excessive exercise. Others need a specialized diet and extra personal daily care to keep them healthy, such as wrinkle and tail cleaning. To make matters worse, they also have an extremely high pain threshold which can mask underlying problems. For all these reasons, the breed is not recommended for first-time and inexperienced dog owners.

On the other hand, if you answer YES to the next set of questions, then the Bulldog could be just the dog for you.

1. Are you looking for a companion dog?

2. Do you want a dog that is good with children or old people?

3. Have you got the finances to cover medical problems which may run into thousands of dollars – or pounds? (Not all conditions may be covered by insurance).

4. Are you prepared to put in the time to train your dog – even if he is a bit stubborn?

5. Are you prepared to clean your dog's eyes, ears, skin folds and tail area regularly – i.e. nearly every day?

6. Does everyone in your house like Bulldogs?

7. Are you around a lot of the time?

The Bulldog's stand-out feature – apart from his unique good looks - is his deeply affectionate and relatively undemanding companionship (as long as you are around and he is not left alone for long periods). He will enjoy nothing more than snuggling up and snoring away happily.

The breed is suitable for the elderly, as most Bulldogs are house dogs which require relatively little exercise, although it all depends on what they have become used to as a puppy. A dog accustomed to two daily walks will come to expect them, whereas another which has only lived in the house and yard or had 20 minutes a day in the park since puppyhood will probably be equally as content.

Bulldogs are renowned for being good with children. They have protective instincts and will take care of them, play with them and patiently allow children to do what children do, which is poke and prod and stroke and play with them. A word of warning, a Bulldog may weigh 50lb or more and can sometimes play rough; if you have small children you must train your dog not to be too boisterous around them.

Bulldogs can suffer from a range of inherited illnesses, some of which are due to their trademark large heads and flat faces. They have been listed as one of the top five most expensive breeds of dog when it comes to veterinary bills. Good breeding is helping to improve the health of individual dogs, but you would be a rare owner indeed if you did not need to visit the veterinarian several times during your Bulldog's life - and that's in addition to his annual injections and check-up.

Bulldog training is an art in itself. If you expect your Bully to jump to your every command, you're in for a disappointment. Bulldogs prefer to consider the command, and then ruminate on it a little longer before deciding whether to respond. Patience is the key if your little treasure is proving to be a tad strong willed.

Before getting any breed of dog, it is important that all the family wants this new member of the household. There are far too many Bulldogs who become surplus to requirements and end up in rescue shelters or looking for a new home through no fault of their own.

Becoming a Bulldog Owner

If you've definitely decided that the Bulldog is the canine for you, then you had better brush up on a few of the special terms used by lovers of the breed. To begin with, you are not a Bulldog owner, you have become a Bulldogger! Your dog hasn't just got wrinkles, he has got a roll or rope over his nose and his cheeks are known as chops or flews. A corkscrew isn't something with which to open a bottle of wine while you sit back and watch his amusing antics, it's a type of tail to be avoided.

You should also know that many owners succumb to the temptation of becoming wardrobe assistants to their Bulldog -they just can't help but dress up their beloved pets in a variety of outfits.

Most Bulldogs do not object to being put into costumes, but if you do feel compelled to put Buster into a Batman outfit, make sure that it does not restrict his breathing, vision or hearing and that it is not too hot for him. Avoid dangly or small accessories that he could chew and choke on.

One thing the Bulldog does probably better than any other breed is sleep. Any time, any place anywhere. He can sleep on his tummy, his side or his back, he loves to doze with his humans, big and small. If you are ever feeling sad, visit the website YouTube and type in "Bulldogs sleeping, " the results are sure to cheer you up.

The Bulldog is a unique breed of dog whose health and happiness rely on a special kind of owner. Are you ready for the challenge? Read on to find out.

2. Complete History of the Bulldog

Few breeds have a history as long and as colorful as the Bulldog. To trace its true origins we have to journey back in time through many centuries and even millennia.

There is some controversy over the exact roots of the breed, with some historians suggesting that the Pug was involved way back in the mists of time to reduce the size of the Bulldog - although this is strongly contested by other experts. However, we can be pretty sure about the development of the breed over the last hundred years, as there are many literary references and historical documents referring to Bulldogs and Old English Bulldogs, a breed which is now officially extinct, but which was the forerunner of today's Bulldog.

The Beginning

The generally accepted theory is that the Bulldog is one of the breeds descended from the

Caucasian Shepherd Dog

Alaunt, a war dog and protector of livestock and caravans. It was bred by the Alani tribes of the central Asian steppes, who were known as superb warriors, herdsmen and breeders of horses and dogs.

The Alaunt became extinct in the 17th century, but we know it resembled today's Caucasian Shepherd Dog, a breed with primitive origins going back over 2,000 years. The Russian name for the breed is Volkodav, which means wolf dog.

Some of the Alaunt's ancestors lie with not so much a breed, but a category of dog: the Mastiff, which was also known as the Molosser or Molossus. The Mastiff originated in ancient times with the Molossis people in the mountainous regions of north west Greece and southern Albania. They were known as ferocious hounds, used by shepherds to guard their flocks in the mountains.

Some scholars describe the Molossus as having a wide, short muzzle and a heavy dewlap (similar to modern Mastiff breeds) and believe it was used to fight tigers, lions, elephants, and even men in battle. A Roman copy of a Greek sculpture of a guard dog known as The Jennings Dog (below) is generally considered to represent an ancient Molossus and can be seen at the British Museum in London.

There are many literary references to the Molossus. Former professor of ancient history, Jan Libourel, has written an interesting article for the American Bulldog Review at: http://www.american-bulldog.com/BHCol.html

He says: "The true Molossus dog was undeniably one of the most famous dogs of classical (Greco-Roman) antiquity. It is variously mentioned as a premier hunting dog, an aggressive guard dog and as a guardian and herder of cattle and sheep by many of the greatest writers in Greek and Latin literature over a period of 800 years."

The ancient Greek poet Virgil wrote of the Molossus more than 2,000 years ago: "Never, with them on guard need you fear for your stalls a midnight thief, or onslaught of wolves, or Iberian brigands at your back." Aristotle also mentions them in his History of Animals written in the 4th century BC: "Of the Molossian breed of dogs, such as are employed in the chase are pretty much the same as those elsewhere - but the sheep-dogs of this breed are superior to the others in size, and in the courage with which they face the attacks of wild animals."

The poet Grattius, who lived around the time of Jesus, wrote: "...when serious work has come, when bravery must be shown, and the impetuous War-god calls in the utmost hazard, then you could not but admire the renowned Molossians so much."

Today the term Molosser is still used by breeders to refer to a group of dogs. There is even a Molosser forum, which lists large breeds including the Bullmastiff, Fila Brasileiro, Spanish Mastiff, Neapolitan Mastiff, Tibetan Mastiff, Great Dane, Dogo Argentino, Boerboel, Dogue de Bordeaux, Cane Corso, and Japanese Tosa Inu. Just to confuse matters, none of these dogs are true "Mastiffs." This word used in its correct sense refers only to the English Mastiff.

Although the Bulldog is smaller, it is today still regarded as a Molosser, along with other diminutive breeds such as the American Bulldog, Staffordshire Bull Terrier, Pug and French Bulldog, to name but a few.

The Romans

The Romans invaded Britain in 55BC and their historians described the fierce Molossian dogs and the "pugnace britannicii" - fighting dogs of Britain - used in battles. These dogs were known as the "broad-mouthed dogs of Britain" and according to 1930s Bulldog historian R.H. Voss: "There is very little doubt that they were the original and remote ancestors of our Mastiff and Bulldog."

The Romans were mightily impressed with these fighting dogs, but whether they ever took them back to fight in the Roman amphitheatres is a matter of some conjecture, although it has been stated that they appointed an officer to select British dogs and export them to Rome. The "pugnaces" of Britain were later mentioned around 390AD by the poet Claudian who distinguished them from all other dogs as being able to pull down a bull.

It was around this time that the Alaunt dogs spread from central Asia to Europe with the Western Alani tribes when they invaded Europe. The fierce Alaunts influenced many breeds in France, Spain, Portugal, England and other countries, spreading the use of the Alaunt name. Because of all the new bloodlines introduced into the original breed, the word "Alaunt" came to describe a type of working dog rather than a specific breed. And through breeding with various scent hounds and sight hounds, the Alaunt became a valued large game hunting dog in Europe, with different types being bred locally for different purposes.

It was classified into three distinct types based on their physical appearance and duties. The Alaunt Gentil was a light greyhound-type hunting dog, the Alaunt Vautre (Veantre) was an aggressive hunting type, also called the running Mastiff, known for hunting boars, and the Alaunt de Boucherie was the traditional Mastiff-type used with livestock, which was also crucial in the development of the baiting dogs of France.

It is this third type, known as "the Alaunt Butchers" in England, which many believe was the ancestor of today's Bulldog and other "bull breeds," as they were used to control and defend herds of cattle. However, some historians, including Jan Libourel, believe that the Bulldog's ancestor was not the huge Mastiff-type of Molossus, but the lighter, faster version used for hunting and herding, more like a greyhound or modern American Pit Bull Terrier.

It is highly likely that the Bulldog originated from the ancient Alaunt mixed with bloodlines of the fighting dogs of England. However, as you can see from the previous photos, today's Bulldog bears very little resemblance to its ancient ancestors. One theory is that the descendants of these large ancient dogs were bred with the Pug to create the smaller breed of Bulldog, but this is hotly disputed by some scholars.

What most breed historians do agree on is that Bulldogs owe their name to the fact that they were once used to guard, control and bait bulls. (To bait is to taunt or harass).

Bull-Baiting

If we move forward in time from the Alani's western invasion of the 4th century to the Norman Conquest of England in 1066, we can see how the Bulldog's ancestors began to change shape to fulfill a specific function: the baiting of bulls. At this time the training of bulls, bears, horses and other animals for the purpose of baiting them with dogs was practiced by jugglers brought from France by the Norman conquerors.

As early as 1154 in the time of Henry II, bear and bull-baiting by dogs was a popular amusement in England. There are also several literary references from the Middle Ages to the sport of bull-baiting and the dogs which took part. Around 1406 the Duke of York wrote "Mayster of Game" in which he described the Alaunt, or Allen, as a dog with a large, short and thick head and short muzzle, which was remarkable for his courage. When he attacked an animal he hung on, and this dog was used in bull-baiting.

In the 1570s physician and naturalist John Caius wrote a book called "***Of Englishe Dogges: The Diuersities, the Names, the Natures, and the Properties***" in which he described the "Mastvve" or "Bandigge," (Bandog) as a vast, huge, stubborn, ugly and eager dog with a heavy and burdenous body, serviceable to "bait and take the bull by the ear." Two dogs at most were sufficient for that purpose, however untamable the bull might be. It was during the late 1500s that these prized "Bandogs" were exported to Spain to bait bulls there for the amusement of the Spanish aristocracy.

During the reigns of Mary, Elizabeth, James I, and Charles I (1553 to 1649), the baiting of bulls and full-

BULL BAITING

grown bears by dogs was a very popular sport in England. But it was not until 1631 in the reign of Charles I that the name "Bulldog" was first mentioned. This was in a letter written by an Englishman called Prestwich Eaton from St. Sabastian in Spain to his friend George Wellingham in St. Swithin's Lane, London. He asked for "a good Mastive dog, a case of liquor and I beg you to get for me some good bulldoggs" to be sent out to him. This is proof that the Bulldog and the Mastiff were then becoming separate breeds.

Over the centuries, many crosses were made using Mastiffs and Bandogs, as well as various other breeds. In those days, bull-baiting and bear-baiting was the sport of kings, who used to regale ambassadors and other foreign dignitaries with the sport. There was a theatre built for the purpose in London called the Bankside Bear Garden where very large dogs were used for baiting the bull; historians believe they may have weighed around 90lbs.

When James II came to the throne in 1685, the sport was shunned by the nobility. And from then until bull-baiting was banned in 1835, the rules changed so that the dog only had to "pin" the bull, which was now tethered, not roaming free. Specially trained dogs were set upon the bull one at a time, a successful attack resulting in the dog fastening his teeth strongly in the bull's nose. The Bulldog was bred especially for this sport.

The great dogs used when bull-baiting was the sport of kings were no longer wanted, or affordable to the common folk who now ran the sport. Much can happen to change any dog by selective breeding and it was during this time that the Bulldog's trademark features emerged and the size of the dog was reduced to around 50lb.

The following description given by the French Advocate Mission, who lived in England during the late 1600s, is taken from Chamber's Book of Days: "After a coming Bull-baiting had been advertised, the bull, decorated with flowers or coloured ribbons would be paraded round the streets of the town, and the dog which pulled off the favours in the subsequent baiting would be especially cheered by the spectators. The parade ended, the bull, with a rope tied round the root of his horns, would be fastened to a stake with an iron ring in it, situated in the centre of the ring."

This new system of bull-baiting suited a medium sized, active dog of moderately low stature with well laid-back nose and a protruding underjaw. From early writers' descriptions, we know that the Bulldog had a short muzzle, a massive head and a broad mouth. The big, heavy head and powerful jaws gave the dogs a vice-like grip on the bull, as well as helping to prevent the enraged beast from shaking the dog around and breaking its back.

The underjaw projected beyond the upper to enable the dog to grasp the bull and to give him a firmer hold. The thick and strong lower jaw gave the mouth the appearance of curving upwards across the middle of the face.

The top of the nose inclined backwards to allow free passage of air into the nostrils while still holding on to the bull with its powerful jaws. The rope – or fold of skin across the face - channeled the blood away from the Bulldog's eyes. During bull-baiting, the dog would flatten itself to the ground, creeping as close to the bull as possible, then dart out and try to bite the bull on the nose or head. The bull would be tethered by a collar and rope to a stake in the ground. As the dog darted at the bull, the beast would try to catch the dog with his head and horns and throw it into the air.

Most of these fearless dogs were so tenacious that they would hold on to the bitter end and be tossed off rather than let go as the bulls swung them around violently in the air. A great many dogs were killed, more were badly maimed and some held so fast that by the bull swinging them, their teeth were often broken out. Often the men were tossed as well as the dogs.

During my research, I have come across historical reports written at or near the time of bull-baiting events which describe in some detail the gory fates which met these incredibly brave dogs when they refused to give up, even when they were dying. They are distressing to read and I have chosen to omit them.

By the time Queen Anne came to the throne in England in 1702, the cruel blood sport of bull-baiting was practiced twice a week at a place called Hockley-in-the-Hole (now Clerkenwell), London.

It was also fairly common in provincial towns. At Stamford in Lincolnshire and Tutbury, Staffordshire, a bull was tied to an iron stake so that it could only move within a 30 feet radius. The aim was for the dogs to immobilize the bull. Before the event started, the bull's nose was blown full of pepper to enrage the animal, which was often placed in a hollow in the ground.

Bull baiting may have begun as early as the 13th century in Lincolnshire. The ancient text "Survey of Stamford" describes one theory as to how it began in that town: "William, Earl Warren, lord of this town in the time of King John (A.D.1199 to 1216), standing upon the castle walls of Stamford, saw two bulls fighting for a cow in the meadow till all the butchers' dogs, great and small, pursued one of the bulls (being maddened with noise and multitude) clean through the town.

"This sight so pleased the said earl that he gave all those meadows (called the Castle Meadows) where first the bull duel began for a common to the butchers of the town, after the first grass was eaten, on condition they find a mad bull the day six weeks before Christmas Day for the continuance of that sport every year."

Bull-baiting was not only practiced as a form of entertainment. In early modern England, many towns had by-laws regulating the sale of meat, which stipulated that bulls' flesh should be baited before any bull was slaughtered and sold. The practice was based on what seems to us nowadays a rather strange belief that the meat would be more tender and nutritious if the animal had been baited. This belief was so strong that the meat from a bull which had not been baited was considered improper for consumption, and a butcher who sold it was liable to a penalty.

A graphic description of the Bulldog can be found in the 1800 Cynographia Britannica written by Sydenham Edwards: "...head round and full, muzzle short, ears small... chest wide, body round, with the limbs very muscular and strong; the tail... rarely erected (...) the most striking character is the under-jaw almost uniformly projecting beyond the upper..."

The Bulldog was the breed of choice for dog fighting throughout the 1700s. But in the 1800s, the followers of this barbaric sport wanted a quicker dog in the pit and so crossed the Bulldog with various types of larger terriers used to kill rats and foxes. These dogs became known as Bull Terriers and combined the alertness and speed of the terrier with the indomitable courage and fighting instinct of the Bulldog.

America and Bull-Baiting

England wasn't the only country to host the bloodthirsty spectacle of bull-baiting. In the 18th century it was also one of America's favorite pastimes. The journal of the American Revolution states that in 1774 the cruel blood sport of bull-baiting had crossed the Atlantic along with other customs and was still practiced long after the American Revolution ended.

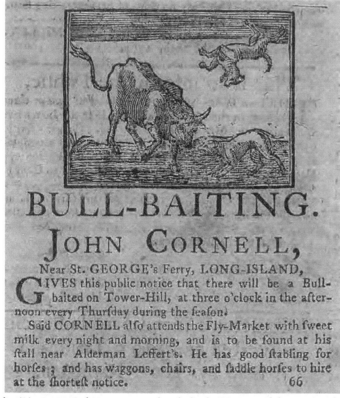

According to Jennie Holliman's **American Sports 1785-1835**: "British troops stationed in America during the Revolution and until 1783 played a part in establishing certain English sports in the States, an impetus being given to bull baiting and cockfighting during this time.

"...For the purpose of the sport, dogs of undisputed pedigree were kept, usually bull dogs. Many butchers kept dogs and buffaloes for animal baiting. The wildest and fiercest bulls of the neighborhood were selected for a bull bait."

Large crowds of spectators gathered behind a circular enclosure as a chained bull would face off against six to eight bull dogs, which oftentimes were immediately killed, Holliman explains. In his July 28, 1774, **New-York Gazetteer**, printer James Rivington published a bull-baiting advertisement for John Cornell. Apparently the blood sport had such a draw that a "season" of weekly bull-baiting matches was scheduled. Pictured here is the original public notice.

However, the Bulldog's early role was not limited to sport in America. In mid-17th century New York, they were used as a part of a city-wide round-up effort led by Richard Nicolls, the first English colonial governor of New York province. Because cornering and leading wild bulls was dangerous, Bulldogs were trained to seize a bull by its nose long enough for a rope to be secured around the animal's neck.

Bull-baiting began to decline in England in the early 19th century. In the Parliamentary Record of April 18th, 1800 William Wyndham, the Secretary of War, spoke in defense of the Bulldog in the debate on bull-baiting.

Bulldog 1802
Philip Reinagle

The record states: "He certainly admitted that the practice of bull-baiting was very different from the manly, athletic exercises he had just mentioned, because there was some degree of cruelty in tormenting an animal; but even this had its use; it served to cultivate the qualities and keep up the breed of those useful animals called bull-dogs—a breed which he was sorry to see degenerating very much, so as to be nearly lost.

"England had long been famous for this breed of dog, and they were mentioned by Grattius so early as the days of Augustus; even some of our ships had taken their names from those animals. But the practice of bull-baiting was objected to on the ground of its cruelty, and that too by the very men who gave their sanction to the game laws, and monopolized to themselves the noble practice of shooting."

Lion-Baiting

One other bizarre sport which was occasionally organized for the amusement of the public was lion-baiting. There were some interesting characters involved in the sport and Bulldog breeding in the 19th century, some of whom appear to have stepped straight out of the pages of a Charles Dickens novel.

Bill George (1802–1881) was an well-known dog dealer who started out as a butcher's boy, then bare-knuckle prizefighter before becoming apprentice to Old English Bulldog dealer Ben White, from a rough area in north London known as Kensal New Town. Although now officially extinct, in those days the Old English Bulldog was a muscular fighting dog around 15 inches tall weighing some 45lbs. It was no doubt the forerunner of today's Bulldog,

NOTE: Olde English Bulldogge is an American breed (not recognized by the American Kennel Club) which dates back to the 1970s when David Leavitt, of Coatesville, PA, set about trying to recreate the "Regency Period Bull Baiter." His aim was to breed a dog with the look, health and athleticism of the original bull-baiting dogs, but with a mellow temperament. The foundation crosses were half Bulldog and half a mix of Bullmastiff, American Pit Bull Terrier and American Bulldog. These dogs, although not officially recognized as a breed, do physically look more akin to the athletic Bulldog of 200 years ago. On January 1st 2014, the United Kennel Club in the USA adopted a breed standard for the Olde English Bulldogge.

In 1825, White and George provided the dogs for two lion-baiting contests organized by a promoter called Wombwell. The event held on July 26th involved three Old English Bulldogs and a lion named Nero in an enclosure at the Old Factory Yard near Warwick. The dogs were fallow colored – reddish brown – and were named Captain, Tiger and Turk.

Spectators paid a small fortune to watch the sorry, cruel spectacle. The Bulldogs were incredibly brave, they rushed at Nero, "pinning" him by the nose and face. Although the gently-natured lion repeatedly roared with pain and fended off the dogs with his paws, he refused to bite them.

After two dogs were taken away maimed, Turk, the lightest of the three Old English Bulldogs, showed incredible courage for which the Old English Bulldog was famous in those days:

"Left entirely alone with an animal twenty times its weight, (he) continued the battle with unabated fury and though bleeding all over from the effect of the lion's claws, seized and pinned him by the nose at least half a dozen times; when, at length, releasing himself with a desperate effort, the lion flung his whole weight upon the dog and held him lying between his fore paws for more than a minute, during which time he could have bitten his head off a hundred times over, but did not make the slightest effort to hurt him.

"Poor Turk was then taken away by the dog-keepers, grievously mangled but still alive and seized the lion, for at least the twentieth time, the very same moment that he was released from under him."

The public were outraged at the promotion of such baiting spectacles, and the matter was raised in Parliament and Wombwell's lion baits were the last to be staged in the United Kingdom.

Birth of the Modern Breed

Earlier, in 1802, a bill to abolish bull-baiting was issued in the House of Commons. But the sport continued legally until 1835 when the Cruelty to Animals Act was passed in Parliament outlawing "Blood Sport" in Great Britain – although the practice continued illegally in large towns and cities for about another 45 years.

With the banning of bull-baiting the Bulldog's work was suddenly over. The breed had also acquired a reputation for being vicious - indeed, it had been bred for its bravery and tenacity, to fight to the death - and the Bulldog rapidly went into decline.

The Natural History of Dogs, Volume X printed in 1840, just five years after the banning of bull-baiting, very graphically describes the strength and ferocity of these early Bulldogs. Their bravery and tenacity was second to none. They sometimes wore leather armor for hunting and there is reference to the spiked collar, which has become synonymous with the Bulldog today:

"In stature the present race is of moderate size, but entirely moulded for strength and elasticity; the head is large; the forehead sinks between the eyes, and the line of the nose rises again at a considerable angle ; the lower jaw projects beyond the upper, often showing the teeth, which altogether, with the frequent redness about the eyelids, produces a most forbidding aspect ; the ears are partially drooping, unless the terrier blood is crossed in the animal; and the tail is carried high.

"The present breed is commonly ochry or reddish buff with the nose and chops alone black. Formerly when the brindled breed, always preferred on the Continent, was ex-ported for strengthening the wolf and boar packs of hounds, the ears were always cropped; and we have seen leather armour, consisting of a breast-piece and cap, with holes for the eyes, made of studded leather, which were used, along with a spiked collar, for some valuable dogs to engage the boar or wolf, and protected them effectually; in-deed such a defence, where the breed was scarce, may have been necessary, from the unceremonious mode of attacking and indomitable pertinacity the dogs evince when once excited; never letting go the hold they have, even if mutilated, as if there was some spasm in the jaws to prevent their un-locking.

"The bull-dog differs from all others, even from the mastiff, in giving no warning of his attack by barking; he grapples his opponent without in the least estimating their comparative weight or powers. We have seen one pinning an American bison and holding his nose down, till the animal gradually brought forward its hind feet, and, crushing the dog to death, tore his muzzle out of the fangs, most dreadfully mangled.

"We have known another hallooed on to attack a disabled eagle; the bird, unable to escape, threw himself on the back, and, as the dog sprang at his throat, struck him with his claws, one of which penetrating the skull, killed him instantly, and caused the butcher, his master, the loss of a valued animal, and one hundred dollars in the wager."

If it had not been for some keen enthusiasts, the breed may have died out completely. But interest in the Bulldog remained among a number of working class men who began carefully breeding them, with attention to their trademark physical features, but at the same time breeding out the dog's aggressive nature.

They organized small evening shows in public houses, where their dogs paraded on the sanded floors of tap rooms. The landlord usually provided the prizes, though sometimes the working men themselves clubbed together to contribute a handsome silver collar or similar prize.

At this time, the Bulldog was far more of a functional dog than today's Bulldog. It had longer legs, neck and tail, a longer muzzle and was sleeker, more athletic in build. *Crib and Rosa* is an 1817 painting by Samuel Raven (left) which depicts two famous Old English Bulldogs. Both dogs had deep chests, extremely well-defined muscle tone, roach backs and low tails.

The painting was frequently referred to by the new Bulldog exhibitors as an ideal form of the breed, and Rosa was regarded as the foundation for the modern Bulldog. Through an engraving, this painting became the best-known and most reproduced painting of any dogs from that period.

In Hugh Dalziels's book (c.1879) ***British Dogs, their Varieties, History, Characteristics, Breeding, Management and Exhibition,"*** Mr. F.G.W. Crafer, Honorary Secretary of the Bulldog Club, wrote: "The outline of Rosa, in the well-known print of "Crib and Rosa," is considered to represent perfection in the shape, make, and size of the ideal type of the bulldog.

"The only exception that has ever been taken is that it has been alleged to be deficient in wrinkles about the head and neck, and also in substance of bone in the limbs. This, however, does not alter the fact of its being a correct representation of the true type of the old-fashioned bulldog. Some allowance should be made for her sex - never as grand and well developed as dogs - and her position in the drawing."

This is a description of the ideal body shape of the 19th century Bulldog from the same book: "The body of the dog is (like that of man) broad and deep in the shoulders and chest, and small in the waist, the forelegs appearing short on account of the deep chest and muscular shoulders.

"The back short and strong, long-backed animals being weak, slow, and unwieldy, easily fatigued, and having a loose, shuffling, and disjointed manner of moving. The hind legs large and muscular, with plenty of propelling power and, like the greyhound's, long in proportion to his forelegs, raising the loins into an arch higher than the shoulders, so as to bring his hind legs well under him, and enable him to spring quickly high off the ground. The belly small and well gathered up; and the flank, under the loins, hollow to lighten him as much as possible of useless weight.

"The wrinkles on the head, the length of the tail, the colour, and other minor points much insisted on by modern fanciers, however much to be admired, were, and ought still to be, of secondary importance to (instead of taking precedence of) a correct general formation, and especially of the square protruding lower jaw, the broad mouth, and receding nose."

One of the 19th century Bulldog breeders was Bill George. When his employer, dog dealer Ben White, died in the same year that bull-baiting was outlawed, George bought the premises from his widow and renamed them Canine Castle. Aware that he would have to create a new clientele for the business to continue, George shifted the focus from the Bulldog as a fighter to the Bulldog as a companion animal, giving the breed new life.

In 1840, he imported Big Headed Billy, one of the large Spanish Bulldogs used for bull-baiting on the Iberian peninsula. Billy was brindle pied (white and brindle) in color and his grandson was George's famous white dog, Dan, which weighed 65 lbs and was sold for the huge sum of £100. The photo on the right shows one of today's fierce-looking Spanish Bulldogs (still called Alano Espanols) with cropped ears.

The Alano Espanol is believed to be directly descended from the dogs used for bull-baiting in Spain hundreds of years ago. Incredibly it has kept the name Alano, from the Alani tribe which invaded Europe more than 1,600 years ago. Today the breed weighs anything up to 90lb and is massively bigger than the (English) Bulldog of the 21st century.

French Bulldogs

Back in the mid 1800s, George was breeding Bulldogs in three sizes. One of these was a new line of "Toy Bulldogs" which began to be exhibited once dog shows started in 1860. At the same time, lace workers from Nottingham in England no longer had work at home due to the Industrial Revolution. Many left and settled in Normandy, France, taking their dogs, including many miniature Bulldogs with them. These dogs sparked a craze, and English breeders like George sent over Bulldogs that they considered to be too small, or with faults such as pricked up ears.

A decade or two later, there were few miniature Bulldogs left in England, such was their popularity in France. These dogs were highly fashionable and sought after by everyone from

society ladies to Parisian prostitutes! They also became popular with creative types such as artists, writers and fashion designers.

The small Bulldog type gradually became thought of as a breed, and received a name, the Bouledogue Francais - or French Bulldog. (Incidentally, in France "dogue" means Mastiff or Molosser.) French Bulldogs were introduced to the United States in 1885 when they were imported in order to set up an American-based breeding program. They were mostly owned by society ladies, who first displayed them at the Westminster Kennel Club Dog Show in 1896.

On April 29th, 1899 Country Life Magazine stated: "Some five-and-thirty years ago in fact, [i.e. about 1864], the small-sized or light-weight Bulldog was common in this country; so much so that dogs of the breed that scaled over 28 lbs were not encouraged at such shows as Birmingham, which was at that period the most important exhibition of its kind in England.

"Then by some freak of fashion the Toy Bulldog became all the rage in Paris, with the result that the celebrated Bill George, of Canine Castle, Kensal New Town, the most eminent dog dealer of his or any other day, received carte blanche commissions from French customers to procure them light-weight Bulldogs, and by this means England was denuded of all the best specimens."

George became famous for his Bulldogs during his lifetime, being featured in Punch magazine (previous page) and Charles Dickens is believed to have visited him when researching Bull's Eye, Bill Sikes' Bulldog in Oliver Twist (1837-39).

But the Bulldog's true salvation came with the arrival of the era of the conformation dog show, which began in 1859, although a Bulldog was not present at the first show.

Dog Shows – the Bulldog's Salvation

The Bulldog fell into decline and disappeared in great numbers after the end of bull-baiting in 1835. But the small group of dedicated Bulldog fanciers kept the breed alive and the breed experienced a new surge of interest and lease of life with the introduction of conformation dog shows.

James Hinks is credited with being one of the first Bulldog exhibitors. One of the first shows where he exhibited was held at the Birmingham Agricultural Hall in December 1860. The show attracted an entry of 40 Bulldogs, including the famous red male, King Dick – also known as Old King Dick - owned by Jacob Lamphier. King Dick had a very successful show career and went on to become the first show champion.

These original show Bulldogs came in three types and sizes:

1. The dog which had been specifically bred to bait the bull from 1735 "when this dog first attained a very definite type" until bull baiting was abolished in 1835 and which since 1835 had maintained its existence by reason, first of a dog fighter and later of pot house shows. These dogs generally varied from 45lb to 50lb in weight, similar to today's Bulldog.

2. The big Mastiff-type dogs (the remnants of the original 90lb Bulldogs), which had by now been reduced to 60lb. These dogs received a stimulus by the importation of the famous Spanish Bulldog, Big-Headed Billy, in 1840.

3. Small dogs weighing 12lb to 25lb which had been produced by inbreeding smaller Bulldogs (and probably by crossing these with Pugs from 1835 to 1845) and which went on to provide the foundation of the French Bulldog.

In 1864, the first Bulldog Club was formed by a man with the marvelous name of R.S. Rockstro with the motto 'Stranglehold', or 'Hold Fast' and had about 30 members. Their declared aim was: "the perpetuation and improvement of the Old English Bulldog." Unfortunately, the club only lasted three years, but this was long enough for the 'Philo-Kuon' Breed Standard to be written, named after the nom-de-plume of its author, Samuel Wickens. (Philo kuon means 'dog lover' in Greek.)

The original Bulldog was a ferocious fighting dog, and the breeders who stuck to the Philo Kuon standard bred a dog which retained some of these pugilistic qualities, but which were also suitable as companions. These dogs would attack on command and became known as excellent family protectors, but they were also easy to control.

The printed Philo Kuon Breed Standard stated: "The English Bulldog is a majestic, ancient animal, very scarce, much maligned and as a rule, very little understood. ....but brought up in kindness, constant communication and attention from the owner, the dog is calm and docile, but if it is on the circuit without attention, it becomes far less sociable and obedient, but excited, can burn up so much that it becomes very dangerous for the environment. Dogs of this breed are excellent guards, excellent swimmers, are very valuable for breeding with terriers, Pointer, hounds, Greyhound, etc, to give them courage and endurance. This is the most bold and determined animal.

"...Venturesome, daring and fearless, he will fight to the last drop of blood. This noble dog becomes degenerate abroad – in truth he is a national animal, and is perfectly identified with old England – and he is a dog of which Englishmen may be proud."

The Philo Kuon standard also stated that the Bulldog should be least 20lb (9kg) and rarely exceed 60lb (27kg). Owners tested these athletic Bulldogs extensively in various activities, such as throwing wooden planks into a churning ocean from 15 foot cliffs. The Philo-Kuon Bulldogs would plunge off the cliffs into white caps and drag the planks to shore. It is interesting to note that the Bulldog was a good swimmer, whereas the physical conformation of today's dog, with its heavy body and short legs, does not lend itself to swimming; indeed, many Bulldogs cannot.

The Philo-Kuon Bulldog was used to create many fine bull breeds around the world. English breeders sold top dogs to the Germans, and the modern Boxer is at least 50% descended from Philo-Kuon bloodlines.

The picture on the previous page is T. Wood's portrait of Captain G. Holdworth's white Bulldog Sir Anthony, listed date of birth January 1st, 1873 (although he would have been born some time the previous year). His sire was Crib by Duke II out of Rush, his dam was Meg by Old King Dick out of Old Nell. Sir Anthony took first prize in the open class at the Crystal Palace, 1874.

At this point it is worth noting that among historians, there is some confusion about the dog Crib. Some saying that all Bulldogs were based on Rosa from Samuel Raven's 1817 painting, and others saying that the modern Bulldog was based on Crib. And if you read that Sir Anthony was sired by Crib, you might wonder how a dog which was painted in 1817 lived to father another dog some 56 years later, a remarkable feat - even for a determined Bulldog!

The answer, I believe, is simple - there were two Cribs; the name was not uncommon among Bulldogs at that time. And in fact, the conformation of the modern Bulldog is based on the ideals of Rosa in the early painting as well as the bloodlines of the champion show dog of the 1870s called Crib. This dog was also known as Turton's Crib after its owner, Mr. T. Turton.

The dog is listed in the "English Bulldog Pedigree Database" (an unofficial register for mainly Bulldog bloodlines in Europe) as being born in 1871 and bred by Fred Lamphier , son of the famous Bulldog breeder Jacob Lamphier. Turton's Crib was never beaten in the show ring and went on to become English Champion. The picture on the left is of Turton's Crib, which you will see is a completely different color and slightly different shape to the Crib of 1817. It is known that four of the Bulldog's foundation bloodlines originated with Crib. These were through the following dams:

- ❖ Rose (owned by Mr. Berrie) which gave rise to the Monarch champion show dogs
- ❖ Meg (owned by Fred Lamphier), whose bloodlines produced the brindle male Tiger, which in turn bred the champions Richard the Lionheart, Redova, the white bulldog Sir Anthony (pictured on the pervious page) and many others
- ❖ Miss Smiff (owner P. Rust), who bred Sancho Panza, L'Ambassador, the first champion of the American-bred champion Rodney Stone, and many others.
- ❖ Kit (owner V. Beckett), bred the champion lines of Dryads and Dimbulah

Amongst the finest champions and stud dogs of the day were: Mr. Raper's Tiger - full brother to Sir Anthony, Mr. Berrie's Monarch, Mr. Shirley's Sancho Panza, Mr. Pearl's Duke, Mr. Benjamin's Smasher, Mr. Shaw's Sepoy, Mr. Verinder's Slenderman, Mr. Ball's Lord Nelson, Capt. Holdsworth's Doon Brae, Mr. Webb's Faust, and especially Mr. Donkin's Byron (right) and Mr. Raper's Richard Coeur de Lion.

BULLDOG.
Mr. B. H. Donkin's Byron. Sire, Mr. Gibbon's Dan, out of Rose, by Tiger out of Rush; Tiger by Crib.

They were particularly admired: "for their possession of the broad lower jaw, with the six front teeth in an even row - the chief bulldog point to be produced and transmitted, and in which too many of Crib's descendants show a deplorable deficiency."

The Original Breed Standard

April 4, 1873 saw the formation of The Kennel Club which set up the world's first register of pedigree dogs. One of its priorities was the Kennel Club Stud Book and the Bulldog was listed in the first-ever version of this. The first Bulldog to be named in the register was a dog named Adam (Adamo), born in 1864. Adam belonged to Mr. R. Heathfield and was bred by Jacob Lamphier.

Imports of Spanish Bulldogs continued, boosting the number and making the large Bulldogs even bigger, although only four or five kennels used these imported studs. These Spanish dogs greatly incensed the Bulldog breeders of England who swore by their by-now 50lb dogs, and this was one of the main factors which led to the formation of The Bulldog Club, the world's oldest single breed association, at the Blue Post Inn on London's Oxford Street in 1875.

The Club held its annual exhibition of Bulldogs in London, and also offered trophies and medals for competition among members in other cities. The new Bulldog Club drew up a breed standard very similar to the Philo Kuon standard (see below). This breed standard remained largely unchanged in the UK for over a century. However, since 2008, the breed standard has been slightly revised in the UK to soften some of the Bulldog's trademark features in order to improve the health of the breed.

The ultimate aim of the original breed standard was to preserve the distinctive features of the Bulldog which had been bred for a specific purpose over hundreds of years. And even though that purpose was now defunct, the Bulldog had acquired a unique and distinctive look which enthusiasts were keen to preserve. They also set about breeding the aggression out of the dog – a task at which they were particularly successful.

Here is the original 1870s breed standard laid down by the Bulldog Club. The number in brackets is the maximum number of points out of 100 that the show judges of the day could award for perfection, and you will see that great importance was placed on the size of the head, and also that black, which had once been a popular Bulldog color, was no longer desirable:

1. "General appearance (10) – The general appearance of the bulldog is that of a smooth coated thick set dog, rather low in stature, about 18in. high at the shoulder, but broad, powerful, and compact. Its head strikingly massive, and very large in proportion to the dog's size. Its face extremely short, with nose almost between the eyes. Its muzzle very broad, blunt, truncated, and inclined upwards. Its body short and well knit; the limbs stout and muscular. Its hind quarters very high and strong, but rather lightly made in comparison with its massive fore parts. The dog conveys an impression of determination, strength, and activity, similar to that suggested by the appearance of a thick set Ayrshire or Highland bull.

2. Skull. (15) The head (or skull) should be very large - the larger the better - and in circumference should measure round in front of the ears at least the height of the dog at the shoulder. Viewed from the front, it should be very high from the corner of the lower jaw to the apex of the skull; it should also be broad and square. The cheeks should be well rounded, and extend sideways beyond the eyes. Viewed at the side, the head should be very high, and very short from its back to the point of the nose. The forehead should be flat, neither prominent, rounded, nor overhanging the face; and the skin upon it and about the head very loose, hanging in large folds or wrinkles.

3. Stop. (5) The temples or frontal bones should be very prominent, broad, square, and high, causing a groove between the eyes. This indentation is termed the ' Stop,' it should be both broad and deep, and extended up the middle of the forehead, dividing the head vertically, and be traceable at the top of the skull.

4. Eyes. (5) The eyes (seen from the front), should be situated low down in the skull, as far from the ears as possible. Their corners should be in a straight line at right angles with the stop, and quite in front of the head. They should be as wide apart as possible, provided their outer corners are within the outline of the cheeks. They should be quite round in shape, of moderate size, neither sunken nor prominent, and in colour should be as dark as possible, showing no white when looking directly forward.

5. Ears. (5) The ears should be set on high, i.e., the front inner edge of each ear should (as viewed from the front) join the outline of the skull at the top corner of such outline, so as to place them as wide apart and as high and far from the eyes as possible. In size they should be small and thin. The shape termed 'rose ear' is the most correct. The 'rose ear' folds inwards at its back, the upper or front edge, curving over outwards and backwards, showing part of the inside of the burr.

6. Face. (5) The face, measured from the front of the cheek bone to the nose, should be as short as possible; its skin should be deeply and closely wrinkled. The muzzle should be short, broad, square, not pointed, turned upwards, and very deep from the corner of the eye to the corner of the mouth. The nose should be large, broad, and black its top should be deeply set back, almost between the eyes. The distance from the inner corner of the eye (or from the centre of the stop between the eyes) to the extreme tip of the nose should not exceed the length from the tip of the nose to the edge of the under lip. The nostrils should be large, wide, and black, with a well defined straight line between them.

7. Chop. (5) The flews, called the 'chop,' should be thick, broad, pendent, and very deep, hanging completely over the lower jaw at the side (not in front). They should join the under lip in front and quite cover the teeth, which should not be seen when the mouth is closed.

8. Mouth. (5) The jaws, more especially the lower, should be broad, massive, and square, not in any way pinched or pointed, the canine teeth, or tusks, wide apart. The lower jaw should project considerably in front of the upper, and turn up. It should be very broad and square, and have the six small front teeth between the canines in an even row. The teeth should be large and strong.

9. Neck and Chest. (5) The neck should be moderate in length, rather short than long, very thick, deep, and strong. It should be well arched at the back, with much loose, thick, and

wrinkled skin hanging about the throat, forming a double dewlap on each side from the lower jaw to the chest. The chest should be very wide laterally, round, prominent, and deep, making the dog appear very broad and short-legged in front.

10. Shoulders. (5) The shoulders should be broad, slanting, deep, and very powerful.

11. Body. (5) The barrel should be capacious, round, and deep. It should be very deep from the top of the shoulders to its lowest part, where it joins the chest, and be well let down between the fore legs. It should be large in diameter, and round behind the fore legs (not flat-sided, the ribs being well rounded). The body should be well ribbed up behind, with the belly tucked up, and not pendulous.

12. Back. (5) The back should be short, broad, and strong, very broad at the shoulders and comparatively narrow at the loins. There should be a slight fall in the back close behind the shoulders (its lowest part), whence the spine should rise to the loins (the top of which should be higher than the top of the shoulder), thence curving again more suddenly to the tail, forming an arch - (a distinctive characteristic of the breed) - termed ' roach back,' or, more correctly, ' wheel back.'

13. Tail. (5) The tail, termed the 'stern,' should be set on low, jut out rather straight, and then turn downwards, the end pointing horizontally. It should be quite round in its whole length, smooth, and devoid of fringe or coarse hair. It should be moderate in length - rather short than long - thick at the root, and tapering rather quickly to a fine point. It should have a downward carriage (not having a decided upward curve at the end or being screwed or deformed), and the dog should, from its shape and position, not be able to raise it over his back.

14. Fore Legs. (5) The fore legs should be very stout and strong, set wide apart, thick, muscular, and straight, with well-developed calves, presenting a rather bowed outline, but the bones of the legs should be large and straight, not bandy or curved. They should be rather short in proportion to the hind legs, but not so short as to make the back appear long, or to detract from the dog's activity and so cripple him. The elbows should be low and stand well away from the ribs. The ankles, or pasterns, should be short, straight, and strong. The fore feet should be straight, and turn very slightly inwards; they should be of medium size, and moderately round. The toes short, compact, and thick, being well split up, making the knuckles prominent and high.

15. Hind Legs. (5) The hind legs should be large and muscular, and longer in proportion than the fore legs, so as to elevate the loins. The hocks should be very slightly bent and well let down, so as to be long and muscular from the loins to the point of the hock. The lower part of the leg should be short, straight, and strong. The stifles should be round, and turn slightly outwards away from the body. The hocks are thereby made to approach each other, and the hind feet to turn outwards. The latter, like the fore feet, should be round and compact, with the toes short, well split up and the knuckles prominent. From his formation, the dog has a peculiar heavy, slouching, and constrained gait, appearing to walk with short quick steps on the tips of his toes, his hind feet not be lifted high, but appearing to skim the ground, and often running with the one shoulder rather advanced, similar to the manner of a horse in cantering.

16. Size. (5) The most desirable size for the bulldog, and at which excellence is mostly attained, is about 50lb.

17. Coat and Colour. (5) The coat should be fine in texture, short, close, and smooth (hard only from its shortness and closeness, not wiry or woolly). The colour should be whole or smut, that is, a whole colour with a black mask or muzzle. It should be brilliant and pure

of its sort. As 'a good horse cannot be of a bad colour,' the same may be said of the dog if perfect in other points. The colours, in their order of merit, if bright and pure, are, first smuts, and whole brindles, reds, white, with their varieties, as whole fawns, fallows, etc.; second, pied and mixed colours. Black, which was once most esteemed, is now considered undesirable."

The Bulldog Arrives in the United States

In the late 1870s and 1880s, Bulldogs began to be imported to the United States. One of the first dogs to be shown was Donald, a brindle-and-white exhibited by Sir William Verner in the 1880 New York dog show. According to the famous judge Enno Meyer: "Donald lacked somewhat in substance, but he had a rather good head".

The leading imported Bulldogs of the day were two littermates: Colonel John E. Thayer's Robinson Crusoe and his sister and English champion, Britomartis. She took first place at the New York shows from 1885 to 1890, and Robinson Crusoe was the first national champion in 1888.

Another famous dog of the period was Handsome Dan. In 1889, Andrew B. Graves saw a Bulldog sitting in front of a New Haven blacksmith shop. Graves was an Englishman in the Yale class of 1892 and a member of the crew team as well as a footballer.

He offered $50 for the dog, the blacksmith countered with $75 and they settled on $65. Graves cleaned up the dog and named him "Handsome Dan." The dog (right) followed him everywhere around campus, including to sporting events, and the Yale students quickly adopted him as their mascot.

Handsome Dan is believed to be the first live mascot in the world. Since the original, a further 16 dogs have held the position of Yale mascot. Dan's modern successors are selected on the basis of their ability to tolerate bands and children, cleanliness and, most importantly, their negative reaction to the color crimson and tigers - the symbols of rivals Harvard and Princeton!

On April 1, 1890, The Bulldog Club of America was founded in the Mechanics Hall, Boston, by H.D. Kendall of Lowell, Massachusetts. Its aim was the "Unification of efforts to support the deliberate and serious breeding of bulldogs in America, preserving the purity of form, to improve the quality of the local population, as well as to put an end to the unwanted bias, in the public mind in relation to this wonderful breed" and to encourage "the thoughtful and careful breeding of the English Bulldog in America."

The Club was originally composed of a small group of men in the north eastern United States, but membership soon grew country-wide. Six years later members came to the conclusion that the English breed standard was not sufficiently clear, and so they wrote their own version for America, which, with a few minor refinements, is today's breed standard. In 1950 the structure of The Bulldog Club of America was revamped to make it a national organization. And in 1907, the Bulldog Club of Philadelphia became the first regional club to be recognized.

THE BULLDOGS THE GRAVEN IMAGE, HOLY TERROR, AND BATHOS

In the 1890s, the only major dog show in America was the Westminster Kennel Club's annual event held at the old Madison Square Garden in New York City. For the first 10 or 15 years, the Bulldog entry was an indifferent collection entered by scattered breeders, generally running from five to ten exhibits in all. But in 1891 the newly-formed Bulldog Club of America backed the show in an organized fashion. The Club offered the unheard of total of 16 cups, medals, and cash prizes for the breed and the Bulldog entry jumped to 51, several times the number of specimens ever before exhibited at a single dog show.

At this time, the American bloodlines relied on the importation of pedigree champions from top producers in England. Three of the most famous were imported by R.B. Sawyer; they were Harper, a male from the champion British Monarch; the arrival of this great dog caused a sensation in Bulldog circles as well as receiving considerable attention in the press. Harper became the first winner of one of two historic silver trophies awarded by the BCA, the Parke Cup (renamed the Grand Trophy).

The females Graven Image and Holy Terror were also brought in, they are pictured above with another top dog, Bathos, to the right of them. In 1901, Richard Croker's newly imported champion Rodney Stone, won the Grand Trophy, he became the first Bulldog ever to command a price of $5,000, when he was bought by controversial Irish-American political figure Richard Croker. The BCA's introduction of prestigious trophies and prizes triggered the heyday for Bulldog showing, which culminated in 1904 when Bulldogs led the entries at all the major USA dog shows.

The great champion La Roche won the Grand Trophy in 1905 and repeated the win in 1906. In 1913, Strathway Prince Albert, the only Bulldog ever to win best in show at Westminster, won the cup and returned to win it again in both 1914 and 1915.

The Bulldog Club of America initially hampered efforts to establish other bulldog clubs in order to maintain a monopoly on the breed. Regional organizations were denied recognition and there were many heated debates. These finally culminated in the successful recognition of the Philadelphia Bulldog Club in 1907. During these early days, there were many scandals and allegations of fraud and rigged prize-giving in the United States! After several unsuccessful attempts, the Chicago Bulldog Club was finally allowed to conduct its own show in 1916, followed in 1923 by the Pacific Coast Club.

In 1972, the BCA first published a quarterly magazine entitled "The Bulldogger" which is the name given to fans of the breed. Today the organization has eight regional divisions.

Incidentally, the American Bulldog has an entirely different - and even longer - history in the Americas. In the Depression of the early 1700s, British immigrants arrived, bringing their dogs with them. Many of them settled on farms in Georgia and used their Bulldogs as versatile working dogs to protect property, pen cattle and even to hunt wild boar. The farmers selected the biggest and strongest dogs to breed from.

The Changing Temperament of the Bulldog

Although the ideal size and shape of the Bulldog was hotly contested by the various fanciers and breeders in the mid to late 19th century, it is clear that their efforts to rid the Bulldog of its ferocity and aggression and turn it into a companion dog were highly successful. It is interesting to note two things: firstly that the Bulldog's character trait of being wonderful with children dates back more than 125 years. Secondly, at that time, the Bulldog was still regarded as an excellent guard dog.

F.G.W. Crafer wrote about the Bulldog of the day in the book "**British Dogs; Their Varieties, History, Characteristics, Breeding, Management and Exhibition**" published around 1879. He says: "...it may be said that the manners also make the dog; if a dog is capable of being trained to the perfection of canine intelligence and fidelity, he ought not to be undeservedly condemned. There are many people who can testify and prove that the bulldog can be so trained "precisely."

"Several owners of bulldogs have assured me that in their opinion it is the only kind of dog that can with perfect safety be trusted alone to the mercy of children, than which there can hardly be a greater trial of patience and good temper. Having from my earliest recollection been accustomed to dogs, and having possessed specimens of almost every breed of dog, I consider myself, from experience, competent to contradict the statements made to the disparagement of this breed, whose cause I now advocate.

"In proof I can show one which for nine years has been the constant companion and playfellow of my only child. It succeeded in my household a fine Mount St. Bernard, and has proved itself in every way fully, if not more than, equal to any of its predecessors in endurance, fidelity, and sagacity (wisdom).

"When first brought home the dog was chained to a kennel in the garden, whence my little child, then not three years old, brought it indoors to play with. It has since remained always loose in the house, and has, with others of the same breed, daily sustained trials which none but a bulldog could endure without showing its teeth.

Dryad and British Monarch, 1891 pencil drawing

"Food or bones can be taken away from them without any exhibition of ill temper, whilst they are as good watch dogs as possible, and under the most complete control. I could adduce plenty of little anecdotes in proof of the bulldog's intelligence; but as every dog owner can do the same of his own dog, and not having space for such, I will only repeat that there are many people who can corroborate my assertion that the bulldog is inferior to no other dog, and that ferocity is not natural to this more than any other breed."

He goes on to criticize the 19th century breeders for not paying as much attention to the color of Bulldogs as to the other features of the dog: "It is a matter of surprise that bulldog breeders have not the good taste to take the same pains to study the art of breeding for colour which they take to produce the broad mouth, short face, and other points by which the dog is judged.

"By so doing they would remove the prejudice impressed on the admirers of other breeds by the pied specimens. The colour is the most conspicuous point to a casual observer, and when a bulldog is white and unevenly pied with brindled patches and a patch over one eye and ear, and appears red and raw round its eyes, and wherever its coat is thin, it is no wonder that fanciers of

Pomeranians, Italian greyhounds, and other breeds so diametrically opposed, should decline to admit the bulldog's claim to beauty.

"But when of uniform colour brindle, red, or fawn the bulldog is in many respects more attractive than several other canine pets ; for example, the modern King Charles spaniel, and if its colour be whole and a "smut," like the pug whose 'Mouth was black as a bulldog's at the stall,' it is in every way to be preferred to that dog, being handsomer as well as more useful, faithful, and intelligent. White animals have not generally as strong constitutions as dark coloured ones, and are, therefore, much more liable to disease. When bred together they frequently produce "ricketty" or deaf whelps."

In a testament to the Bulldog's guarding abilities, Mr. Crafer said that a Staffordshire farmer had written in a newspaper that "two good bulldogs always loose in his yard do much more towards making his neighbours honest than all the parson's preaching."

He added: "The bulldog has been described as stupidly ferocious, but this is untrue, he being an excellent watch and as a guard unequalled . . . far from quarrelsome. ... If once the pure breed is allowed to drop, the best means of infusing fresh courage into degenerate breeds will be finally lost ... for I believe that every kind of dog possessed of very high courage owes it to a cross with the bulldog. ... I am sure my brother sportsmen will see the bad taste of running down a dog which with all its faults is not only the most courageous dog, but the most courageous animal in the world.

"I think this alone is sufficient testimony in the bulldog's favour, and fully endorse the words of the poet Smart:

Well! of all dogs, it stands confessed, Your English bulldogs are the best! I say it and will set my hand to it; Cambden records it, and I'll stand to it."

The Great Bulldog Race

Towards the end the 19th century, there was much dispute and discussion as to exactly how the Bulldog should look. We already know that there were three sizes of Bulldogs, although eventually the very small type was dropped, and it was around this time that the term "sourmug" was used for the first time to describe a particular type of Bulldog.

The sourmug had an extremely short muzzle and its legs were bowed. Its chest was so wide that it was no longer highly mobile, but moved in a less agile manner. In short, it looked much more

like today's Bulldog. The Philo-Kuon breeders, who were breeding towards the idealized athletic conformation of Rosa, declared it an abomination against nature. However, the sourmug-type began to have increasing success in the show ring when competing against the Philo-Kuon ideal.

There was much bad feeling between the two groups, with the breeders of sourmugs accusing the Philo-Kuon fanciers of being unpatriotic, as some were using the Spanish Bulldog (whose bloodlines actually originated in England) to breed a larger dog.

There was also criticism that some Philo-Kuon Bulldogs were aggressive and would attack cats and other dogs. However, others were mellower and with training made excellent guard dogs which would attack a person or animal on command, but which remained easy for the owner to control.

The event that followed was to determine the look of today's Bulldog. In 1893 the two top Bulldogs of the day were King Orry and Dockleaf, and it was decided to hold a 10-mile race to see which dog would win. Dockleaf (left) was a three-year-old sourmug owned by Mr. Sam Woodiwiss and was condemned as a deformed "cripple' by his detractors, yet he won prize after prize at dog shows, becoming the English champion. The four-year-old King Orry (next page), owned by Mr. George Murrell, was reminiscent of the original fighting Bulldogs, being lighter boned with a sleeker, more athletic body and smaller head.

Rawdon Lee describes the background to the race **in "The History of Modern Dogs of Great Britain and Ireland (Nonsporting Division)"** (1894):

"I must write of dogs as I find them at the present time, and, to show the state to which an endeavour to breed for exaggeration in certain points has brought the bulldog, reproduce the following account of a walking match between two crack bench winners, which took place in the summer of 1893.

"There had been a brindled dog shown with extraordinary success at that time, for which his owner, Mr. S. Woodiwiss, was reported to have given £250—the greatest amount of money ever paid for a dog of this variety. In the opinion of many persons he was so much a cripple as to be unable to stand properly in the ring, which was a fact.

"However, the judges under whom the dog in question came, appeared blind to his defects, and time after time he was placed over more perfect animals. Then a match was made between Dockleaf the dog above alluded to, and another well-known prize-winning bulldog, called King Orry owned by Mr. G. R. Murrell."

Here is his account of the race: "Each dog (is) to be led and make the best of the way from the Roebuck Hotel, Lewisham, to Bromley Town Hall and back, the distance being about ten miles. "The competitors might have as much rest as appeared desirable, but 'lifting' from the ground was disqualification.

" At seven o'clock, when the start was made, a big crowd was in attendance, a portion of which accompanied the dogs on their journey. King Orry went off with the lead, and was nearly 400 yards ahead when a mile or more had been traversed. Soon after Dockleaf showed signs of fatigue, but continued on his journey to a couple of miles from the start, when, being fairly beaten, Mr. Woodiwiss withdrew him from further competition; his opponent was then far in front, and 'going well'. Mr. Murrell's dog, after a rest of seven minutes, arrived at Bromley Town Hall, and then set off on the return journey, Lewisham being duly reached at 9.25 p.m.

"Both animals had been in training for the match, and the winner showed no signs of distress after the accomplishment of what some modern admirers of the bulldog consider a great feat, but which we consider any bulldog ought to do equally satisfactorily. The loser occupied a trifle under forty minutes in covering his two miles, and, exclusive of stoppages, the winner progressed at the rate of some four and a half miles in the hour."

Although beaten, the sourmug breeders and supporters of Dockleaf retaliated, saying that perhaps the new sourmug was no ball of fire, but at least it was not polluted with Spanish blood and a media campaign was directed against the Philo-Kuon breeders and King Orry. The Press campaign and anti-Spanish feelings were very strong and resulted in a moral victory for the pro-Dockleaf campaign.

It was, therefore, Dockleaf – and not King Orry - that breeders chose as the ideal conformation and which forms the basis of Bulldogs today. The drawings of Rosa and Crib were torn from the breed standard and ground under a boot heel as the victorious sourmug breeders had their final revenge for being humiliated in the race.

At the turn of the 19th century there were almost no Philo-Kuon Bulldogs left in England. The result of this was that within 20 years of the Kennel Club being formed and an official breed standard being laid down, the supremely athletic Bulldog had been so interbred that it was no longer able to walk more than a couple of miles without difficulty.

Controversy

The new Bulldog was not without its detractors. Many dog fanciers and experts were saddened at the changes within the breed and the fact that the national dog of England, once known for its immense bravery, strength and athleticism, had become a physical weakling.

Even in these early days, difficulties with breathing, stamina and whelping (giving birth to puppies) were recorded. One such was Edgar Farman, Honorary Member of the Bulldog Club and Editor of the Kennel Gazette, who said in his book *"The Bulldog - A Monograph"*, (The Stock Keeper Co, Ltd 1899): "He is a manufactured article, a mass of show points."

In *"The Book Of Dogs– An Intimate Study Of Mankind's Best Friend"* (National Geographic Society, 1919) Ernest Baynes and Louis Fuertes wrote: "The bulldog of today is a grotesque deformity – short-legged, short-winded, short-lived, and barely able to reproduce its kind.

"It is chiefly useful for infusing courageous blood into other breeds, for adding variety to a dog show, and as an example (to be avoided) of what can be done by senseless breeding to spoil a perfectly good dog. But they haven't quite spoiled him, for he still retains his old-time dauntless courage, and he has a homely smile that would melt the hearts of even the few unfortunates who boast that they hate dogs.

"And here is an appropriate place to register a friendly protest against the arbitrary fixing of points for which dog owners must breed in order to win at the dog shows. There is tendency in the very proper enthusiasm over dog shows and show dogs to forget that the primary object of breeding most dogs is to produce animals which are useful in different fields of activity, and not to conform to a particular standard unless that standard is the one most likely to develop dogs fitted in mind and body for the work required of them."

"With the idea of making as ugly and surly looking a beast as possible, the present (interpretation of the) standard for the bulldog demands a type that is all but unfitted for existence."

The picture above is J. Hay Hutchison's illustration from "***The Perfect Bulldog in Word and Picture; A Guide for Exhibitors, Breeders and Judges,***" printed in the Illustrated Kennel News, London, 1908. It is a dog like this which retains the stand-out features of the Bulldog, but in a rather more athletic form, that some modern Bulldog breeders are working towards.

The 20th Century Onwards

In the 20th century, the Bulldog increased in popularity, not only in Britain, but also in Europe, Russia, North and South America, Australia, New Zealand, South Africa and Japan. During the Second World War, the Bulldog once again came to the fore, as it was portrayed on posters and photographs as the indomitable national dog of Britain. Our pictures show a propaganda photo from WWII (top) and Venus (below), mascot of the 1941 Royal Navy destroyer HMS Vansittart.

Since 2000, the Bulldog has enjoyed a further resurgence, becoming one of the most popular dogs in both the USA and UK. It is not only the breed's unique look which has attracted new "bulldoggers," but also the modern Bulldog's reputation as having an agreeable and gentle temperament and being an excellent companion dog for all ages, but second to none when it comes to children.

Today, the Bulldog is no longer classed as a working or sporting dog, but in the Non-Sporting Group by the AKC and the Utility Group in the UK. In 2013, the breed was the fifth most popular dog in the whole of the USA, being number one dog in many cities. In the UK there were nearly 6,000 registrations of Bulldogs in 2013.

Numerous references were used in the research of this history, in particular:

- The R.H. Voss article "Our Dogs" magazine, Dec. 15, 1933, University of California Digital Library
- "British Dogs: Their Varieties, History, Characteristics, Breeding, Management, And Exhibition," Hugh Dalziel
- "The History of Modern Dogs of Great Britain and Ireland (Nonsporting Division" (1894), Rawdon Lee
- "The Perfect Bulldog in Word and Picture; A Guide for Exhibitors, Breeders and Judges"
- "The Book Of Dogs – An Intimate Study Of Mankind's Best Friend" (National Geographic Society, 1919)
- "The Bulldog - A Monograph"
- Wikipedia
- Chest of Books www.chestofbooks.com
- "American Sports 1785-1835," Jennie Holloman
- "The Natural History of Dogs, Volume X"

3. Bulldog Breed Standard

The **breed standard** is a blueprint for not only how each breed of dog should look, but also how it moves and what sort of temperament it should have.

It is laid down by the breed societies, and the Kennel Clubs keep the register of purebred (pedigree) dogs. The dogs entered in shows run under Kennel Club rules are judged against this ideal list of attributes, and breeders approved by the Kennel Clubs agree to breed puppies to the breed standards.

The breed standard can vary over time and from country to country, and this is certainly true of the Bulldog, whose breed standard has changed dramatically over the last 50 years. In the UK, the Kennel Club has slightly revised its list of ideal attributes following public pressure from the media which heavily criticised the breeding guidelines for some dogs - including the Bulldog - for causing health problems.

The new Bulldog standard in Britain calls for a "relatively" short face, a slightly smaller head and less-pronounced facial wrinkling. The Bulldog Club of America (BCA), which owns the copyright to the American breed standard, still calls for a "massive, short-faced head," a "heavy, thick-set, low-swung body," a "very short" face and muzzle and a "massive" and "undershot" jaw.

Breed Watch

In 2014 the Kennel Club (UK) launched its **Breed Watch Fit For Purpose** campaign. It identified a number of breeds and designated them as Category Three on Breed Watch. Category Three is classed as: "High Profile Breeds - Breeds where some dogs have visible conditions or exaggerations that can cause pain or discomfort. The Kennel Club provides additional support for these breed representatives. Best of Breed (BOB) Veterinary Health checks at General and Group Shows are required."

The Bulldog is on this list, along with the following breeds: Basset Hound, Bloodhound, Chow Chow, Clumber Spaniel, Dogue de Bordeaux, German Shepherd, Mastiff, Neapolitan Mastiff, Pekingese, Pug, Shar-Pei, and Saint Bernard.

The KC states: "The Kennel Club works closely with the clubs for these breeds in identifying key issues to be addressed within the breed, obtaining the opinion of breed experts on the issues identified, advising on how breed clubs can effectively address health and conformational issues and investigating how the Kennel Club can assist."

And this is what it has to say about Bulldogs: "Particular points of concern for individual breeds may include features not specifically highlighted in the breed standard including current issues. In some breeds, features may be listed which, if exaggerated, might potentially affect the breed in the future.

"Prior to 2014 the features listed below derived from a combination of health surveys, veterinary advice, a meeting of Kennel Club Group judges, feedback from judges at shows or consultation with individual breed club(s)/councils via the breed health coordinators.

"From 2014 the structure of Breed Watch will allow for a greater involvement by judges in the reporting on and monitoring of the points of concern.

"Points of concern (with the Bulldog) for special attention by judges: Excessive amounts of loose facial skin with conformational defects of the upper and/or lower eyelids so that the eyelid margins are not in normal contact with the eye when the dog is in its natural pose (e.g. they turn in, or out, or both abnormalities are present).

> Hair loss or scarring from previous dermatitis
> Heavy overnose wrinkle (roll)
> Inverted tail
> Lack of tail
> Pinched nostrils
> Significantly overweight
> Sore eyes due to damage or poor eyelid conformation
> Tight tail
> Unsound movement"

The Kennel Club lists the Bulldog in the Utility Group, which is where many of the non-sporting dogs are found. Other UK Utility Group dogs include the Akita, Boston Terrier, Chow Chow, Dalmatian, French Bulldog, Lhasa Apso, Miniature Schnauzer (which is classed as a Terrier in the USA) and all Poodles. This is the KC's description of the Bulldog:

"One of Britain's oldest indigenous breeds, the Bulldog is known as the national dog of Great Britain and is associated throughout the world with British determination and the legendary John Bull. The Bulldog was first classified as such in the 1630s, though there is earlier mention of similar types referred to as bandogs, a term reserved today for a type of fighting dog.

"Used originally for bull-baiting, the Bulldog also fought its way through the dog pits, but after 1835 it began to evolve into the shorter-faced, more squat version we know today. It entered the show ring in 1860 and the ensuing years saw a big personality change.

"The pugilistic expression of this delightfully ugly dog belies his loving, affectionate nature to family and friends. He has a reputation for tenacity and is very courageous, strong and powerful. Although he is a little bit stubborn by nature, he is good-tempered with children, of whom he is also very protective. The impression he gives of being slow and sluggish is completely contradicted by the great bursts of speed that he can and does produce when the occasion demands. His mood can be dignified, humorous or comical, and he has many endearing ways."

UK Breed Standard

General Appearance - Smooth-coated, fairly thick set, rather low in stature, broad, powerful and compact. Head, fairly large in proportion to size but no point so much in excess of others as to destroy the general symmetry, or make the dog appear deformed, or interfere with its powers of motion. Face relatively short, muzzle broad, blunt and inclined upwards although not excessively so. Dogs showing respiratory distress highly undesirable. Body fairly short, well knit, limbs stout, well muscled and in hard condition with no tendency towards obesity. Hindquarters high and strong. Bitches not so grand or well developed as dogs.

Characteristics - Conveys impression of determination, strength and activity.

Temperament - Alert, bold, loyal, dependable, courageous, fierce in appearance, but possessed of affectionate nature.

Head and Skull - Skull relatively large in circumference. Viewed from front appears high from corner of lower jaw to apex of skull; also broad and square. Cheeks well rounded and extended sideways beyond eyes. Viewed from side, head appears very high and moderately short from back to point of nose. Forehead flat with skin on and about head slightly loose and finely wrinkled without excess, neither prominent nor overhanging face. From defined stop, a furrow extending to middle of skull being traceable to apex.

Face from front of cheek bone to nose, relatively short, skin may be slightly wrinkled. Muzzle short, broad, turned upwards and deep from corner of eye to corner of mouth. Nose and nostrils large, broad and black, under no circumstances liver colour, red or brown.

Distance from inner corner of eye (or from centre of stop between eyes) to extreme tip of nose should not be less than distance from tip of the nose to edge of the underlip. Nostrils large wide and open, with well defined vertical straight line between. Flews (chops) thick, broad and deep, covering lower jaws at sides, but joining underlip in front.

Teeth not visible. Jaws broad, strong and square, lower jaw slightly projecting in front of upper with moderate turn up. Over nose wrinkle, if present, whole or broken, must never adversely affect or obscure eyes or nose. Pinched nostrils and heavy over nose roll are unacceptable and should be heavily penalised.

Viewed from front, the various properties of the face must be equally balanced on either side of an imaginary line down centre.

Eyes - Seen from front, situated low down in skull, well away from ears. Eyes and stop in same straight line, at right angles to furrow. Wide apart, but outer corners within the outline of cheeks. Round, of moderate size, neither sunken nor prominent, in colour very dark – almost black – showing no white when looking directly forward. Free from obvious eye problems.

Ears - Set high – i.e. front edge of each ear (as viewed from front) joins outline of skull at top corner of such outline, so as to place them as wide apart, as high and as far from eyes as possible. Small and thin. 'Rose ear' correct, i.e. folding inwards back, upper or front inner edge curving outwards and backwards, showing part of inside of burr.

Mouth - Jaws broad and square with six small front teeth between canines in an even row. Canines wide apart. Teeth large and strong, not seen when mouth closed. When viewed from front under jaw directly under upper jaw and parallel.

Neck - Moderate in length, thick, deep and strong. Well arched at back, with some loose, skin about throat, forming slight dewlap on each side.

Forequarters - Shoulders broad, sloping and deep, very powerful and muscular giving appearance of being 'tacked on' body. Brisket round and deep. Well let down between forelegs. Ribs not flat-sided, but well rounded.

Forelegs very stout and strong, well developed, set wide apart, thick, muscular and straight, bones of legs large and straight, not bandy nor curved and short in proportion to hindlegs, but not so short as to make back appear long, or detract from dog's activity. Elbows low and standing well away from ribs. Pasterns short, straight and strong.

Body - Chest wide, prominent and deep. Back short, strong, broad at shoulders. Slight fall to back close behind shoulders (lowest part) whence spine should rise to loins (top higher than top of shoulder), curving again more suddenly to tail, forming slight arch – a distinctive characteristic of breed. Body well ribbed up behind with belly tucked up and not pendulous.

Hindquarters - Legs large and muscular, slightly longer in proportion than forelegs. Hocks slightly bent, well let down; legs long and muscular from loins to hock. Stifles turned very slightly outwards away from body.

Feet - Fore, straight and turning very slightly outward; of medium size and moderately round. Hind, round and compact. Toes compact and thick, well split up, making knuckles prominent and high.

Tail - Set on low, jutting out rather straight and then turning downwards. Round, smooth and devoid of fringe or coarse hair. Moderate in length – rather short than long – thick at root, tapering quickly to a fine point. Downward carriage (not having a decided upward curve at end) and never carried above back.

Lack of tail, inverted or extremely tight tails are undesirable.

Gait/Movement - Appearing to walk with short, quick steps on tips of toes, hind feet not lifted high, appearing to skim ground, running with one or other shoulder rather advanced. Soundness of movement of the utmost importance.

Coat - Fine texture, short, close and smooth (hard only from shortness and closeness, not wiry).

Colour - Whole or smut, (i.e. whole colour with black mask or muzzle). Only whole colours (which should be brilliant and pure of their sort) viz., brindles, reds with their various shades, fawns, fallows etc., white and pied (i.e. combination of white with any of the foregoing colours). Dudley, black and black with tan highly undesirable.

Size - Dogs: 25 kgs (55 lbs); bitches: 23 kgs (50 lbs).

Faults - Any departure from the foregoing points should be considered a fault and the seriousness with which the fault should be regarded should be in exact proportion to its degree and its effect upon the health and welfare of the dog.

Note - Male animals should have two apparently normal testicles fully descended into the scrotum.

American Breed Standard

In the USA the Bulldog is in the Non-Sporting Group, alongside such other breeds as the Bichon Frise, Boston Terrier, Chinese Shar-Pei, Chow Chow, Dalmatian, Finnish Spitz, French Bulldog, Lhasa Apso, Poodle, Tibetan Spaniel and Tibetan Terrier.

According to the AKC, non-sporting dogs are a diverse group. They are a varied collection in terms of size, coat, personality and overall appearance.

The **AKC Meet the Breeds** states: "Known for their loose-jointed, shuffling gait and massive, short-faced head, the Bulldog is known to be equable, resolute and dignified. A medium-sized dog, they are not your typical lap dog, but would like to be!

"They are one of the most popular breeds according to AKC Registration Statistics due to their lovable and gentle dispositions and adorable wrinkles. The Bulldog may be brindle, white, red, fawn, fallow or piebald."

The AKC goes on to state: "Bulldogs are recognized as excellent family pets because of their tendency to form strong bonds with children. They tend to be gentle and protective. The breed requires minimal grooming and exercise. Their short nose makes them prone to overheating in warm weather, so make sure to provide a shady place to rest."

In 2012 and 2013 the Bulldog was the fifth most popular breed of dog in the United States. Here is the full American breed standard:

General Appearance - The perfect Bulldog must be of medium size and smooth coat; with heavy, thick-set, low-swung body, massive short-faced head, wide shoulders and sturdy limbs. The general appearance and attitude should suggest great stability, vigor and strength. The disposition should be equable and kind, resolute and courageous (not vicious or aggressive), and demeanor should be pacific and dignified. These attributes should be countenanced by the expression and behavior.

Size, Proportion, Symmetry - *Size*--The size for mature dogs is about 50 pounds; for mature bitches about 40 pounds. *Proportion*--The circumference of the skull in front of the ears should measure at least the height of the dog at the shoulders. *Symmetry*--The "points" should be well distributed and bear good relation one to the other, no feature being in such prominence from either excess or lack of quality that the animal appears deformed or ill-proportioned. *Influence of Sex* In comparison of specimens of different sex, due allowance should be made in favor of the bitches, which do not bear the characteristics of the breed to the same degree of perfection and grandeur as do the dogs.

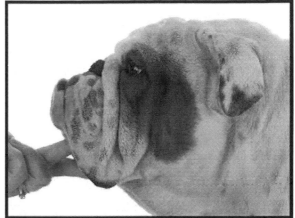

Head - *Eyes and Eyelids*--The eyes, seen from the front, should be situated low down in the skull, as far from the ears as possible, and their corners should be in a straight line at right angles with the stop. They should be quite in front of the head, as wide apart as possible, provided their outer corners are within the outline of the cheeks when viewed from the front. They should be quite round in form, of moderate size, neither sunken nor bulging, and in color should be very dark. The lids should cover the white of the eyeball, when the dog is looking directly forward, and the lid should show no "haw."

Ears--The ears should be set high in the head, the front inner edge of each ear joining the outline of the skull at the top back corner of skull, so as to place them as wide apart, and as high, and as far from the eyes as possible. In size they should be small and thin. The shape termed "rose ear" is the most desirable. The rose ear folds inward at its back lower edge, the upper front edge curving over, outward and backward, showing part of the inside of the burr. (The ears should not be carried erect or prick-eared or buttoned and should never be cropped.)

Skull--The skull should be very large, and in circumference, in front of the ears, should measure at least the height of the dog at the shoulders. Viewed from the front, it should appear very high from the corner of the lower jaw to the apex of the skull, and also very broad and square. Viewed at the side, the head should appear very high, and very short from the point of the nose to occiput. The forehead should be flat (not rounded or domed), neither too prominent nor overhanging the face.

Cheeks--The cheeks should be well rounded, protruding sideways and outward beyond the eyes. *Stop*--The temples or frontal bones should be very well defined, broad, square and high, causing a hollow or groove between the eyes. This indentation, or stop, should be both broad and deep and extend up the middle of the forehead, dividing the head vertically, being traceable to the top of the skull.

Face and Muzzle--The face, measured from the front of the cheekbone to the tip of the nose, should be extremely short, the muzzle being very short, broad, turned upward and very deep from the corner of the eye to the corner of the mouth.

Nose--The nose should be large, broad and black, its tip set back deeply between the eyes. The distance from bottom of stop, between the eyes, to the tip of nose should be as short as possible

and not exceed the length from the tip of nose to the edge of underlip. The nostrils should be wide, large and black, with a well-defined line between them. Any nose other than black is objectionable and a brown or liver-colored nose shall **disqualify**.

Lips--The chops or "flews" should be thick, broad, pendant and very deep, completely overhanging the lower jaw at each side. They join the underlip in front and almost or quite cover the teeth, which should be scarcely noticeable when the mouth is closed.

Bite--Jaws--The jaws should be massive, very broad, square and "undershot," the lower jaw projecting considerably in front of the upper jaw and turning up.

Teeth The teeth should be large and strong, with the canine teeth or tusks wide apart, and the six small teeth in front, between the canines, in an even, level row.

Neck, Topline, Body - *Neck* -- The neck should be short, very thick, deep and strong and well arched at the back.

Topline -- There should be a slight fall in the back, close behind the shoulders (its lowest part), whence the spine should rise to the loins (the top of which should be higher than the top of the shoulders), thence curving again more suddenly to the tail, forming an arch (a very distinctive feature of the breed), termed "roach back" or, more correctly, "wheel-back."

Body--The brisket and body should be very capacious, with full sides, well-rounded ribs and very deep from the shoulders down to its lowest part, where it joins the chest. It should be well let down between the shoulders and forelegs, giving the dog a broad, low, short-legged appearance. *Chest*--The chest should be very broad, deep and full.

Underline--The body should be well ribbed up behind with the belly tucked up and not rotund.

Back and Loin--The back should be short and strong, very broad at the shoulders and comparatively narrow at the loins. *Tail*--The tail may be either straight or "screwed" (but never curved or curly), and in any case must be short, hung low, with decided downward carriage, thick root and fine tip. If straight, the tail should be cylindrical and of uniform taper. If "screwed," the bends or kinks should be well defined, and they may be abrupt and even knotty, but no portion of the member should be elevated above the base or root.

Forequarters - *Shoulders*--The shoulders should be muscular, very heavy, widespread and slanting outward, giving stability and great power.

Forelegs--The forelegs should be short, very stout, straight and muscular, set wide apart, with well developed calves, presenting a bowed outline, but the bones of the legs should not be curved or bandy, nor the feet brought too close together.

Elbows--The elbows should be low and stand well out and loose from the body. *Feet*-- The feet should be moderate in size, compact and firmly set. Toes compact, well split up, with high knuckles and very short stubby nails. The front feet may be straight or slightly out-turned.

Hindquarters - *Legs*--The hind legs should be strong and muscular and longer than the forelegs, so as to elevate the loins above the shoulders. Hocks should be slightly bent and well let down, so as to give length and strength from the loins to hock. The lower leg should be short, straight and strong, with the stifles turned slightly outward and away from the body. The hocks are thereby made to approach each other, and the hind feet to turn outward.

Feet--The feet should be moderate in size, compact and firmly set. Toes compact, well split up, with high knuckles and short stubby nails. The hind feet should be pointed well outward.

Coat and Skin - *Coat*--The coat should be straight, short, flat, close, of fine texture, smooth and glossy. (No fringe, feather or curl.) *Skin*--The skin should be soft and loose, especially at the head, neck and shoulders.

Wrinkles and Dewlap--The head and face should be covered with heavy wrinkles, and at the throat, from jaw to chest, there should be two loose pendulous folds, forming the dewlap.

Color of Coat - The color of coat should be uniform, pure of its kind and brilliant. The various colors found in the breed are to be preferred in the following order: (1) red brindle, (2) all other brindles, (3) solid white, (4) solid red, fawn or fallow, (5) piebald, (6) inferior qualities of all the foregoing.
Note: A perfect piebald is preferable to a muddy brindle or defective solid color. Solid black is very undesirable, but not so objectionable if occurring to a moderate degree in piebald patches.

The brindles to be perfect should have a fine, even and equal distribution of the composite colors. In brindles and solid colors a small white patch on the chest is not considered detrimental. In piebalds the color patches should be well defined, of pure color and symmetrically distributed.

Gait - The style and carriage are peculiar, his gait being a loose-jointed, shuffling, sidewise motion, giving the characteristic "roll." The action must, however, be unrestrained, free and vigorous.

Temperament - The disposition should be equable and kind, resolute and courageous (not vicious or aggressive), and demeanor should be pacific and dignified. These attributes should be countenanced by the expression and behaviour.

In the show ring, here is how the judging points are awarded:

General Properties		
Proportion and symmetry	5	
Attitude	3	
Expression	2	
Gait	3	
Size	3	
Coat	2	
Color of coat	4	**22**
Head		
Skull	5	
Cheeks	2	
Stop	4	
Eyes and eyelids	3	
Ears	5	
Wrinkle	5	
Nose	6	
Chops	2	
Jaws	5	
Teeth	2	**39**
Body, Legs, etc.		
Neck	3	

Dewlap	2	
Shoulders	5	
Chest	3	
Ribs	3	
Brisket	2	
Belly	2	
Back	5	
Forelegs and elbows	4	
Hind Legs	3	
Feet	3	
Tail	4	**39**
Total		**100**

Disqualification
Brown or liver-colored nose.

Approved July 20, 1976. Reformatted November 28, 1990

4. Bulldog Puppies

Are You Ready?

Apart from getting married or having a baby, getting a puppy is one of the most important, demanding, expensive and life-enriching decisions you will ever make. Just like babies, puppies will love you unconditionally - but there is a price to pay. In return for their loyalty and devotion, you have to fulfill your part of the bargain.

In the beginning you have to be prepared to devote several hours a day to your new Bulldog puppy. You have to feed, exercise (lightly) and train him every day as well as take care of his health and welfare. A point particularly worth considering with Bulldogs is that you also have to be prepared to part with hard cash for regular healthcare, and even more money in veterinary bills in the case of illness.

If you are not prepared, or unable, to devote the time and money to a new arrival – or if you are out at work all day – then now might not be the right time for you to consider getting a puppy. Bulldogs, more than most dogs, are extremely faithful creatures; they are above all companion dogs and love being with their people.

If you are out at work all day these are NOT the dogs for you. To leave a Bulldog on his own for long periods is just not fair on this lovable dog that is happiest lounging around near you. Bulldog puppies are great chewers and if they are left for too long, may become destructive or stubborn. Just because your pup may seem calm and laid back doesn't mean he doesn't need training. He does. Bullies are very trainable – although don't expect them to jump through hoops at your every command - but they also need plenty of mental and physical stimulation to stop them getting bored and becoming destructive, especially when young.

Getting a puppy is definitely a long-term commitment. Before getting a puppy, ask yourself some questions:

Have I Got Enough Time?

In the first days after leaving his - or her - mother and littermates, your puppy will feel very lonely and maybe even a little afraid. You and your family have to spend time with your new arrival to make him feel safe and sound. Ideally, for the first few days you will be around all of the time to help your puppy settle into his new home and to start bonding with him. Book time off work in the beginning if necessary, but don't just get a puppy and leave him alone in the house a couple of days later.

After the initial period, you will need to spend time housetraining and then behavior training. Although Bulldogs generally do not need a lot of exercise, it is still a good idea to get into the habit of taking him out of the house and yard (once he is safe to do so after his vaccinations) for a short walk every day. These new surroundings will stimulate his interest and help to stop him from becoming bored and stubborn.

You'll also have to feed your dog daily, in fact several times a day with a young puppy and more than with any other breed, feeding your Bulldog the right diet is of paramount importance. He or she will also require regular care in the form of eye, ear, wrinkle and possibly even tail cleaning, as well as light grooming. You will also need time to visit the veterinary surgery for regular healthcare visits and annual vaccinations.

How Long Can I Leave Him For?

This is a question we get asked all of the time and one which causes a lot of debate among owners and prospective owners. All dogs are pack animals; their natural state is to be with others. Being alone is not normal for a dog, although many have to get used to it.

Another issue is the toilet; the Bulldog is not a breed with a large bladder, so leaving him unattended all day is not an option. All Bulldogs have smaller bladders than humans. Forget the emotional side of it, how would you like to be left for eight hours without being able to visit the bathroom?

So how many hours can you leave a dog alone for? Well, a useful guide comes from the rescue organizations. In the UK, they will not allow anybody to adopt if they are intending leaving the dog alone for more than four or five hours a day.

Dogs left at home alone all day become bored and, in the case of Bulldogs and other breeds which are highly dependent on human company for their happiness, they may well become sad or depressed. Some of it will, of course, depend on the character and temperament of your dog. But a lonely Bulldog may display signs of unhappiness by being destructive or displaying poor behavior when you return home.

A puppy or fully-grown dog must NEVER be left shut in a crate all day. It is OK to leave a puppy or adult dog in a crate if they are happy there, but the door should never be closed for more than two or three hours. A crate is a place where a puppy or adult should feel safe, not a prison.

Ask yourself why you want a dog – is it for selfish reasons or can you really offer a good home to a young puppy and then adult dog for up to a next decade, or if you are lucky, even longer? Would it be more sensible to wait until you are at home more?

Is My Home Suitable?

If you have decided to get a puppy, then choose one which will fit in with your living conditions. All dogs, even Bulldogs with low energy levels, need some time out of doors. If you live in a small apartment on the 10th floor of a high rise block with an intermittent elevator service, then a Bulldog would not be a good choice. However, Bulldogs can be suitable for people living in apartments, and indeed are the most popular breed in New York and Los Angeles.

Successful apartment living for canine involves having easy access to the outside and to spend time housetraining. This may mean training the dog to use a pad or a tray as an indoor bathroom. If you can regularly take your Bulldog out at least three or four times a day to do what he needs to do, there is no need to indoor housetrain him. If you live in a house and have a yard, do not leave your Bulldog unattended there for long periods – Bulldogs love to sunbathe and they can easily overheat. They may also wander off through a gap in the fence and, at $2,000 to $3,000 a time, they are sadly targets for thieves.

Bully-proofing your home should involve moving anything breakable or chewable - including your shoes! - out of reach to sharp little teeth. Make sure he can't chew electrical cords – lift them off the floor if necessary, and block off any off-limits areas of the house, such as upstairs or your bedroom, with a child gate or barrier, especially as he will probably be following you around the house in the first few days. If you have a yard or garden, make sure there are no poisonous plants or chemicals he could eat or drink.

Family and Children

What about the other members of your family, do they all want the puppy as well? A puppy will grow into a dog which will become a part of your family for many years to come. If you have children, they will, of course, be delighted.

One of the wonderful things about Bulldogs is how naturally good they are with children; many seem to have a natural affinity or attraction to kids and babies, get excited when they see them and love to be around them. Years ago Julie, a friend of mine, chose the breed because it is generally excellent with children - she and her husband had narrowed it down to a Bully or a Labrador, but went with the Bulldog because he needs less exercise. They fell in love with the breed and its gentle and comical nature and have recently got their third, Teddy. Whenever Julie took her first Bulldog and young son to the playground, Winston would think he was in seventh heaven, he just loved being with the children so much.

Make sure your puppy gets enough time to sleep – which is most of the time in the beginning, so don't let your children constantly pester him. Sleep is very important to puppies, just as it is for babies. One of the reasons some Bulldogs end up in rescue centers is that the owners are unable to cope with the demands of small children AND a dog.

Remember that dogs are very hierarchical, in other words, there is a pecking order. Although Bulldogs are not regarded as one-person dogs, here is usually one human that the puppy will regard as pack leader (alpha), usually the person who feeds him or who spends most time with him.

Puppies will often regard children as being on their own level, like a playmate, and so they might chase, jump and nip at them with sharp teeth. This is not aggression; this is normal play for puppies. Be sure to supervise play time and make sure the puppy doesn't get too boisterous, train him to be gentle with the children, as when he's roughhousing at 40lb or 50lb he can cause some damage.

Fortunately, Bulldogs do not bark much and they spend most of their life indoors, so they are not likely to cause a problem for your neighbors, like some noisy dogs do.

Older People

If you are older or have elderly relatives living with you, the good news is that Bulldogs are great company. They love to be with people and are affectionate in a laid back way. Nobody has told the Bulldog that he is not a lapdog and is happiest when snoozing on a chair or on you.

Bear in mind that larger dogs may be too much for a senior citizen, especially if they haven't been trained properly. They may pull on the leash or be boisterous or destructive in the house (the dog, not the old person!) If you are older, make sure your energy levels are up to those of a young puppy. Ask yourself if you are fit enough to take your dog for at least one short walk every day.

Dogs can be great for older people. My father is in his 80's, but takes his dog out walking for an hour every day – even in the rain or snow. It's good for him and it's good for the dog, it keeps both of them fit and socialized! They get fresh air, exercise and the chance to communicate with other dogs and their humans.

Dogs are also great company at home – you're never alone when you've got a dog. Many older people get a puppy after losing a loved one (a husband, wife or previous much-loved dog). A dog gives them something to care for and love, as well as a constant companion. With Bulldogs in particular, health may become an issue, so it's important the older person can afford annual pet insurance or veterinary fees.

Some Bulldogs will survive perfectly well by only going out into the garden or yard, but there is no substitute in most dogs' minds for a walk away from the home at least once a day – even a short one. Take out the leash and see how your dog reacts, you'll soon find out if he'd rather go for a walk or stay at home.

Single People

Many single adults own dogs, but if you live alone, having a puppy will require a lot of dedication from you. There will be nobody to share the tasks of daily care, exercise, grooming and training, so taking on a dog requires a huge commitment and a lot of your time if the dog is to have a decent life. If you are out of the house all day as well, it is not really fair to get a puppy, or even an adult dog. Left alone all day, they will feel isolated, bored and sad. However, if you work from home or close to home or are at home all day and you can spend considerable time with the puppy every day, then great! Bulldogs make excellent companions.

Other Pets

If you already have other pets in your household, spend time to introduce them gradually to each other. If you have other dogs, supervised sessions from an early age will help the dogs to get along and chances are they will become the best of friends. Bulldogs are generally very placid by nature and do well with other pets, provided the introductions are done properly. With another dog, it is important to introduce the two on neutral territory, rather than in areas one pet deems as his own. You don't want one dog to feel he has to protect his territory. Walking the dogs parallel to each other before heading home for the first time is a good idea to get them used to each other.

Cats can sometimes be more of a problem; most dogs' natural instinct is to chase a cat. However, it's also true that most Bulldogs are not like Spike (the Bully in the Tom and Jerry cartoons who spent his life chasing cats) and many live very happily alongside other pets, including cats. Bulldogs love attention and may see the cat as a threat and in a minority of cases it may take a long time (if ever) to accustom them to small pets.

The fact that a dog has lived with one cat will not guarantee that it will tolerate a different, strange cat. Other Bulldogs will have no problems at all with a cat and will even protect them. A lot will depend on the temperament of the individual dog and at what age he is introduced to the other animal(s) – the earlier, the better. Your chances of success are greater if your cat is strong-willed and your dog is docile, fortunately most Bulldogs are! If your cat is timid and your dog is alert, young and active, then your job will be more difficult.

Supervised sessions and patience are the answer. A pup may tease a cat, but in the end will probably learn to live with it. Make sure the cat does not attack the puppy. Take the process slowly, if your cat is stressed and frightened he may decide to leave. Our feline friends are notorious for abandoning home because the food and facilities are better down the road. Until you know that they can get on together, don't leave them alone.

For a dog to get on with a cat, you are asking him to forget some of his natural instincts and to respond to your training. But do not despair, it can be done very successfully with Bulldogs.

Due to its sensitivities and healthcare needs, the Bulldog is not a breed suitable to be left for long periods. If you do leave a young dog alone for any length of time, you may want to leave a newspaper or wee pad on the floor in case of an accident. If you decide to use a crate, only leave your pup in it for short periods initially and only after he has accepted it and is comfortable there.

The ideal scenario is to leave the pup in his open crate, block off other rooms or areas, so he has a small area he can wander round in, but remember to remove any wooden objects or furniture so he can't chew them. If you're still determined to have a Bully when you're out for several hours at a time, here are some useful points:

Top 10 Tips For Working Bulldog Owners

1. Either come home during your lunch break to let your dog out or employ a dog walker (or neighbor) to take him out for a walk in the middle of the day.

2. Do you know anybody you could leave your dog with during the day? Consider leaving the dog with a friend, relative or elderly neighbor who would welcome the companionship of a Bulldog without the full responsibility of ownership.

3. Take him for a walk before you go to work – even if this means getting up at the crack of dawn – and spend time with him as soon as you get home.

Exercise generates serotonin in the brain and has a calming effect. A dog that has been exercised will be less anxious and more ready for a good nap. Remember that most Bulldogs cannot tolerate very strenuous exercise, so don't go jogging with him.

4. Leave him in a place of his own where he feels comfortable. If you use a crate, leave the door open, otherwise his favorite dog bed or chair. If possible, leave him in a room with a view of the outside world. This will be more interesting than staring at four blank walls.

5. VERY IMPORTANT WITH BULLDOGS: Make sure that it does not get too hot during the day and there are no cold draughts in the place where you leave him. Your dog can die if he overheats, so in very hot weather he may well need an air conditioned room.

6. Food and drink. Remove his food and put it down at specific meal times. If the food is there all day, he may become a fussy eater or 'punish' you for leaving him alone by refusing to eat. Make sure he has access to water at all times. Dogs cannot cool down by sweating; they do not have many sweat glands (which is why they pant, but this is much less efficient than perspiring) and can die without sufficient water.

7. Leave toys available for him to play with to prevent boredom and destructive chewing (the favorite occupation of a bored Bulldog or one suffering from separation anxiety.) Stuff a Kong toy with treats to keep him occupied for a while. Choose the right size of Kong for your dog and then put a treat inside. You can even smear the inside with peanut butter or another favorite to keep him occupied for longer.

8. Consider getting a companion for your Bulldog - another dog or even a cat. This will involve even more of your time and twice the expense, and if you have not got time for one dog, you have hardly time for two. A better idea is to find someone you can leave the dog with during the day; there are also dogsitters and doggie day care for those who can afford them.

9. Consider leaving a radio or TV on very softly in the background. The 'white noise' can have a soothing effect on some pets. If you do this, select your channel carefully – try and avoid one with lots of bangs and crashes or heavy metal music!

10. Stick to the same routine before you leave your dog home alone. This **will** help him to feel secure. Before you go to work, get into a daily habit of getting yourself ready, then feeding and exercising your Bulldog. Dogs love routine. But don't make a huge fuss of him when you leave, this can also stress the dog; just leave the house calmly.

Similarly when you come home. Your Bulldog will feel starved of attention and be pleased to see you. Greet him normally, but try not to go overboard by making too much of a fuss of him as soon as you walk through the door. Give him a pat and a stroke then take off your coat and do a few other things before turning your attention back to him. Lavishing your Bulldog with too much attention the second you walk through the door may encourage demanding behavior or **separation anxiety -** see our section on this.

Puppy Stages

It is important to understand how a puppy develops into a fully grown dog. This knowledge will help you to be a good owner to your puppy. The first few months and weeks of a puppy's life will have an effect on his behavior and temperament for the rest of his life. This Puppy Schedule will help you to understand the early stages:

Birth to seven weeks	A puppy needs sleep, food and warmth. He needs his mother for security and discipline and littermates for learning and socialization. The puppy learns to function within a pack and learns the pack order of dominance. He begins to become aware of his environment. During this period, puppies should be left with their mother.
Eight to 12 weeks	A puppy should not leave his mother before eight weeks. At this age the brain is fully developed and he now needs socializing with the outside world. He needs to change from being part of a canine pack to being part of a human pack. This period is a fear period for the puppy, avoid causing him fright and pain.
13 to 16 weeks	Training and formal obedience should begin. He needs socializing with other humans, places and situations. This period will pass easily if you remember that this is a puppy's change to adolescence. Be firm and fair. His flight instinct may be prominent. Avoid being too strict or too soft with him during this time and praise his good behavior.
Four to eight months	Another fear period for a puppy is between seven to eight months of age. It passes quickly, but be cautious of fright or pain which may leave the puppy traumatized. The puppy reaches sexual maturity and dominant traits are established. Your dog should now understand the commands 'sit', 'down', 'come' and 'stay'.

Plan Ahead

Puppies usually leave the litter for their new homes when they are eight weeks or older (toy breeds may stay with the mother for up to 12 weeks.) Like all dogs, Bulldog puppies learn the rules of the pack from their mothers. Most continue teaching their pups the correct manners and do's and don'ts until they are around eight weeks old.

Breeders who allow their pups to leave before this time may be more interested in a quick buck than a long-term puppy placement. Top breeders often have waiting lists. If you want a well-bred Bulldog puppy, it pays to plan ahead. If you have decided you are definitely going to have a Bulldog puppy, then the next step is one of the most important decisions you will make: **choosing the right breeder**.

Like humans, your puppy will be a product of his or her parents and will inherit many of their characteristics. His temperament and how healthy your puppy will be now and throughout his life will largely depend on the genes of his parents.

It is essential that you select a good, responsible breeder. They will have checked out the temperament and health records of the parents and will only breed from suitable stock. Some

Bulldog breeders have their own websites, particularly in the USA, and many are trustworthy and conscientious. You have to learn to spot the good ones from the bad ones.

With the cost of a Bulldog puppy running into two or three thousand dollars - and over £1,000 if you are in the UK - unscrupulous breeders with little knowledge of the breed have sprung up, tempted by the prospect of making easy cash. A healthy Bulldog will be your companion for the  next decade if you are lucky. You wouldn't choose a good friend without screening them first and getting to know them, so why buy an unseen puppy, or one from a pet shop or general advertisement? Good Bulldog breeders do not sell their dogs on general purpose websites or in pet shops. In fact they usually have a waiting list of prospective owners.

At the very minimum you MUST visit the breeder personally and follow our **Top 10 Tips for Selecting a Good Breeder** to help you make the right decision. Buying a poorly-bred puppy may save you a few hundred dollars or pounds in the short term, but could cost you thousands in extra veterinary bills in the long run, not to mention the terrible heartache of having a sickly dog.

Rescue groups know only too well the dangers of buying a poorly-bred dog. Many years of problems can arise, usually these are health issues with Bulldogs, but behavior problems can also result from poor breeding, causing pain and distress for both dog and owner. All rescue groups strongly recommend taking the time to find a good breeder.

There's certainly a Bulldog breeder with the right puppy for you - but how do you find them? Everybody knows you should get your puppy from "a good breeder." But how can you tell the good guys from the bad guys?

The Kennel Club in your country is a great place to start as they have lists of approved breeders. In the USA, the American Kennel Club has an online Breeder Classifieds section for each breed. Here is the link for Bulldogs:

www.akc.org/classified/search/landing_puppy.cfm?breed_code=302

The Kennel Club in the UK has an Assured Breeder scheme. Here is the link for the KC breeders, only the ones with the rosette symbol are "assured", which means they have been personally visited and approved by the KC:

http://www.thekennelclub.org.uk/services/public/findapuppy/display.aspx?breed=4084&area=0

You might have had a personal recommendation, or like the look of a friend's handsome Bulldog and want to have one which looks the same. If that's the case, make sure you ask all the right questions of the breeder regarding how they select their breeding stock and ask to see the parents' health certificates, or at the very least what health screening the dam and sire have had.

Another good place to start looking is the breed association in your country. The Bulldog Club of America says this: "The Bulldog Club of America's ("BCA") On-Line Breeder Referral Program is an opt-in member privilege created to assist potential puppy owners in making contact with BCA members in good standing who agree to follow BCA's Breeder Code of Ethics. The BCA strongly recommends that all representations, promises, statements, warranties and guarantees made by either party be in writing and signed by both parties."

Of course, there are no cast iron guarantees that your puppy will be healthy and have a good temperament, but choosing an approved breeder who conforms to a code of ethics is a very good place to start. On the BCA website you can search by geographical state and background information is also given on individual breeders as to whether they carry out health checks and whether their pups are bred from champions. Here is the BCA link for Bulldog breeders:

http://www.bulldogclubofamerica.org/bca.aspx?id=188

In the UK the Bulldog Breed Council recommends looking for a breeder by contacting the secretary of your local Bulldog club, which is listed on the website here:

http://bulldogbreedcouncil.co.uk/contact.html

It also suggests visiting Bulldog shows and chatting with breeders, reminding potential new owners that reputable breeders do not have to advertise, such is the demand for their puppies - so it's up to you to do your research to find a really good breeder.

If, for whatever reason, you're not able to buy a puppy from one of these accredited breeders and you've never bought a Bulldog puppy before, how do you avoid buying one from a "backstreet breeder" or puppy mill? These are people who just breed puppies for profit and sell them to the first person who turns up with the cash. Unhappily, this can end in heartbreak for a family months or years later when their puppy develops health or temperament problems due to poor breeding.

Good Bulldog breeders will only breed from dogs which have been carefully selected for health, temperament, physical shape and lineage. There are plenty out there, it's just a question of finding one. The good news is that there are signs that can help the savvy buyer spot a good breeder.

Top 10 Tips for Choosing a Good Bulldog Breeder

1. They keep the dogs in the home and as part of the family - not outside in kennel runs or in the garage/outbuildings. Check that the area where the puppies are kept is clean and that the puppies themselves look clean.

2. They have Bulldogs which appear happy and healthy. The dogs are alert, excited to meet new people and don't shy away from visitors.

3. A good dog breeder will encourage you to spend time with the puppy's parents - or at least the pup's mother - when you visit. They want your entire family to meet the puppy and are happy for you to make more than one visit.

4. They breed only one, or maximum two, types of dogs, such as Bulldogs and Pugs or French Bulldogs, and they are very familiar with the **breed standards**.

5. Bulldogs can have genetic weaknesses. Check that the puppy has wide nostrils and clean eyes with no discharge and that he or she does not seem breathless. A good breeder will explain the extra care a Bulldog needs. Ideally, they will have OFA certificates (or equivalent in countries outside the US) to prove that both parents are free from genetic defects. The requirements for minimum health screenings in the US have been defined by BCA as covering the heart, patella (knee cap), thyroid and hip dysplasia. If no health certificates are available – and these are optional – check what health screening has been done.

6. Responsible Bulldog breeders should provide you with a written contract and health guarantee and allow you plenty of time to read it. They will also show you records of the puppy's visits to the vet, vaccinations, worming medication, etc. and explain what other vaccinations your puppy will need.

7. They feed their adults and puppies high quality 'premium' dog food – a good diet is especially important for Bulldogs. A good breeder will give you guidance on feeding and caring for your puppy and will be available for advice even after you take your puppy home.

8.. They don't always have puppies available, but will keep a list of interested people for the next available litter.

9. They don't overbreed their females. A Bulldog bitch should not have her first litter until two or three years old. Some vets think back-to-back breedings are acceptable (i.e. a litter every heat cycle), but many good breeders will only allow one litter a year from their females, and then only three litters in her lifetime. Bulldogs have a relatively short lifespan, typically eight to 10 years, and breeding from older females can be detrimental to their health.

10. And finally … good Bulldog breeders want to know their beloved pups are going to good homes and will ask YOU a lot of questions about your suitability as owners. DON'T buy a puppy from a website or advert where a Paypal or credit card deposit secures you a puppy without any questions. Puppies are not inanimate objects, they are warm-blooded, living breathing creatures and you need to make sure that the one you select will be suitable. A good breeder will, if asked, provide references of other people who have bought their puppies, make sure you call at least one before you commit. They will also agree to take a puppy back within a certain time frame if it does not work out for you, or if there is a health problem.

Healthy, happy puppies and adult dogs are what everybody wants. Taking the time now to find a responsible and committed breeder with well-bred Bulldog puppies is time well spent. It could save you a lot of time, money and heartache in the future and help to ensure that you and your chosen puppy are happy together for many years.

The Most Important Questions to Ask a Breeder

Many of these points have been covered in the previous section, but here's a reminder and checklist of the questions you should be asking.

1. Have the parents been health screened? Ask to see original copies of heart, hip and any other health certificates. If no certificates are available, ask what guarantees the breeder

is offering in terms of genetic illnesses, and how long these guarantees last – 12 weeks, a year, a lifetime? It will vary from breeder to breeder, but good ones will definitely give you some form of guarantee – always ask for this in writing.

They will also want to be informed of any hereditary health problems with your puppy, as they may choose not to breed from the dam or sire (mother or father) again. Some breeders keep a chart documenting the full family health history of the pup – ask if one exists and if you can see it.

2. Can you put me in touch with someone who already has one of your puppies?

3. Are you a member of one of the Bulldog associations or clubs, and are you listed as a recommended breeder? (If not, why not?)

4. How long have you been breeding Bulldogs? You are looking for someone who has a track record with the breed.

5. How many litters has the mother had? Female Bulldogs should not have litters until they are two or three years old and then only have perhaps three litters in their lifetime. Many more and the breeder may be a "puppy mill", churning out cute – and expensive - pups for a fast buck.

6. Do you breed any other types of dog? Buy from a Bulldog specialist.

7. What is so special about this litter? You are looking for a breeder who has used good breeding stock and his or her knowledge to produce **healthy, handsome dogs with good temperaments**, not just dogs with massive heads and wide shoulders. All Bulldog puppies look cute, don't buy the first one you see – be patient and pick the right one. If you don't get a satisfactory answer, look elsewhere.

8. What do you feed your adults and puppies? Bulldogs do not do well on cheap feed bulked up with corn. A reputable breeder will certainly feed a top quality dog food and advise that you do the same.

9. What special care do you recommend? Your Bulldog will probably need all or some of the following: regular eye, ear, tail and wrinkle cleaning.

10. What is the average life span of your Bulldogs? Generally, pups bred from healthy stock and those which are free whelped (born naturally) live longer.

11. Why aren't you asking me any questions? A responsible breeder will be committed to making a good match between the new owners and their puppies. If the breeder spends more time discussing money than the welfare of the puppy and how you will care for him,

you can draw your own conclusions as to what his or her priorities are – and they probably don't include improving the breed. Walk away.

TOP TIPS: Take your puppy to a veterinarian – always try and find one who knows Bulldogs – to have a thorough check-up **within 48 hours** of purchase. If your vet is not happy with the health of the dog, no matter how painful it may be, return the pup to the breeder. Keeping an unhealthy puppy will only cause more distress and expense in the long run.

If you are buying a purebred (pedigree) Bulldog, the puppy will have official AKC or Kennel Club papers; make sure you are given original copies of these. If they are not available, then the puppy is not a true purebred/pedigree registered with the Kennel Clubs - no matter what the breeder says. Some top breeders may place restrictions on the sale. For example they may say that you cannot breed from your Bulldog, or that if your female has puppies, they have first pick of the litter.

In the UK, ask if the puppy is being sold with a Bulldog Breed Council Puppy Contract. These protect both buyer and seller by providing information on diet, worming, vaccination and veterinary visits from the birth of the puppy until it leaves the breeder.

Do your research before you go to see the litter, as once you are there the cute Bulldog puppies will undoubtedly be irresistible, and you will buy with your heart rather than your head. If you have any doubts at all about the breeder or the puppy, WALK AWAY.

Top 12 Tips for Choosing a Healthy Bulldog Puppy

1. Bulldogs are chunky and your puppy should have a well-fed appearance. They should NOT, however, have a distended abdomen (pot belly) as this can be a sign of worms (or Cushing's disease in adults.) The ideal puppy should not be too thin either. You should not be able to see his ribs.

2. His nostrils should be round, not slits, enabling him to breathe more easily and quietly. His nose should be cool, damp and clean with no discharge. Avoid choosing a puppy with very heavy skin folds/rolls around his nose, sometimes they will get proportionately smaller as the pup grows, but if they remain large they will need regular, even daily, cleaning as they become a breeding ground for bacteria.

3. Eye problems are not uncommon. The pup's eyes should be bright and clear with no discharge or tear stain. Steer clear of a puppy which blinks a lot, this could be the sign of a problem.

4. The pup's ears should be clean with no sign of discharge, soreness or redness.

5. Many breeds' appearance changes a great deal between puppyhood and adulthood – wrinkles disappear, noses and legs grow long and they generally look much different after a couple of years. Bulldogs do not; the puppy looks a lot like the adult dog. If your pup has big facial

wrinkles and very short legs, for example, he will have these as an adult. Pick one displaying the physical traits you want.

6. Gums should be clean and a healthy pink color.

7. Check the puppy's bottom to make sure it is clean and there are no signs of diarrhea. What sort of tail has he got? In the UK, a straight tail is recommended rather than a tight tail – although the straight tail is not as common in the US. In all events, avoid a corkscrew tail, the hidden pocket underneath will require regular cleaning to prevent infection.

8. A Bulldog's coat should be clean with no signs of ticks or fleas. Red or irritated skin or bald spots could be a sign of infestation or a skin condition. Also check between the toes of the paws for signs of redness or swelling, the breed is prone to interdigital cysts.

9. The puppy should breathe normally with no coughing or wheezing. Watch him run around and then listen to his breathing – does it sound normal or labored?

11. Choose a puppy that is solid in build and moves freely without any sign of injury or lameness. The Bulldog's gait (movement) is unusual. He walks or skips with short, quick steps, keeping low – appearing to skim across the ground. He may also lead with one shoulder, like a horse in canter. It is sometimes referred to as "a rolling gait" and however unusual, it should be a fluid movement, not jerky or stiff, which could be a sign of joint problems.

10. When the puppy is distracted, clap or make a noise behind him - not too loud- to make sure he is not deaf.

12. Finally, ask to see veterinary records to confirm your puppy has been wormed and had his first injections. If you are unlucky enough to have a health problem with your pup within the first few months, a reputable breeder will allow you to return the pup. Also, if you get the Bulldog puppy home and things don't work out for whatever reason, good breeders should also take the puppy back. Make sure this is the case before you commit.

Choosing the Right Temperament

If you've decided that a Bulldog is the ideal dog for you, then here are two important points to bear in mind at the outset:

1. Find a responsible breeder with a good reputation, we can't stress that enough.

2. Secondly, take your time. Choosing a puppy which will share your home and your life for the next decade is an important decision. Don't rush it.

You've picked a Bulldog because you really like the way these dogs look and their temperament, and maybe because they are one of the very few impressive-looking breeds which doesn't need a huge amount of exercise and is suited to apartment living. Presumably you're planning on spending a lot of time with your new puppy, as Bulldogs love being with humans.

Individuals - The next thing to remember is that while different Bulldogs may share many characteristics and temperament traits, each puppy also has his own individual character, just like humans.

The generally placid temperament of the Bulldog suits most people. However, if you are buying a puppy, visit the breeder more than once to see how your chosen pup interacts and get an idea of his character in comparison to his littermates. If you are rescuing or adopting an adult dog, make sure you are ready to cope with any health or behavior problems – such as chewing – which may arise.

Some Bulldog puppies will run up to greet you, pull at your shoelaces and playfully bite your fingers. Others will be more content to stay in the basket sleeping. Watch their behavior and energy levels. Which puppy will be most suitable?

Submissive or Dominant? - A submissive dog will by nature be more passive, less energetic and also possibly easier to train. A dominant dog will usually be more energetic and lively. They may also be more stubborn and need a firmer hand when training or socializing with other dogs.

There is no good or bad, it's a question of which type of character will best suit you and your lifestyle. Here are a couple of quick tests to try at the breeder's to see if your puppy has a submissive or dominant personality:

❖ Roll the Bulldog puppy gently on to his or her back in the crook of your arm (or on the floor). Then rest a hand on the pup's chest and look into his eyes for a few seconds. If he immediately struggles to get free, he is considered to be **dominant**. A puppy that doesn't struggle, but is happy to stay on his or her back has a more **submissive** character.

❖ A similar test is the suspension test. Gently lift the puppy at arm's length under the armpits for a few seconds while allowing his hind legs to dangle free. A dominant pup will kick and struggle to get free. A puppy that is happy to remain dangling is more submissive.

Useful Tips

Here are some other useful signs to look out for –

❖ Watch how he interacts with other Bulldog puppies in the litter. Does he try and dominate them, does he walk away from them or is he happy to play with his littermates? This may give you an idea of how easy it will be to socialize him with other dogs.

❖ After contact, does the pup want to follow you or walk away from you? Not following may mean he has a more independent nature.

❖ If you throw something for the puppy is he happy to retrieve it for you or does he ignore it? This may measure their willingness to work with humans.

❖ If you drop a bunch of keys behind the Bulldog puppy, does he act normally or does he flinch and jump away? The latter may be an indication of a timid or nervous disposition. Not reacting could also be a sign of deafness.

Decide which temperament would fit in with you and your family and the rest is up to you. A Bulldog that has constant positive interactions with people and other animals during the first three to four months of life will be a happier, more stable dog. In contrast, a puppy plucked from its family and isolated at home alone for weeks on end will be less happy, less socialized and may well have behavior problems later on.

Puppies are like children. Being properly raised contributes to their confidence, sociability, stability and intellectual development. The bottom line is that a pup raised in a warm, loving environment with people is likely to be more tolerant and accepting and less likely to develop behavior problems.

For those of you who prefer a scientific approach to choosing the right puppy, we are including the full **Volhard Puppy Aptitude Test (PAT).** This test has been developed by the highly respected Wendy and Jack Volhard who have built up an international reputation over the last 30 years for their invaluable contribution to dog training, health and nutrition. Their philosophy is: "We believe that one of life's great joys is living in harmony with your dog."

They have written several books and the Volhard PAT is regarded as the premier method for evaluating the nature of young puppies. Jack and Wendy have also written the excellent **Dog Training for Dummies** book. Visit their website at www.volhard.com for details of their upcoming dog training camps, as well as their training and nutrition groups.

The Volhard Puppy Aptitude Test

Here are the ground rules for performing the test:

- The testing is done in a location unfamiliar to the puppies. This does not mean they have to taken away from home. A 10-foot square area is perfectly adequate, such as a room in the house where the puppies have not been.

- The puppies are tested one at a time.

- There are no other dogs or people, except the scorer and the tester, in the testing area

- The puppies do not know the tester.

- The scorer is a disinterested third party and not the person interested in selling you a puppy.

- The scorer is unobtrusive and positions himself so he can observe the puppies' responses without having to move.

- The puppies are tested before they are fed.

- The puppies are tested when they are at their liveliest.

- Do not try to test a puppy that is not feeling well.

- Puppies should not be tested the day of or the day after being vaccinated.

Only the first response counts! *Tip: During the test, watch the puppy's tail. It will make a difference in the scoring whether the tail is up or down.*

The tests are simple to perform and anyone with some common sense can do them. You can, however, elicit the help of someone who has tested puppies before and knows what they are doing.

Social attraction - the owner or caretaker of the puppies places it in the test area about four feet from the tester and then leaves the test area. The tester kneels down and coaxes the puppy to come to him or her by encouragingly and gently clapping hands and calling. The tester must coax the puppy in the opposite direction from where it entered the test area. Hint: Lean backward, sitting on your heels instead of leaning forward toward the puppy. Keep your hands close to your body encouraging the puppy to come to you instead of trying to reach for the puppy.

Following - the tester stands up and slowly walks away encouraging the puppy to follow. Hint: Make sure the puppy sees you walk away and get the puppy to focus on you by lightly clapping your hands and using verbal encouragement to get the puppy to follow you. Do not lean over the puppy.

Restraint - the tester crouches down and gently rolls the puppy on its back for 30 seconds. Hint: Hold the puppy down without applying too much pressure. The object is not to keep it on its back but to test its response to being placed in that position.

Social Dominance - let the puppy stand up or sit and gently stroke it from the head to the back while you crouch beside it. See if it will lick your face, an indication of a forgiving nature. Continue stroking until you see a behavior you can score. Hint: When you crouch next to the puppy avoid leaning or hovering over it. Have the puppy at your side, both of you facing in the same direction.

Tip: During testing maintain a positive, upbeat and friendly attitude toward the puppies. Try to get each puppy to interact with you to bring out the best in him or her. Make the test a pleasant experience for the puppy.

Elevation Dominance - the tester cradles the puppy with both hands, supporting the puppy under its chest and gently lifts it two feet off the ground and holds it there for 30 seconds.

Retrieving - the tester crouches beside the puppy and attracts its attention with a crumpled up piece of paper. When the puppy shows some interest, the tester throws the paper no more than four feet in front of the puppy encouraging it to retrieve the paper.

Touch Sensitivity - the tester locates the webbing of one the puppy's front paws and presses it lightly between his index finger and thumb. The tester gradually increases pressure while counting to ten and stops when the puppy pulls away or shows signs of discomfort.

Sound Sensitivity - the puppy is placed in the centre of the testing area and an assistant stationed at the perimeter makes a sharp noise, such as banging a metal spoon on the bottom of a metal pan.

Sight Sensitivity - the puppy is placed in the centre of the testing area. The tester ties a string around a bath towel and jerks it across the floor, two feet away from the puppy.

Stability - an umbrella is opened about five feet from the puppy and gently placed on the ground.

During the testing, make a note of the heart rate of the pup, this is an indication of how it deals with stress, as well as its energy level.

Puppies come with high, medium or low energy levels. You have to decide for yourself, which suits your life style. Dogs with high energy levels need a great deal of exercise, and will get into mischief if this energy is not channeled into the right direction.

Finally, look at the overall structure of the puppy. You see what you get at 49 days age (seven weeks). If the pup has strong and straight front and back legs, with all four feet pointing in the same direction, it will grow up that way, provided you give it the proper diet and environment. If you notice something out of the ordinary at this age, it will stay with puppy for the rest of its life. He will not grow out of it.

Scoring the Results

Following are the responses you will see and the score assigned to each particular response. You will see some variations and will have to make a judgment on what score to give them –

Test	Response	Score
SOCIAL ATTRACTION	Came readily, tail up, jumped, bit at hands	1
	Came readily, tail up, pawed, licked at hands	2
	Came readily, tail up	3
	Came readily, tail down	4
	Came hesitantly, tail down	5
	Didn't come at all	6
FOLLOWING	Followed readily, tail up, got underfoot, bit at feet	1
	Followed readily, tail up, got underfoot	2
	Followed readily, tail up	3
	Followed readily, tail down	4
	Followed hesitantly, tail down	5
	Did not follow or went away	6
RESTRAINT	Struggled fiercely, flailed, bit	1
	Struggled fiercely, flailed	2

	Settled, struggled, settled with some eye contact	3
	Struggled, then settled	4
	No struggle	5
	No struggle, strained to avoid eye contact	6
SOCIAL DOMINANCE	Jumped, pawed, bit, growled	1
	Jumped, pawed	2
	Cuddled up to tester and tried to lick face	3
	Squirmed, licked at hands	4
	Rolled over, licked at hands	5
	Went away and stayed away	6
ELEVATION DOMINANCE	Struggled fiercely, tried to bite	1
	Struggled fiercely	2
	Struggled, settled, struggled, settled	3
	No struggle, relaxed	4
	No struggle, body stiff	5
	No struggle, froze	6
RETRIEVING	Chased object, picked it up and ran away	1
	Chased object, stood over it and did not return	2
	Chased object, picked it up and returned with it to tester	3
	Chased object and returned without it to tester	4
	Started to chase object, lost interest	5
	Does not chase object	6
TOUCH SENSITIVITY	8-10 count before response	1
	6-8 count before response	2
	5-6 count before response	3
	3-5 count before response	4
	2-3 count before response	5
	1-2 count before response	6
SOUND SENSITIVITY	Listened, located sound and ran toward it barking	1
	Listened, located sound and walked slowly toward it	2
	Listened, located sound and showed curiosity	3
	Listened and located sound	4
	Cringed, backed off and hid behind tester 5	5
	Ignored sound and showed no curiosity	6
SIGHT SENSITIVITY	Looked, attacked and bit object	1
	Looked and put feet on object and put mouth on it	2
	Looked with curiosity and attempted to investigate, tail up	3
	Looked with curiosity, tail down	4
	Ran away or hid behind tester	5
	Hid behind tester	6
STABILITY	Looked and ran to the umbrella, mouthing or biting it	1
	Looked and walked to the umbrella, smelling it cautiously	2
	Looked and went to investigate	3
	Sat and looked, but did not move toward the umbrella	4
	Showed little or no interest	5
	Ran away from the umbrella	6

The scores are interpreted as follows:

Mostly 1s - Strong desire to be pack leader and is not shy about bucking for a promotion. Has a predisposition to be aggressive to people and other dogs and will bite. Should only be placed into a very experienced home where the dog will be trained and worked on a regular basis.

Tip: Stay away from the puppy with a lot of 1's or 2's. It has lots of leadership aspirations and may be difficult to manage. This puppy needs an experienced home. Not good with children.

Mostly 2s - Also has leadership aspirations. May be hard to manage and has the capacity to bite. Has lots of self-confidence. Should not be placed into an inexperienced home. Too unruly to be good with children and elderly people, or other animals. Needs strict schedule, loads of exercise and lots of training. Has the potential to be a great show dog with someone who understands dog behavior.

Mostly 3s - Can be a high-energy dog and may need lots of exercise. Good with people and other animals. Can be a bit of a handful to live with. Needs training, does very well at it and learns quickly. Great dog for second-time owner.

Mostly 4s - The kind of dog that makes the perfect pet. Best choice for the first time owner. Rarely will buck for a promotion in the family. Easy to train, and rather quiet. Good with elderly people, children, although may need protection from the children. Choose this pup, take it to obedience classes, and you'll be the star, without having to do too much work!

Tip: The puppy with mostly 3's and 4's can be quite a handful, but should be good with children and does well with training. Energy needs to be dispersed with plenty of exercise.

Mostly 5s - Fearful, shy and needs special handling. Will run away at the slightest stress in its life. Strange people, strange places, different floor or surfaces may upset it. Often afraid of loud noises and terrified of thunderstorms. When you greet it upon your return, may submissively urinate. Needs a very special home where the environment doesn't change too much and where there are no children. Best for a quiet, elderly couple. If cornered and cannot get away, has a tendency to bite.

Mostly 6s - So independent that he doesn't need you or other people. Doesn't care if he is trained or not - he is his own person. Unlikely to bond to you, since he doesn't need you. A great guard dog for gas stations! Do not take this puppy and think you can change him into a lovable bundle - you can't, so leave well enough alone.

Tip: Avoid the puppy with several 6's. It is so independent it doesn't need you or anyone. He is his own person and unlikely to bond to you.

The Scores - Few puppies will test with all 2's or all 3's, there'll be a mixture of scores.

For that first time, wonderfully easy to train, potential star, look for a puppy that scores with mostly 4's and 3's. Don't worry about the score on Touch Sensitivity - you can compensate for that with the right training equipment.

It's hard not to become emotional when picking a puppy - they are all so cute, soft and cuddly. Remind yourself that this dog is going to be with you for eight to 16 years. Don't hesitate to step back a little to contemplate your decision. Sleep on it and review it in the light of day.

Avoid the puppy with a score of 1 on the Restraint and Elevation tests. This puppy will be too much for the first-time owner.

It's a lot more fun to have a good dog, one that is easy to train, one you can live with and one you can be proud of, than one that is a constant struggle.

Getting a Dog From a Shelter

Don't overlook an animal shelter as a source for a good dog. Not all dogs wind up in a shelter because they are bad. After that cute puppy stage, when the dog grows up, it may become too much for its owner. Or, there has been a change in the owner's circumstances forcing him or her into having to give up the dog.

Most of the time these dogs are housetrained and already have some training. If the dog has been properly socialized to people, it will be able to adapt to a new environment. Bonding may take a little longer, but once accomplished, results in a devoted companion.

A Dog or a Bitch (Male or Female)?

When you have decided to get a Bulldog puppy and know how to find a good breeder, the next decision is whether to get a male or female.

The differences within the sexes are greater than the differences between the sexes. In other words, you can get a dominant female and a submissive male, or vice versa. There are, however, some general traits which are more common with one sex or another.

Bulldogs are sociable dogs and, unless they have had a bad experience, are not normally aggressive. However, un-neutered males – referred to as 'dogs' – are more likely to display aggression if confronted by aggression from other male dogs. The Bulldog will not pick a fight, but he will defend himself and whatever he regards as his territory – and this may include you or your children. An entire (un-neutered) male is also more likely to go wandering off on the scent of a female.

However, if it is the classic looks of the Bulldog which you love, then the huge head and chunky build are more apparent in the male, as females tend to be slightly smaller.

If you take a male Bulldog for a walk, you can expect him to stop at every lamp-post, trash can and interesting blade of grass to leave his mark by urinating. A female will tend to urinate far less often on a walk.

Female dogs, or bitches, generally tend to be less aggressive towards other dogs, except when they are raising puppies. With some breeds, families consider a female if they have young children, as a bitch may be more tolerant towards young creatures. However, virtually all Bulldogs, regardless of their gender, love children.

Female Bulldogs can be messy when they come into heat every six months, due to the blood loss. If your princess is not spayed, you will also have the nuisance of becoming a magnet for all the free-wandering male dogs in your neighborhood.

Unless you bought your Bulldog specifically for breeding, it is recommended you have your dog neutered, or spayed if she is a female. If you plan to have two or more Bulldogs living together, this is even more advisable. Bear in mind that when you select your puppy, you should also be looking out for the right temperament as well as the right sex.

Puppy Checklist

Here's a list of things you ought to think about getting before bringing your puppy home:

- ✓ A dog bed or basket

- ✓ Bedding – old towels or a blanket which can easily be washed

- ✓ If possible, a towel or piece of cloth which has been rubbed on the puppy's mother to put in his bed

- ✓ A collar and leash

- ✓ An identification tag for the puppy's collar

- ✓ Food and water bowls, preferably stainless steel

- ✓ Lots of newspapers for housetraining (potty training)

- ✓ Poo(p) bags

- ✓ Puppy food – find out what the breeder is feeding

- ✓ Puppy treats

- ✓ Toys and chews suitable for puppies

- ✓ A puppy coat if you live in a cool climate

- ✓ A crate if you decide to use one

- ✓ Old towels for cleaning your puppy and covering the crate.

- AND PLENTY OF TIME!

Later on you'll also need a larger collar, a longer lead, a grooming brush, dog shampoo and flea and worming products and maybe other items such as a harness or a travel crate.

Vaccinations

When your new puppy arrives home, you need to make an appointment with your veterinarian to have your puppy checked over. He will also need to complete his vaccinations if he hasn't already had them all. All puppies need these shots.

The usual schedule is for the pup to have his first vaccination at or after seven weeks old. This will protect him from a number of diseases in one shot. These may include Canine Parvovirus (Parvo), Distemper, Infectious Canine Hepatitis (Adenvirus), Leptospirosis and Kennel Cough. In the USA, puppies may also need vaccinating separately against Rabies and Lyme Disease.

He will need a second and maybe a third vaccination a few weeks later to complete his immunity. Consult your vet to find out exactly what injections are needed for the area you live in.

Diseases such as Parvo and Kennel Cough are highly contagious and you should not let your puppy mix with other dogs - unless they are your own and have already been vaccinated - until he has completed his vaccinations, otherwise he will not be fully immunized. You also shouldn't take him to places where unvaccinated dogs might have been, like the local park.

Your dog will need a booster injection every year of his life. Your vet should give you a record card or send you a reminder, but it's a good idea to keep a note of the date in your diary.

Vaccinations are generally quite safe and side effects are uncommon. If your puppy is unlucky enough to be one of the very few that has an adverse reaction to the shots, here are the signs to look out for, a pup may have one or more of these:

Mild Reaction - Sleepiness, irritability and not wanting to be touched. Sore or a small lump at the place where he was injected. Nasal discharge or sneezing. Puffy face and ears.

Severe Reaction - Anaphylactic shock. A sudden and quick reaction, usually before leaving the vet's, which causes breathing difficulties. Vomiting, diarrhea, staggering and seizures.

A severe reaction is extremely rare. There is a far, far greater risk of your puppy being ill and spreading disease if he does not have the vaccinations.

All puppies need worming. Usually the breeder will give the puppies their first dose of worming medication before they leave the litter. Get the details and inform the vet exactly what treatment, if any, your pup has already had.

Bringing a New Puppy Home

First of all, make sure that you have puppy-proofed your home. Most Bulldog puppies are mini chewing machines and so remove anything breakable and/or chewable within the puppy's reach – including wooden furniture. Obviously you cannot remove your kitchen cupboards, doors, skirting boards and other fixtures and fittings, so don't leave him unattended for any length of time where he can chew something which is hard to replace, or build a barrier or use a baby gate to confine him to one room.

You may also want to remove your precious oriental rugs and keep the pup off your expensive carpets until he is fully housetrained and has stopped chewing everything in sight. Not all Bulldog puppies chew a lot, but most do. Giving him something he can chew will help – but don't give him old shoes and slippers, or he will think your footwear is fair game.

Designate a place within your home which will be the puppy's area. An area with a wooden or tiled floor would be a good start until he or she is housetrained. Make sure that the area is warm enough, but not too warm. Bullies are extremely sensitive to temperature fluctuations and cannot tolerate heat (it does not have to be baking hot for a Bulldog to overheat), nor can they tolerate cold. Make sure he is out of any drafts and if you live in a hot climate, he may need to be in an air conditioned room.

It should not take your new arrival too long to get used to his new surroundings, but the first few days will be very traumatic and he will probably whine a lot. Imagine a small child being taken away from his mother; that is how your Bulldog pup will feel.

If you have a garden or a yard that you intend letting your puppy roam in, make sure that every little gap has been plugged. You'd be amazed at the tiny holes they can escape through. Also, don't leave him unattended, Bullies are highly sought-after and can be targeted by unscrupulous thieves.

In order for your puppy to grow into a well-adjusted dog, he has to feel comfortable and relaxed in his new surroundings. He is leaving the warmth and protection of his mother and littermates and so for the first few days at least, your puppy will feel very sad. It is important to make the transition from the birth home to your home as easy as possible.

His life is in your hands. How you react and interact with him in the first few days and weeks will shape your relationship and his character for the years ahead.

The First Few Days

This can be a very stressful time for a Bulldog puppy and a worrying time for new owners. Your puppy has just been taken away from his mother, brothers and sisters and is feeling very sorry for himself. Our website receives many emails from worried new owners. Here are some of the most common concerns:

❖ My puppy sleeps all the time, is this normal?

❖ My puppy won't stop crying or whining

❖ My puppy is shivering

❖ My puppy won't eat

❖ My puppy is very timid

❖ My puppy follows me everywhere, she won't let me out of her sight

Most of the above are quite common. They are just a young pup's reaction to leaving his mother and littermates and entering into a strange new world. It is normal for puppies to sleep most of the time, just like babies.

It is also normal for some puppies to whine a lot during the first few days. Make your new pup as comfortable as possible, ensuring he has a warm, quiet place which is his, where he is not pestered by children or other pets. Talk in a soft, reassuring voice to him and handle him gently, while giving him plenty time to sleep.

Unless they are especially dominant, most puppies will be nervous and timid for the first few days. They will think of you as their new mother and may follow you around the house. This is also quite natural, but after a few days, start to leave your puppy for a few minutes at a time, gradually building up the time. If you are never parted, he may develop separation anxiety when you do have to leave him. (See our section on **Separation Anxiety in Chapter 9)**

What is Normal?

If your routine means you are normally out of the house for a few hours during the day, try to get your puppy on a Friday or Saturday so she has at least a couple of days to adjust to her new surroundings. A far better idea is to book at least a week off work to help your puppy settle in. If you don't work, leave your diary free for the first couple of weeks. Getting a new pup and helping him settle in properly is virtually a full-time job in the beginning.

Before you collect your Bulldog, let the breeder know when you are coming and ask him or her not to feed him for three or four hours beforehand. He will be less likely to be car sick and should be hungry when he arrives in his new home. The same applies to an adult dog moving to a new home.

It is normal for a new puppy to sleep for most of the time when you bring him home. Make sure he gets plenty of rest and if you have children, don't let them constantly waken the pup, he needs his sleep. Don't invite friends round to see your new puppy for at least 24 hours, preferably longer. However excited you are, he needs a quiet day or two with you or you and your family.

It is a frightening time for your puppy. Talk softly to him and gently stroke him. If you can, bring home a piece of cloth which has been rubbed with his mother's scent and put it in his bed. Is your puppy shivering with cold or is it nerves? Make sure he is in a warm, safe, quiet place away from any draughts and loud noises. Talk to him and stroke him gently, he needs plenty of reassurance.

If your puppy won't eat, spend time gently coaxing him to eat something. If he leaves his food, take it away and try it later. Do not leave it down for him all of the time or he may get used to turning his nose up at food. The next time you put something down for him, he is more likely to be hungry.

The puppy is following you as you have taken the place of his mother. Encourage him to follow you by patting your leg and calling him and when he does, praise him for doing so – but remember to start leaving him for a few minutes after a few days.

If your puppy is crying, it is probably for one of the following reasons:

- ❖ he's hungry or lonely
- ❖ he wants attention from you
- ❖ he needs to go to the toilet

If it is none of these, then check his body to make sure she hasn't picked up an injury.

Try not to fuss over him, if he whimpers, just reassure him with a quiet word. If he cries loudly and tries to get out, he probably needs to go to the toilet. Get up (yes, sorry, this IS best) and take him outside. Praise him if he goes to the toilet and take him back inside until you are ready to get up.

The strongest bonding period for a puppy is between eight and 12 weeks of age. The most important factors in bonding with your puppy are TIME spent with him and PATIENCE, even when he makes a mess in the house or chews your furniture.

Remember, he is just a baby and it takes time to learn not to do these things. Spend the time to love and train your Bulldog pup and you will have a loyal friend for life who will always be there for you and never let you down.

Where Should He Sleep?

Bulldogs have a strong instinct to want to bond with humans. That emotional attachment between you and your Bulldog may grow to become one of the most important aspects of your - and his - life.

You have to think carefully about where you want your Bully to sleep – and before you immediately say "the bedroom," bear in mind the following: Bulldogs generally snore, they snuffle, belch and fart! If he is to sleep outside your bedroom, put him in a comfortable bed of his own, or a crate if you train him (a dog should never be imprisoned in a crate) – and then block your ears for the first couple of nights. He will almost certainly whine and whimper, but this won't last long and he will soon get used to sleeping on his own, without his littermates or you.

Don't let your pup sleep on the bed. He will not be housetrained and he will grow into an adult weighing anything from 40lb to 55lb. Dogs are very hierarchical and a puppy needs to learn his place in the household – and it has to be below you in the pecking order if you don't want him to rule your life. If you decide to let him on the bed later, that's up to you.

If you want your pup to sleep in your bedroom, initially put him in a crate with a soft blanket or in a high-sided cardboard box he can't climb out of. Put newspapers underneath, as he will not be able to last the night without urinating. Some owners do allow their dogs to sleep on the bed, but it is not conducive to a good night's sleep – especially if you have a large male Bulldog who will eventually take up most of the bed. It may also create problems with separation anxiety later on.

You could consider letting him sleep in the bedroom for a couple of nights until he gets used to your home, but some breeders do not recommend this as it is then harder to turf him out later. Bite the bullet, get some earplugs and make his bed separate from yours.

Crate Training

If you are unfamiliar with them, crates may seem like a cruel punishment for a dog. On the other hand some people, including some trainers, breeders and people who show dogs, recommend their use to train a puppy and make him feel secure. It's true to say they are used more in the USA than elsewhere.

If you use a crate, then remember that it is NOT a prison to restrain the dog. It should only be used in a humane manner and time should be spent to make the puppy feel like the crate is his own safe little haven. If the door is closed on the crate, your Bulldog must ALWAYS have access to water while inside his crate. He also needs bedding in there and it's a good idea to put a chew in as well.

We tried our dog with a crate when he was a young puppy and he howled and whined every time he went in. In the end, we couldn't bear to hear the noise and so we abandoned it. It is now in the porch at our house and makes a very useful storage place for Wellington boots and running shoes. Now, several years later, having heard from so many of our American readers about how much their dogs love their crates, perhaps we gave up too easily. If used correctly and if time is spent getting the puppy used to the crate, it can be a valuable tool. But crates are not for every Bulldog and they should NEVER be used as a means of imprisoning the dog because you are out of the house all day.

Bulldogs are not like hamsters or pet mice which can adapt to life in a cage. They are pack animals and companion dogs which thrive on physically being close to their human owners. Being caged all day is a miserable existence for them.

If you do decide to use a crate, maybe to put your dog in for short periods while you leave the house to stop him chewing, or at night, the best place to locate it is in the corner of a room away from cold draughts or too much heat. Bulldogs like to be near their pack - which is you. Leave him where he can hear you. Some owners make the crate their dog's only bed, so he feels comfortable and safe in there.

The crate should be large enough to allow your dog to stretch out flat on his side without being cramped, be able to turn round easily and to sit up without hitting his head on the top. The crate in our photo is only just big enough for the dog, a larger one would be better. The sides are also covered, which could make this crate too hot for a Bulldog. Air should be able to circulate around the crate. Bear in mind that a Bulldog is chunky, rather than flexible, so needs enough room to turn round comfortably.

The Association of Pet Dog Trainers suggests a crate size of around 42 inches and a width of 30 inches to 36 inches high for Bulldogs. Dogs do not like to foul their sleeping quarters, a large crate may allow your dog to eliminate at one end and sleep at the other, but this may slow down his housetraining. If you are buying a crate for your puppy buy big enough for a fully-grown Bulldog, get adjustable crate dividers to block part of it off while he is small so that he feels safe and secure.

Crates aren't for every owner or dog. But, used correctly, a crate can help to:

- ❖ Housetrain (potty train) your dog

- ❖ Keep your dog safe when travelling

- ❖ Create a doggie bedroom or place where your Bulldog feels safe

If you decide to use one, you'll need to know a couple of things regarding Bulldogs. Firstly, only consider a wire crate where the air can pass easily through. Do not get a plastic crate as your Bully might easily overheat. Secondly, make doubly sure that the crate is not left in bright sunlight inside the house – ensure that the chosen place is shady throughout the day.

Once you've got your crate, you'll need to learn how to use it properly so that it becomes a safe, comfortable haven for your dog and not a prison. Here is one tried-and-tested method of getting your puppy firstly to accept it, and then to actually want to spend time in there.

Initially a pup might not be too happy about going inside, but he will be a lot easier to crate train than an adult dog, which may have got used to having the run of your house. These are the first steps:

- ❖ Drop a few tasty puppy treats around and then inside the crate

- ❖ Put your puppy's favorite bedding in there

- ❖ Keep the door open

- ❖ Give all of your puppy's meals to him inside the crate. Again, keep the door open.

Place a chew or treat INSIDE the crate and close the door while your puppy is OUTSIDE the crate. He will be desperate to get in there. Open the door, let him in and praise him for going in. Fasten a long-lasting chew inside the crate and leave the door open. Let your puppy go inside to spend some time eating the chew.

After a while, close the crate door and feed him some treats through the mesh while he is in there. At first just do it for a few seconds at a time, then gradually increase the time. If you do it too fast, he will become distressed.

Slowly build up the amount of time he is in the crate. For the first few days, stay in the room, then gradually leave for a short time, first one minute, then three, then 10, 30 and so on.

Next Steps

- ❖ Put your dog in his crate at regular intervals during the day - maximum two hours

- ❖ Don't crate only when you are leaving the house. Place the dog in the crate while you are home as well. Use it as a "safe" zone

- ❖ By using the crate both when you are home and while you are gone, your dog becomes comfortable there and not worried that you won't come back, or that you are leaving him alone. This helps to prevent separation anxiety later in life

- ❖ Give him a chew and remove his collar, tags and anything else which could become caught in an opening or between the bars

- ❖ Make it very clear to any children that the crate is NOT a playhouse for them, but a "special room" for the dog

- ❖ Although the crate is your dog's haven and safe place, it must not be off-limits to humans. You should be able to reach inside at any time.

The next point is important if crate training is to succeed:

- ❖ Do not let your dog immediately out of the crate if he barks or whines, or he will think that this is the key to opening the door. Wait until the barking or whining has stopped for at least 10 seconds before letting him out

If you do decide to use a crate, remember that a dog is not normally a caged animal. Use the crate for limited periods and only if your dog is comfortable in there. NEVER force a dog to go in and then lock him in for hours on end. Better to find him a new, happier home.

Following these guidelines is a good start – but it is only the beginning. Read the other chapters on how to care for and train your puppy so that you and your new best friend can have many years of happiness together.

5. Feeding Your Bulldog

Your Bulldog may appear extremely sturdy, but that tough exterior is covering a delicately balanced interior. And to keep his or her whole biological machine in good working order, your Bully needs the right fuel, just like a finely-tuned sports car.

Feeding the correct diet is more important with Bulldogs that with most other breeds, which is why most Bulldog breeders provide new owners with a feeding chart and a quantity of puppy food. **The correct diet is an essential part of keeping your Bulldog fit and healthy.**

However, the topic of feeding your dog the right diet is something of a minefield. Owners are bombarded with endless choices as well as countless adverts from dog food companies, all claiming that theirs is best.

There is not one food that will give every single dog the brightest eyes, the shiniest coat, the most energy, the best digestion, the longest life and stop him from scratching or having skin problems. Dogs are individuals just like people, which means that you could feed a premium food to a group of dogs and find that most of them do great on it, some not so well, while a few may get an upset stomach or even an allergic reaction. The question is: "Which food is best for my Bulldog?"

If you have been given a recommended food from a breeder, rescue centre or previous owner, it is best to stick to this. A good breeder will know which food their Bulldogs thrive on. If you do decide - for whatever reason - to change diet, then this must be done gradually.

There are many different food options for dogs. The most popular manufactured foods include dry complete diets, tinned food (with or without a biscuit mixer), and semi-moist. Some dog foods contain only natural ingredients. Then there is the option of feeding your dog a home-made diet; some owners swear by a raw diet, while others feed their dogs vegetarian food.

Within the manufactured options, there are many different qualities of food. Usually you get what you pay for, so a more expensive food is more likely to provide better nutrition for your dog - in terms of minerals, nutrients and high quality meats – rather than a cheap one, which will most likely contain a lot of grain.

Dried foods (also called kibble in the USA) tend to be less expensive than other foods. They have improved a lot over the last few years and some of the more expensive ones are now a good choice for a healthy, complete diet. Dried foods also contain the least fat and the most preservatives.

Our dog Max, who has inhalant allergies, is on a quality dried food called James Wellbeloved. It contains natural ingredients and the manufacturers claim it is "hypoallergenic," i.e. good for dogs with allergies. Max seems to do well on it, but not all dogs thrive on dried food. We tried several other foods first, it is a question of each owner finding the best food for their dog. If you got your dog from a good breeder, they should be able to advise you on this.

TIP: Beware of buying a food just because it is described as '***premium',*** many manufacturers blithely use this word, but there are no official guidelines as to what premium means. Always check the ingredients on any food sack, packet or tin to see which ingredients are listed first, and it should be meat or poultry, not corn or grain. If you are in the USA, look for a dog food which has been endorsed by AAFCO (Association of American Feed Control Officials).

In general, tinned foods are 60-70% water. Often semi-moist foods contain a lot of artificial substances and sugar, which is maybe why some dogs seem to love them!

Choosing the right food for your Bulldog is important, it will certainly influence his health, coat and even temperament. There are also three stages of your dog's life to consider when feeding: puppy, adult and senior (also called veteran). Each of these represents a different physical stage of his life and you need to choose the right food to cope with his body during each particular phase. Also, a pregnant female will require a special diet to cope with the extra demands on her body. This is especially important as she nears the latter stages of pregnancy.

Some Bulldog owners feed two different meals to their dog each day to provide variety. One meal could be dried kibble, while the other might be home-made, with fresh meat, poultry and vegetables. If you do this, speak with your vet to make sure the two separate meals provide a balanced diet and that they are not too rich in protein.

This book will not recommend one brand of dog food over another, but we do have some general tips to help you choose what to feed your Bulldog. There is also some advice for owners of Bulldogs with food allergies. Sufferers may itch, lick or chew their paws and/or legs, or rub their face. They may also get frequent ear infections as well as redness and swelling on their face.

Switching to a grain-free diet can help to alleviate the symptoms, as your dog's digestive system does not have to work as hard. In the wild, a dog or wolf's staple diet would be meat with some vegetable matter from the stomach and intestines of the herbivores (plant eating animals) he ate – but no grains. Dogs do not digest corn or wheat (which are often staples of cheap commercial dog food) very efficiently. Grain-free diets still provide carbohydrates through fruits and vegetables, so your dog still gets all his nutrients.

Top 16 Tips for Feeding your Bulldog

1. If you choose a manufactured food, **don't pick one where meat or poultry content is NOT the first item listed on the bag.** Foods with lots of cheap cereals or sugar are not the best choice for many dogs, particularly finely balanced ones.

2. Some Bulldogs suffer from sensitive skin, "hot spots" or allergies. A cheap dog food, often bulked up with grain, will only make this worse. If this is the case, bite the bullet and **choose a high quality – usually more expensive - food.** You'll probably save money in vets' bills in the long run and your dog will be happier. A food may be described as "hypoallergenic" on the sack, this means "less likely to cause allergies" and is a good place to start.

3. **Feed your Bulldog twice a day**, rather than once. Bullies are gassy dogs and two smaller feeds will reduce flatulence as well as the risk of gastric torsion, or bloat (see **Chapter 9 Health**). Puppies need to be fed more often, discuss exactly how often with the breeder.

4. **Establish a feeding regime and stick to it**. Dogs like routine. If you are feeding twice a day, feed once in the morning and then again at tea-time. Stick to the same times of day. Do not give the last feed too late, or your dog's body will not have chance to process or burn off the food before sleeping. He will also need a walk or letting out in the garden or yard after his second feed to allow him to go to the toilet. Feeding at the same times each day also helps your dog establish a toilet regime.

5. **Take away any uneaten food between meals.** Most Bullies LOVE their food, but they can become fussy eaters if it is available all day. Imagine if your dinner was left on the table for hours until you finished it. Returning to the table two or three hours later would not be such a tempting prospect, but coming back for a fresh meal would be far more appetizing. Also when food is left down all day, some dogs seem to take the food for granted and lose their appetite. Then they begin to leave the food and you are at your wits' end trying to find a food that they will actually eat. Put the food bowl down twice a day and then take it up after 20 minutes – even if he has left some. If he is healthy and hungry, he will look forward to his next meal and soon stop leaving food. If your dog does not eat anything for days, it could well be a sign that something is wrong with him.

6. **Do not feed too many tidbits and treats between meals.** Bulldogs are often greedy and prone to obesity, which is a dangerous condition. Already a chunky breed, your Bully cannot afford to carry extra weight as it will place extra strain on his organs and joints, have a detrimental effect on his health and even his lifespan. It also throws his balanced diet out of the window. Try to avoid feeding your dog from the table or your plate, as this encourages attention-seeking behavior and drooling.

7. **NEVER feed the following items to your dog**: grapes, raisins, chocolate, onions, Macadamia nuts, any fruits with seeds or stones, tomatoes, avocadoes, rhubarb, tea, coffee or alcohol. ALL of these are poisonous to dogs.

8. **If you do feed leftovers to your Bully, feed them INSTEAD of a balanced meal,** not as well as. High quality dog foods are already made up to provide all the nutrients, vitamins, minerals and calories that your dog needs. Feeding tidbits or leftovers may be too rich for your dog in addition to his regular diet and cause him to scratch or have other problems, as well as get fat. You can feed your dog vegetables such as carrots as a healthy low-calorie treat, most dogs love 'em.

9. **Check your dog's weight regularly.** Obesity in Bulldogs, as well as being generally unhealthy, can lead to the development of some serious health issues, such as diabetes. Although the weight will vary from one dog to another, a good rule of thumb is that your Bulldog's tummy should be higher than his rib cage. If his belly hangs down below it, he is overweight.

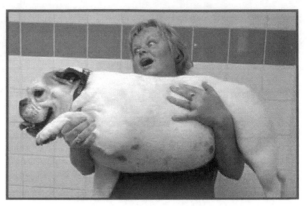

10. **If you switch to a new food, do the transition gradually.** Unlike humans, dogs' digestive systems cannot handle sudden changes in diet. Begin by gradually mixing some of the new food in with the old and increase the proportion so that after seven to eight days, all the food is the new one.

    The following ratios are recommended by Doctors Foster & Smith Inc: Days 1-3 add 25% of the new food, Days 4-6 add 50%, Days 7-9 add 75%, Day 10 feed 100% of the new food. (By the way, if you stick to the identical brand, you can change flavors in one go.)

11. **Check your dog's feces** (aka stools, poo or poop!) If his diet is suitable, the food should be easily digested and produce dark brown, firm stools. If your dog produces soft or light stools, or has gas (even more than usual!) or diarrhea, then the diet may not suit him, so consult your vet or breeder for advice.

12. Bulldogs are prone to overheating, so a good idea is to **get him used to frozen yoghurt or ice pops (popsicles)** while he is young, as these will help him to keep cool throughout the rest of his life. Most dogs like ice cubes – and love popsicles. Just make some beef or chicken broth from a stock cube - low sodium is best - mixed with water and freeze it in ice cube trays. You can also freeze vegetables. Yoghurt is particularly good for gassy dogs and helps with general digestion, many Bulldog owners add a spoonful of (unfrozen) natural yoghurt to one of their pet's daily feeds.

13. **Never give your dog cooked bones,** as these can splinter and cause him to choke or suffer intestinal problems. It's also a good idea to avoid giving him rawhide, as Bulldogs have a tendency to chew and then swallow rawhide, without first bothering to nibble it down into smaller pieces.

14. Feed your dog in stainless steel dishes. Plastic bowls don't last as long and, more importantly, a Bulldog has a sensitive face and they can trigger a reaction in some. Ceramic bowls are best for keeping water cold.

15. **If you have more than one dog, feed them separately**. Bulldogs generally get on well with other pets, especially if introduced at an early age. But they are also greedy and feeding dogs together can lead to dog food aggression from your Bully, either protecting his own food or trying to eat the food designated for another pet.

16. And finally, **always make sure that your Bulldog has access to clean, fresh water.** Change the water and clean the bowl (which gets slimy!) regularly.

Types of Dog Food

We are what we eat. The right food is a very important part of a healthy lifestyle - and this is especially true for Bulldogs. Nutrition can affect general health, coat and skin, energy levels, temperament and even lifespan.

Here are several different types of food you can feed your Bully: dry, semi-moist, canned, frozen or freeze-dried are just some of the options. Or you might decide to feed a home-made or raw diet; this is an option increasingly being considered by owners of Bulldogs with food allergies or skin conditions.

Dry dog food

Often called kibble in the USA, this is a popular choice, particularly for dogs which get through a lot of food. It comes in different flavors and with differing ingredients to suit the various stages of a dog's life, it's also less expensive than many other foods. It's worth paying for a high quality dry food as cheaper ones may contain a lot of grain. Cheap foods are often false economy, particularly if your Bulldog does not tolerate grain/cereal very well. It may also mean that you have to feed larger quantities to ensure he gets sufficient nutrients.

Manufacturer Royal Canin has dried foods specially formulated for Bulldog puppies and adults. The company says of its adult Bulldog food: "Designed for Bulldogs from the age of 12 months, the special formulation helps to maintain the skin and coat of the Bulldog at its optimum condition." It claims that this food helps support healthy joints, has a special kibble to encourage

chewing and reduces stool odor. There are many other high quality manufactured foods popular with Bulldoggers.

Canned food

This is another popular choice – and it's often very popular with dogs too! They love the taste and it generally comes in a variety of flavors. Canned food is often mixed with dry kibble, and a small amount may be added to a dog on a dry food diet if he has lost interest in food. It tends to be more expensive than dried food and many owners don't like the mess.

A part-opened tin may have to be kept in the refrigerator between meals and it can have an overpowering smell when you open the fridge door. As with dry food, read the label closely. Generally, you get what you pay for and the origins of cheap canned dog food are often somewhat dubious. If you choose canned food, you may decide to feed this once daily and then kibble or other food for the second meal.

Semi-Moist

These are commercial dog foods shaped like pork chops, salamis, burgers or other meaty foods and they are the least nutritional of all dog foods. They are full of sugars, artificial flavorings and colorings to help make them visually appealing. Bulldogs don't care what their food looks like, they only care how it smells and tastes, the shapes are designed to appeal to us humans. While you may give your dog one as an occasional treat, they are not a diet in themselves and do

not provide the nutrition that your Bulldog needs. Steer clear of them for regular feeding.

Freeze-Dried

This is made by frozen food manufacturers for owners who like the convenience – this type of food keeps for six months to a year - or for those going on a trip with their dog. It says 'freeze-dried' on the packet and is highly palatable, but the freeze-drying process bumps up the cost.

Home-Cooked

Some dog owners want the ability to be in complete control of their dog's diet, know exactly what their dog is eating and to be absolutely sure that his nutritional needs are being met. Feeding your dog a home-cooked diet is time consuming and expensive, and the difficult thing – as with the raw diet - is sticking to it once you have started out with the best of intentions. But many owners think the extra effort is worth the peace of mind. If you decide to go ahead, you should spend the time to become proficient and learn about canine nutrition to ensure your dog gets all his vital nutrients.

Raw Food

If your dog is not doing well on a commercially-prepared dog food, you might consider a raw diet. There is evidence that they are becoming increasingly popular among owners. Raw food diets emulate the way dogs ate before the existence of commercial dog foods. After all, dry, canned and other styles of cooked food for dogs were mainly created as a means of convenience. Unfortunately, this convenience sometimes can affect a dog's health.

However, raw diets are not without controversy. Supporters argue that a carefully planned raw diet gives the dog numerous health benefits, including a healthier coat, more energy, cleaner teeth and a lack of bad breath and doggy odor.

Some nutritionists believe that dogs that eat raw whole foods tend to be healthier than those on other diets. They say there are inherent beneficial enzymes, vitamins, minerals and other qualities in meats, fruits, vegetables and grains in their natural forms that are denatured or destroyed when cooked. Many also believe dogs are less likely to have allergic reactions to the ingredients on this diet.

Critics say that the risks of nutritional imbalance, intestinal problems and food-borne illnesses, caused by handling and feeding raw meat, outweigh any benefits. Owners must pay strict attention to hygiene when preparing a raw diet. Their dog may also be more likely to ingest bacteria or parasites such as Salmonella, E.coli and Ecchinococcus.

Frozen food can be a valuable aid to the raw diet. The food is highly palatable, made from high quality ingredients and dogs usually love it. The downside is that not all pet food stores stock it and it is expensive.

One type of raw diet is the BARF diet (*Biologically Appropriate Raw Food* or *Bones And Raw Food*), created by Dr Ian Billinghurst. A typical BARF diet is made up of 60-80% of raw meaty bones (bones with about 50% meat, such as chicken neck, back and wings) and 20-40% of fruit and vegetables, offal, meat, eggs or dairy foods.

Another important point for Bulldog owners is that brachycephalic breeds (with short, broad skulls) have jaws and teeth conditions which are not suitable for this type of diet. If you decide you definitely want to feed your Bully a BARF or raw meaty bones diet, then you will have to do some reading and research. Consult your vet and speak to other Bulldog owners to find out exactly what is involved. There are also many discussions on this topic on the internet.

NOTE: Only start a raw diet if you are sure you have the time (and money) to keep it going.

You might also consider feeding two different daily meals to your dog. One dry kibble and one raw diet, for example. If you do, then read up around the subject, and consult your veterinarian to make sure that the two combined meals provide a balanced diet which is not too high in protein, some Bulldogs do not tolerate high protein foods. There are several Bulldog forums; post questions on them to find out what other Bulldoggers are feeding.

Bulldogs and Food Allergies

Symptoms

Dog food allergies affect about one in 10 dogs. They are the third most common canine allergy for after atophy (inhaled allergies) and flea bite allergies. While there's no scientific evidence of links between specific breeds and food allergies, there is anecdotal evidence from Bulldog owners that the breed has a higher-than-normal incidence of food allergies or intolerances.

Food allergies affect males and females in equal measures as well as neutered and intact pets. They can start when your dog is five months or 12 years old - although the vast majority start when the dog is between two and six years old. It is not uncommon for dogs with food allergies to also have other types of allergies.

If your Bulldog is not well, how do you know if the problem lies with his food or not? Here are some common symptoms of food allergies to look out for:

- ❖ Itchy skin (this is the most common). Your Bully may lick or chew his paws or legs and rub his face with his paws or on the furniture, carpet, etc.
- ❖ Excessive scratching
- ❖ Redness and inflammation on the chin and face.
- ❖ Ear infections
- ❖ Hair loss
- ❖ Hot patches of skin
- ❖ Recurring skin infections
- ❖ Increased bowel movements (maybe twice as often as usual)
- ❖ Skin infections that clear up with antibiotics but recur when the antibiotics run out.

Allergies or Intolerance?

There's a difference between dog food **allergies** and dog food **intolerance**:

Typical reactions to allergies are skin problems and/or itching

Typical reactions to intolerance are diarrhea and/or vomiting

Dog food intolerance can be compared to people who get diarrhea or an upset stomach from eating spicy food. Both can be cured by a change to a diet specifically suited to your dog, although a food allergy may be harder to get to the root cause of. As they say in the canine world: "One dog's meat is another dog's poison".

In the canine world generally, certain ingredients are more likely to cause allergies than others. In order of the most common triggers they are:

Beef, dairy products, chicken, wheat, eggs, corn, soy

Unfortunately, these most common offenders are also the most common ingredients in dog foods! By the way, don't think if you put your dog on a rice and lamb dog food diet that it will automatically cure the problem. It might, but then again there's a fair chance it won't. The reason lamb and rice were thought to be less likely to cause allergies is simply because they have not traditionally been included in dog food recipes - therefore less dogs had reactions to them.

It is also worth noting that a dog is allergic or sensitive to an **ingredient**, not to a particular brand of dog food, so it is very important to read the label on the sack or tin. If your Bully has a reaction to beef, for example, he will react to any food containing beef, regardless of how expensive it is or how well it has been prepared.

Symptoms of food allergies are well documented. Unfortunately, the problem is that these conditions may also be symptoms of other issues such as atophy (breathed-in) or contact allergies, flea bite allergies, intestinal problems, mange and yeast or bacterial infections. You can have a blood test on your dog for food allergies, but many veterinarians now believe that this is not accurate enough.

The only way to cure a food allergy or intolerance is complete avoidance. This is not as easy as it sounds. First you have to be sure that your dog does have a food allergy, and then you have to discover which food is causing the reaction. Blood tests are not thought to be reliable and, as far as I am aware, the only true way to determine exactly what your dog is allergic to, is to start a food trial. If you don't or can't do this for the whole 12 weeks, then you could try a more amateurish approach, which is eliminating ingredients from your dog's diet one at a time by switching diets – remember to do this over a period of a week to 10 days.

A food trial is usually the option of last resort, due to the amount of time and attention that it requires. It is also called '**an exclusion diet**' and is the only truly accurate way of finding out if your dog has a food allergy and what is causing it.

Before embarking on one, try switching dog food. A hypoallergenic dog food, either commercial or home-made, is a good place to start. There are a number of these on the market and they all have the word '*hypoallergenic*' in the name. Although usually more expensive, hypoallergenic dog food ingredients do not include common allergens such as wheat protein or soya, thereby minimizing the risk of an allergic reaction. Many may have less common ingredients, such as venison, duck or types of fish.

Here are some things to look for in a high quality food: meat or poultry as the first ingredient, vegetables, natural herbs such as rosemary or parsley, oils such as canola or salmon.

Here's what to avoid: corn, corn meal, corn gluten meal, meat or poultry by-products (as you don't know exactly what these are or how they have been handled), artificial preservatives (including BHA, BHT, Propyl Gallate, Ethoxyquin, Sodium Nitrite/Nitrate and TBHQBHA), artificial colors, sugars and sweeteners like corn syrup, sucrose and ammoniated glycyrrhizin, powdered cellulose, propylene glycol.

If you can rule out all of the above, and you have tried switching diet without much success, then a food trial may be the only option left.

Food Trials

Before you embark on one of these, you need to know that they are a real pain-in-the-you-know-what to monitor. You have to be incredibly vigilant and determined, so only start one if you 100% know you can see it through to the end, or you are wasting your time. It is important to keep a diary during a food trial to record any changes in your Bulldog's symptoms, behavior or habits.

A food trial involves feeding one specific food for 12 weeks, something the dog has never eaten before, such as rabbit and rice or venison and potato. Surprisingly, dogs are typically NOT allergic to foods they have never eaten before. The food should contain no added coloring, preservatives or flavorings.

There are a number of these commercial diets on the market, as well as specialized diets that have proteins and carbohydrates broken down into such small molecular sizes that they no longer trigger an allergic reaction. These are called **'limited antigen'** or **'hydrolyzed protein'** diets.

Home-made diets are another option as you can strictly control the ingredients. The difficult thing is that this must be the **only thing** the dog eats during the trial. Any treats or snacks make the whole thing a waste of time. During the trial, you shouldn't allow your dog to roam freely, as you cannot control what he is eating or drinking when he is out of sight outdoors.

Only the recommended diet must be fed. Do NOT give:

- ❖ Treats
- ❖ Rawhide (you shouldn't feed these to a Bully, anyway)
- ❖ Pigs' ears
- ❖ Cows' hooves
- ❖ Flavoured medications (including heartworm treatments) or supplements
- ❖ Flavored toothpastes
- ❖ Flavored plastic toys

If you want to give a treat, use the recommended diet. (Tinned diets can be frozen in chunks or baked and then used as treats.) If you have other dogs, either feed them all on the trial diet or feed the others in an entirely different location.

If you have a cat, don't let the dog near the cat litter tray. And keep your pet out of the room when you are eating. Even small amounts of food dropped on the floor or licked off of a plate can ruin an elimination trial, meaning you'll have to start all over again.

Bulldogs and Grain

Although beef is the food most likely to cause allergies in the general dog population, there is evidence to suggest that the ingredient most likely to cause a problem in many Bulldogs is grain. Grain is wheat or any other cultivated cereal crop.

Many Bully breeds (such as all types of Bulldog, Boxers, Staffies, Pugs, Bull Terriers, Boston Terriers) are prone to a build-up of yeast in the digestive system. Foods that are high in grains and sugar can cause an increase in unhealthy bacteria and yeast in the stomach. This crowds out the good bacteria in the stomach and can cause toxins to occur that affect the immune system.

When the immune system is not functioning properly the itchiness related to food allergies can cause secondary bacterial and yeast infections, which often show as ear infections, skin disorders, bladder infections and reddish or dark brown tear stains. Symptoms of a yeast infection also include:

- ❖ Itchiness
- ❖ A musty smell
- ❖ Skin lesions or redness on the underside of the neck, the belly or the feet (especially between the toes – interdigital cysts).

Although drugs such as antihistamines and steroids will temporarily help, they do not address the cause. Switching to a grain-free diet may help your dog get rid of the yeast and toxins. Many owners also feed their Bullies a daily spoonful of natural or live yoghurt, as this contains healthy bacteria and helps to balance the bacteria in your dog's digestive system (By the way, it works for humans too!)

Switching to a grain-free diet may help to get rid of yeast and bad bacteria in the digestive system. Introduce the new food over a week to 10 days and be patient, it may take two to three months for symptoms to subside – but you will definitely know if it has worked after 12 weeks.

It is worth noting that some of the symptoms of food allergies - particularly the scratching, licking and chewing and redness - can also be a sign of inhalant or contact (environmental) allergies, which are caused by a reaction to such triggers as pollen, grass or dust. Some dogs are also allergic to flea bites. See **Chapter 10 Bulldog Skin and Allergies** for more details.

If you suspect your Bully has a food allergy, the first port of call should be to the veterinarian to discuss the best course of action.

However, many vets' practices promote specific brands of dog food, which may or may not be the best for your dog. Don't buy anything without first checking every single ingredient on the label. The website www.dogfoodadvisor.com provides useful information with star ratings for grain-free and hypoallergenic dogs foods.

How Much Food?

This is another question which we are often asked on our website. The answer is ... there is no easy answer! The correct amount of food for your dog depends on a number of factors:

- ❖ Breed
- ❖ Gender
- ❖ Age
- ❖ Energy levels
- ❖ Amount of daily exercise
- ❖ Health
- ❖ Environment
- ❖ Number of dogs in house
- ❖ Quality of the food

Some breeds have a higher metabolic rate than others. Bulldogs are generally regarded as dogs with fairly low activity levels, but this is a bit misleading, as energy levels vary tremendously from individual dog to dog. Some Bulldogs, especially young ones, are full of energy.

Generally smaller dogs have faster metabolisms so require a higher amount of food per pound of body weight. Female dogs are slightly more prone to putting on weight than male dogs. Some people say that dogs which have been spayed or neutered are more likely to put on weight, although this is disputed by others. Growing puppies and young dogs need more food than senior dogs with a slower lifestyle.

Every dog is different, you can have two Bulldogs with different temperaments. The energetic dog will burn off more calories. Maintaining a healthy body weight for dogs – and humans – is all about balancing what you take in with how much you burn off. If your Bulldog is exercised a couple of times a day and has play sessions with humans or other dogs, he will need more calories than a couch potato Bulldog.

Certain health conditions such as an underactive thyroid, diabetes, arthritis or heart disease can lead to dogs putting on weight, so their food has to be adjusted accordingly.

Just like us, a dog kept in a very cold environment will need more calories to keep warm than a dog in a warm climate. They burn extra calories in keeping themselves warm. Here's an interesting fact: a dog kept on his own is more likely to be overweight than a dog kept with other dogs, as he receives all of the food-based attention. Cheaper foods usually recommend feeding more to your dog, as much of the food is made up of cereals, which are not doing much except bulking up the weight of the food – and possibly triggering allergies in your Bulldog.

The daily recommended amount of food on the dog food sacks or tins are generally too high – after all, the more your dog eats, they more they sell! Because there are so many factors involved, there is no simple answer. However, below we have listed a broad guideline of the average number of **calories** a Bulldog with medium energy and activity levels needs.

Thanks to *'Better Food for Dogs - A Complete Cookbook and Nutrition Guide'* by D Bastin et al, published by Robert Rose, Inc for the following information and daily feeding guide: ***"The standard weight of each breed is stated in brackets. If your dog falls beyond the standard weight due to under or overfeeding, take the opportunity of diet change as part of your dog's weight management program. Target your dog at the highest acceptable weight of his breed class to begin with if he or she is overweight. On the other hand, if your dog is underweight, target your dog at the lowest acceptable weight of his breed class to begin with. Adjust the energy level gradually toward the middle of the range.***

Note: if your dog's weight problems are caused by certain health problems, pregnancy or other conditions, consult your vet before implementing any weight management program as this must be supervised by your vet."

Disclaimer: This chart is designed to give just a broad guideline, check your dog's ideal weight before embarking on a feeding regime and consult your vet if your dog loses or gains considerable weight.

Canine Calorie Counter

IDEAL ADULT WEIGHT	ENERGY
35lb / 15.8 Kg	875 - 1050 Kcal
40lb / 18.1 Kg	965 - 1158 Kcal
45lb / 20.4 Kg	1056 - 1267 Kcal
50lb / 22.6 Kg	1143 - 1327 Kcal
60lb / 27.2 Kg	1310 - 1537 Kcal

We feed our dog a dried hypoallergenic dog food made by James Wellbeloved in England. Max has seasonal allergies which make him scratch, but he seems to do pretty well on this food. Here are James Wellbeloved's recommended feeding amounts for dogs, listed in kilograms and grams. (**28.3 grams=1 ounce. 1kg=2.2 pounds**)

The number on the left is the dog's **adult weight** in kilograms. An adult Bulldog should weigh somewhere between 40lb (18.14kg) and 55lb (25kg), depending on whether the dog is male or female. The numbers on the right are the amount of daily food in grams that an average dog with average energy levels requires, measured in grams (divide this by 28.3 to get the amount in ounces). For example, a 3-month-old Bulldog puppy which will grow into a 20kg adult would require around 305 grams of food per day (10.75 ounces).

Canine Feeding Chart – Puppy

Size	Expected Adult Body Weight	2 mths	3 mths	4 mths	5 mths	6 mths	> 6 mths
Toy	2kg	50	60	60	60	60	change to adult
Small	5kg	95	115	120	115	115	
Medium	10kg	155	190	195	190	190	change to junior
Medium/Large	20kg	240	305	325	320	315	change to junior /large breed jnr
Large	30kg	300	400	435	435	430	change to large breed junior
Large/Giant	40kg	345	480	530	540	530	
	50kg	390	550	615	630	630*	
Giant	60kg	430	610	690	720*	720*	
	70kg	460	675	765*	800*	810*	

Junior

Size	expected adult body weight (kg)	6 mths	7 mths	8 mths	10 mths	12 mths	14 mths	16 mths
Medium	10	200	195	185	175	change to adult		
Medium/Large*	20	330	325	310	290	300	change to adult/large breed adult	
	30	455	440	430	400	400		
Large*	40	565	555	540	520	485	495	change to large breed adult

Adult

Size	Body Weight (kg)	Daily Serving (g)
Toy	2-5	55-115
Small	5-10	115-190
Medium	10-20	190-320
Medium/Large	20-30	320-430
Large*	30*-40*	430*-520*
Large/Giant*	40*-50*	520*-620*
	50*-60*	620*-710*
Giant*	60*-70*	710*-790*
	70*-90*	790*-950*

Average Weight Table for Growing Bulldog Puppies

One month old – 3kg (6.6lb)

Two months old – 5 kilograms (11lb)

Three months old – 7kg (15.4lb)

Four months old – 11kg (24.2lb)

Five months old – 15kg (33lb)

Six months old – 17kg (37.4lb)

Seven months old – 19kg (41.8lb)

Eight months old – 20kg (44lb)

Nine months old – 21kg (46.2lb)

Ten months old – 22kg (48.4lb)

Eleven months old - 22kg (48.4lb)

Twelve months old - 23kg (50.6lb)

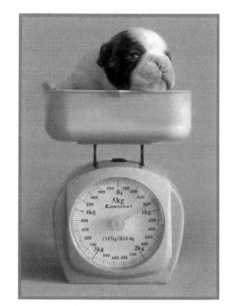

As you will see, a Bulldog puppy puts most of his weight on during the first six months of his life.

NOTE: The above weights are for normal sized male Bulldogs, smaller ones and females will weigh up to 20% less.

Overweight Dogs

It is far easier to regulate your Bully's weight and keep it at a healthy level than it is to try and slim down a voraciously hungry Bully when he becomes overweight. Bulldogs are, however, prone to putting on weight and, sadly, overweight and obese dogs are susceptible to a range of illnesses. According to James Howie, Veterinary Advisor to Lintbells, some of the main ones are:

Joint disease – excessive body weight may increase joint stress which is a risk factor in joint degeneration (arthrosis), as is cruciate disease (knee ligament rupture). Joint disease tends to lead to a reduction in exercise which then increases the likelihood of weight gain which reduces exercise further. A vicious cycle is created. Overfeeding Bulldogs while they are growing can lead to various problems, including the worsening of hip dysplasia. Weight management may be the only measure required to control clinical signs in some cases.

Heart and lung problems – fatty deposits within the chest cavity and excessive circulating fat play important roles in the development of cardio-respiratory and cardiovascular disease.

Diabetes – resistance to insulin has been shown to occur in overweight dogs, leading to a greater risk of diabetes mellitus.

Tumors – obesity increases the risk of mammary tumors in female dogs.

Liver disease – fat degeneration may result in liver insufficiency.

Reduced Lifespan - one of the most serious proven findings in obesity studies is that obesity in both humans and dogs reduces lifespan.

Exercise intolerance – this is also a common finding with overweight dogs, which can compound an obesity problem as fewer calories are burned and are therefore stored, leading to further weight gain.

Obesity also puts greater strain on the respiratory system of Bulldogs, making breathing even more difficult for them.

Most Bullies are very attached to their humans. However, beware of going too far in regarding your dog as a member of the family. It has been shown that dogs regarded as 'family members' (i.e. anthropomorphosis) by the owner are at greater risk of becoming overweight. This is because attention given to the dog often results in food being given as well.

The important thing to remember is that many of the problems associated with being overweight are reversible. Increasing exercise increases the calories burned, which in turn reduces weight. If you do put your dog on a diet, the reduced amount of food will also mean reduced nutrients, so he may need a supplement during this time.

Feeding Puppies

Puppy foods

Feeding your Bulldog puppy the right diet is important to help his young body and bones grow strong and healthy. Puppyhood is a time of rapid growth and development and puppies require different levels of nutrients to adult dogs.

For the first six weeks, puppies need milk about five to seven times a day, which they take from their mother. Generally they make some sound if they want to feed. The frequency is reduced when the pup reaches six to eight weeks old.

Bulldog puppies should stay with their mothers and littermates until at least eight weeks old. During this time, the mother is still teaching her offspring some important rules about life. For the first few days after that, it's a good idea to continue feeding the same puppy food and at the same times as the breeder. Dogs do not adapt to changes in their diet or feeding habits as easily as humans.

You can then slowly change his food based on information from the breeder and your vet. This should be done very gradually by mixing in a little more of the new food each day over a period of seven to 10 days. If at any time your puppy starts being sick, has loose stools or is constipated, slow the rate at which you are switching him over. If he continues vomiting, seek veterinary advice as he may have a problem with the food you have chosen.

Because of their special nutritional needs, you should only give your puppy a food that is approved either just for puppies or for all life stages. If a feed is recommended for adult dogs only, it won't have enough protein, and the balance of calcium and other nutrients will not be right for a pup.

Puppy food is very high in calories and nutritional supplements, so you want to switch to adult food once he begins to approach maturity. With Bulldogs, this is later than with most other breeds, which mature at around two years old. Bullies may not fully mature until they are three years old. Feeding puppy food too long can result in obesity and orthopedic problems – check with your vet on the right time to switch. Getting the amount and type of food right for your pup is important. Feeding too much will cause him to put on excess pounds, and overweight puppies are more likely to grow into overweight adults.

DON'T:

❖ Feed table scraps. Your Bully will get used to begging for food, not an attractive prospect when you end up with a 50lb mound of drooling, adult Bulldog next to you every time you eat. It will also affect a puppy's carefully balanced diet.

❖ Feed uncooked meat or food which may be off. Puppies have sensitive stomachs, stick to a prepared puppy food suitable for Bulldogs.

DO:

❖ Regularly check the weight of your growing puppy to make sure he is within normal limits for his age.

❖ Take your puppy to the vet if he has diarrhea or is vomiting for two days or more.

❖ Remove his food after it has been down for 15 to 20 minutes. Food available 24/7 encourages fussy eaters.

Large puppies

Overfeeding large pups, or feeding too many carbohydrates, promotes too-rapid growth which puts stress on joints and can lead to problems such as hip dysplasia. Puppies grow 20 times faster than adult dogs and so require a special diet to aid their physical development. The average Golden Retriever, for example, grows from 14oz to over 65lb within one year – a 70-fold increase! Human beings take 18 years to do the same thing.

Most pet nutritionists recommend that big, fast growing puppies eat diets containing at least 30% protein and 9% fat (dry matter basis). The calcium content should be around 1.5% (or 3 grams per 1,000 kcal), check the labeling or ask your vet to recommend a feed - but be prepared, he or she may recommend an expensive option available only through them. Do not feed a calcium supplement to a puppy, it may cause the bones to grow too big too fast, resulting in joint problems later in life.

Remember that treats add calories to the overall diet. Make sure the treats are small and do not contain added calcium – get used to giving fruit and vegetables as treats, these are healthier options.

Many manufacturers offer a special formula dog food for puppies and sometimes for large breed puppies. You should not overfeed any Bulldog puppy, and protein, calcium and phosphorus levels may be more critical than with some smaller breeds. It's worth spending time to choose the right fuel to power his healthy development. Think of it as a foundation stone towards future health.

How often?

Puppies have small stomachs but large appetites, so feed them small amounts on a frequent basis. Establishing a regular feeding routine with your puppy is a good idea, as this will also help to toilet train him. Get him used to regular mealtimes and then let him outside to do his business straight away when he has finished. Puppies have fast metabolisms, so the results may be pretty quick!

Don't leave food out for the puppy so that he can eat it whenever he wants. You need to be there for the feeds because you want him and his body on a set schedule. Smaller meals are easier for him to digest and energy levels don't peak and fall so much with frequent feeds.

❖ Up to the age of four months, feed your puppy four times a day,
❖ feed him three times a day until he is six months old,
❖ then twice a day for the rest of his life.

Bulldogs are known for their healthy appetites and will eat most things put in front of them, it's up to you to control his intake and manage his diet. Stick to the correct amount, you're doing your pup no favors by overfeeding him. Unless he is particularly thin, don't give in - no matter how much your cute Bulldog puppy pleads with his big eyes. You must be firm and resist the temptation to give him extra food or treats.

A very broad rule of thumb is to feed puppy food for a year, but some owners start earlier on adult food, while others delay switching until their Bully is 18 months or even two years old. If you are not sure, consult your breeder or your vet.

Pack leader/Alpha

Bulldogs are particularly loyal dogs and the person who feeds the puppy will probably become their pack leader. In other words, this is the person to whom the dog will probably show most loyalty and affection. If your dog is not responding well to a particular family member, a useful tactic is to get that person to feed the dog every day. The way to a dog's heart is often through his stomach!

Something else to bear in mind is that if your mealtimes coincide with those of your puppy or adult dog, you should always eat something from your plate before feeding your Bulldog. Dogs are very hierarchical; they respect the pecking order. In the wild the top dogs eat first. If you feed your puppy before you, he will think that he is higher up the pecking order than you.

If allowed, some Bulldogs can develop a "cocky" attitude and think that they rule the roost. So feeding your dog **after** yourself and your family is an important part of training and discipline. Your dog will not love you any less because you are the boss. In fact, just the opposite.

Feeding Seniors

Once your adolescent dog has switched to an adult diet he will be on this for several years. But unlike most breeds who will have adult food for most of their life, Bulldogs mature slowly and have a relatively short lifespan – eight to 10 years on average.

This means that a Bulldog may switch from puppy to adult food typically at one year to 18 months old, and then start to slow down as early as six years of age, although this will vary from one dog to another. As a dog moves towards old age, his body has different requirements to those of a young dog. This is the time to consider switching to a senior diet.

Dogs are living to a much older age than they did 30 years ago. There are many factors contributing to this, including better vaccines and veterinary care, but one of the most important factors is better nutrition. Generally a dog is considered to be 'older' if he is in the last third of his normal life expectancy.

Some owners of large breeds, such as Great Danes with a lifespan of nine years, switch their dogs from an adult to a senior diet when they are only six or seven years old, as do some Bulldog owners, while other (often smaller) breeds have a longer life expectancy. They may remain relatively youthful for many more years and do not need a senior diet until they are perhaps 10 or older. It all depends on the individual dog, his size, energy levels and general health.

Look for signs of your dog slowing down or having joint problems. That may be the time to talk to your vet about moving to a senior diet. You can describe any changes at your dog's annual vaccination appointment, rather than having the expense of a separate consultation.

As a dog grows older, his metabolism slows down, his joints may stiffen, his energy levels decrease and he needs less exercise, just like with humans. You may notice in middle or old age that your dog starts to put weight on. The adult diet he is on may be too rich and have too many calories, so it may be the time to consider switching.

Even though he is older, keep his weight in check as obesity in old age only puts more strain on his body, especially joints and organs, and makes any health problems even worse. Because of lower activity levels, many older dogs will gain weight and getting an older dog to slim down can be very difficult. It is much better not to let your Bulldog get too chunky than to put him on a diet.

But if he is overweight, put in the effort to shed the extra pounds. This is one of the single most important things you can do to increase your dog's quality and length of life.

Other changes in canines are again similar to those in older humans and might include stiff joints or arthritis, moving more slowly and sleeping more. His hearing and vision may not be so sharp and organs don't all work as efficiently as they used to, his teeth may have become worn down.

When this starts to happen, it is time to feed your old friend a senior diet, which will take these changes into account. Specially formulated senior diets are lower in calories but help to create a feeling of fullness. Older dogs are more prone to develop constipation, so senior diets are often higher in fiber - at around 3% to 5%.

Wheat bran can also be added to regular dog food to increase the amount of fiber (but do not try this if your Bulldog has a low tolerance or intolerance to grain). If your dog has poor kidney function, then a low phosphorus diet will help to lower the workload for the kidneys.

Aging dogs have special dietary needs, some of which can be supplied in the form of supplements, such as glucosamine and chondroitin which help joints. If your dog is not eating a complete balanced diet, then a vitamin/mineral supplement is recommended to prevent any deficiencies. Some owners also feed extra antioxidants to an older dog – ask your vet's advice on your next visit. Antioxidants are also found naturally in fruit and vegetables.

While some older dogs suffer from obesity, others have the opposite problem – they lose weight and are disinterested in food. If your old Bulldog is getting thinner and not eating well, firstly get him checked out by the vet to rule out any possible disease problems. If he gets the all-clear, your next challenge is to tempt him to eat. He may be having trouble with his teeth, so if he's on a dry food, try smaller kibble or moistening it with water. Adding gravy or a small amount of canned food will make it even more appetizing.

Some dogs can tolerate a small amount of milk or eggs added to their food, and home-made diets of boiled rice, potatoes, vegetables and chicken or meat with the right vitamin and mineral supplements can also work well.

Reading Dog Food Labels

A NASA scientist would have a hard job understanding some dog food manufacturers' labels, so it's no easy task for us lowly dog owners. Here are some things to look out for on the manufacturers' labels:

Ingredients: Chicken, Chicken By-Product Meal, Corn Meal, Ground Whole Grain Sorghum, Brewers Rice, Ground Whole Grain Barley, Dried Beet Pulp, Chicken Fat (preserved with mixed Tocopherols, a source of Vitamin E), Chicken Flavor, Dried Egg Product, Fish Oil (preserved with mixed Tocopherols, a source of Vitamin E), Potassium Chloride, Salt, Flax Meal, Sodium Hexametaphosphate, Fructooligosaccharides, Choline Chloride, Minerals (Ferrous Sulfate, Zinc Oxide, Manganese Sulfate, Copper Sulfate, Manganous Oxide, Potassium Iodide, Cobalt Carbonate), DL-Methionine, Vitamins (Ascorbic Acid, Vitamin A Acetate, Calcium Pantothenate, Biotin, Thiamine Mononitrate (source of vitamin B1), Vitamin B12 Supplement, Niacin, Riboflavin Supplement (source of vitamin B2), Inositol, Pyridoxine Hydrochloride (source of vitamin B6), Vitamin D3 Supplement, Folic Acid), Calcium Carbonate, vitamin E Supplement, Brewers Dried Yeast, Beta-Carotene, Rosemary Extract.

❖ The ingredients are listed by weight and the top one should always be the main content, such as chicken or lamb. Don't pick one where grain is the first ingredient, it is a poor quality feed and some Bulldogs can develop grain intolerances or allergies, often it is specifically wheat they have a reaction to.

❖ High up the list should be meat or poultry by-products, these are clean parts of slaughtered animals, not including meat. They include organs, blood and bone, but not hair, horns, teeth or hooves.

❖ Guaranteed Analysis – This guarantees that your dog's food contains the labeled percentages of crude protein, fat, fiber and moisture. Keep in mind that wet and dry dog foods use different standards. (It does not list the digestibility of protein and fat and this can vary widely depending on their sources). While the guaranteed analysis is a start in understanding the food quality, be wary about relying on it too much.

Crude Protein (min)	32.25%
Lysine (min)	0.43%
Methionine (min)	0.49%
Crude Fat (min)	10.67%
Crude Fiber (max)	7.3%
Calcium (min)	0.50%
Calcium (max)	1.00%
Phosphorus (min)	0.44%
Salt (min)	0.01%
Salt (max)	0.51%

One pet food manufacturer made a mock product with a guaranteed analysis of 10% protein, 6.5% fat, 2.4% fiber, and 68% moisture (similar to what's on many canned pet food labels) – the only problem was that the ingredients were old leather boots, used motor oil, crushed coal and water!

❖ Chicken meal (dehydrated chicken) has more protein than fresh chicken, which is 80% water. The same goes for beef, fish and lamb. So, if any of these meals are number one on the ingredient list, the food should contain enough protein.

❖ A certain amount of flavorings can make a food more appetizing for your dog. Chose a food with a specific flavoring, like 'beef flavoring' rather than a general 'meat flavoring', where the origins are not so clear.

❖ Find a food that fits your dog's age, breed and size. Talk to your vet or visit an online Bulldog forum and ask other owners what they are feeding their dogs.

❖ If your Bulldog has a food allergy or intolerance to wheat, check whether the food is gluten free. All wheat contains gluten.

❖ Natural is best. Food labeled **"natural"** means that the ingredients have not been chemically altered, according to the FDA in the USA. However, there are no such guidelines governing foods labeled "holistic" – so check the ingredients and how it has been prepared.

❖ In the USA, dog food that meets minimum nutrition requirements has a label that confirms this. It states: **"[food name] is formulated to meet the nutritional levels established by the AAFCO Dog Food Nutrient Profiles for [life stage(s)]".**

Even better, look for a food that meets the minimum nutritional requirements **"as fed"** to real pets in an AAFCO-defined feeding trial, then you know the food really delivers the nutrients that it is "formulated" to.

AAFCO feeding trials on real dogs are the gold standard. Brands that do costly feeding trials (including Nestle and Hill's) indicate so on the package.

* Dog food labeled **"supplemental"** isn't complete and balanced. Unless you have a specific, vet-approved need for it, it's not something you want to feed your dog for an extended period of time. Check with your vet if in doubt.

If it still all looks a bit baffling, you might find the following website, mentioned earlier, very useful: www.dogfoodadvisor.com run by Mike Sagman. He has a medical background and analyses and rates hundreds of brands of dog food based on the listed ingredients and meat content. You might be surprised at some of his findings. (I have no vested interest in this website, but include it as it is one of the best I have come across in giving unbiased advice on dog foods.)

To recap: no one food is right for every dog. You must decide on the best for your Bulldog. Once you have decided on a food, monitor your puppy or adult. The best test of a food is how well your dog is doing on it.

If your dog is happy and healthy, interested in life, has enough energy, is not too fat and not too thin, and has healthy-looking stools, then...

Congratulations, you've got it right!

6. Bulldog Behavior

Treated well and taught the rules of the household, Bulldogs make wonderful family pets. They are certainly sociable animals and enjoy being around people, forming close bonds with their humans - which is why once you've had a Bully, no other dog seems quite the same.

But sometimes dogs develop behavior problems. There are numerous reasons why a dog might behave badly; each one is an individual with his own character, temperament and environment, all of which influence the way he interacts with you and the world.

Cause and Effect

Poor behavior may result from a number of factors, including:

- ❖ Poor breeding
- ❖ Being badly treated
- ❖ Boredom, due to lack of exercise or stimulation
- ❖ Being left alone too long
- ❖ A change in living conditions
- ❖ Anxiety or insecurity
- ❖ Lack of socialization
- ❖ Fear

Bad behavior may show itself in a number of different ways, such as:

- ❖ Chewing or destructive behavior (common with Bullies, especially young ones)
- ❖ Barking
- ❖ Nipping
- ❖ Biting
- ❖ Jumping up
- ❖ Soiling or urinating inside the house
- ❖ Growling at people
- ❖ Aggression towards other dogs

This chapter looks at some of the more familiar behavior problems. Although every dog is different and requires individual assessment and treatment, some common causes of bad behavior are discussed and general pointers given to help improve the situation.

The best way to avoid poor behavior is to put in the time early on to train your dog and nip any potential problems in the bud. This isn't always possible if, for example, you are rehoming a dog, when more time and patience will be needed.

Whatever the causes, if the bad behavior persists, you should consider consulting a canine professional.

Personality

Just like humans, a dog's personality is made up of a combination of temperament and character.

Temperament is the nature the dog is born with and it is inherited.

This is why getting your puppy from a good breeder is so important. Not only will a responsible breeder produce puppies from physically healthy dams and sires, but they will also look at the temperament of their dogs and only breed from those with good temperament traits.

Character is what develops through the dog's life and is formed by a combination of temperament and environment. How you treat your Bulldog will have a great effect on his or her personality and behavior.

Starting off on the right foot with good routines and training for your puppy is very important. Treat your dog well, spend time with him, exercise him regularly (even if it is only a short walk - new environments and scents keep your dog stimulated), praise good behavior and be firm when he needs discipline. These measures will all help your Bulldog to grow into a happy, well-adjusted and well-behaved adult dog.

If you adopt a rescue Bulldog, you may need a little extra patience. These people-loving dogs may arrive with some baggage. They have been abandoned by their previous owners for a variety of reasons - or perhaps tied up and forced to produce puppies in a puppy mill - and may very well still carry the scars of that trauma. They may feel insecure or fearful, they may not know how to properly interact with a loving owner. Your time and patience is needed to teach these dogs to trust again and to become happy in their new forever homes.

Canine Emotions

In order to understand why your dog behaves like he or she does, we need a little understanding of how the canine mind works.

As pet lovers, we are all too keen to ascribe human traits to our dogs, this is called *anthropomorphism* – "the attribution of human characteristics to anything other than a human being."

One example of this might be that the owner of a male dog might not want to have him neutered because he will "miss sex, " as a human might if he or she were no longer able to have sex.

This is simply not true. A male dog's impulse to mate is entirely governed by his hormones, not emotions. If he gets the scent of a bitch on heat, his hormones (which are just chemicals) tell him he has to mate with her. He does not stop to consider how attractive she is or whether she is the one to produce his puppies.

No, his reaction is entirely physical, he just wants to dive in there and get on with it!

It's the same with females. When they are on heat, a chemical impulse is triggered in their brain making them want to mate – with any male, they aren't at all fussy. So don't expect your little princess to be all coy when she is on heat, she is not waiting for Prince Charming to come along, the hobo down the road or any other scruffy pooch will do! It is entirely physical, not emotional.

Dr Stanley Coren is a psychologist, well known for his work on canine psychology and behavior. He and other researchers believe that in many ways a dog's emotional development is equivalent to that of a young child. (Which does not mean that you should treat your Bully like a baby!)

Dr Coren says: "Researchers have now come to believe that the mind of a dog is roughly equivalent to that of a human who is two to two-and-a-half years old. This conclusion holds for most mental abilities as well as emotions.

"Thus, we can look to the human research to see what we might expect of our dogs. Just like a two-year-old child, our dogs clearly have emotions, but many fewer kinds of emotions than found in adult humans.

"At birth, a human infant only has an emotion that we might call excitement. This indicates how excited he is, ranging from very calm up to a state of frenzy. Within the first weeks of life the excitement state comes to take on a varying positive or a negative flavor, so we can now detect the general emotions of contentment and distress.

"In the next couple of months, disgust, fear, and anger become detectable in the infant. Joy often does not appear until the infant is nearly six months of age and it is followed by the emergence of shyness or suspicion. True affection, the sort that it makes sense to use the label "love" for, does not fully emerge until nine or ten months of age.

"Dogs go through their developmental stages much more quickly than humans do and have all of the emotional range that they will ever achieve by the time they are four to six months of age."

So, our Bulldogs can truly love us – but we knew that already!

According to Dr Coren, they can't feel shame, so if you are housetraining your puppy, don't expect him to be ashamed if he makes a mess in the house, he can't; he simply isn't capable of feeling shame. But he will not like it when you tell him off in a firm voice for making the mess, and he will love it when you praise him for eliminating outdoors. He is simply responding to your reaction with his simplified range of emotions.

Dr Coren also believes that dogs cannot experience guilt, contempt or pride. Some owners will disagree with this – take a Bulldog to a show, watch him parade in front of the judges and then win a rosette- surely his delight is something akin to pride?

Dogs can certainly show empathy ("the ability to understand and share the feelings of another.") This may not be scientifically proven, but there are numerous stories from owners of how their dogs have stayed with an ill or dying relative, of how they have comforted (by licking, staying close or even shedding tears) a human being showing distress.

Another canine emotion is jealousy. An interesting article was published in the PLOS (Public Library of Science) Journal in summer 2014 following an experiment into whether dogs get jealous.

Building on research that shows that six-month old infants display jealousy, the scientists studied 36 dogs in their homes and video recorded their actions when their owners displayed affection to a realistic-looking stuffed canine.

Over three-quarters of the dogs were likely to push or touch the owner when they interacted with the decoy (pictured left). The envious mutts were more than three times as likely to do this for interactions with the stuffed dog compared to when their owners gave their attention to other objects, including a book. Around a third tried to get between the owner and the plush toy, while a quarter of the put-upon pooches snapped at the dummy dog.

"Our study suggests not only that dogs do engage in what appear to be jealous behaviors, but also that they were seeking to break up the connection between the owner and a seeming rival," said Professor Christine Harris from University of California in San Diego.

The researchers believe that the dogs understood that the stuffed dog was real. The authors cite the fact that 86% of the dogs sniffed the toy's rear end, during and after the experiment!

"We can't really speak to the dogs' subjective experiences, of course, but it looks as though they were motivated to protect an important social relationship. Many people have assumed that jealousy is a social construction of human beings - or that it's an emotion specifically tied to sexual and romantic relationships," said Professor Harris.

"Our results challenge these ideas, showing that animals besides ourselves display strong distress whenever a rival usurps a loved one's affection."

Ten Ways to Avoid Bad Behavior

Different dogs have different reasons for exhibiting bad behavior. There is no simple cure for everything. Your best chance of ensuring your Bulldog does not become badly behaved is to start out on the right foot and follow these simple guidelines:

1. **Buy from a good breeder**. A good breeder will only breed Bulldogs (or perhaps a similar breed, such as Pugs or French Bulldogs). They will use their expertise to match suitable breeding couples, taking into account factors such as good temperament and health.

2. **Start training early.** You can't start too soon, like babies, puppies have enquiring minds which can quickly absorb a lot of new information. You can start teaching your puppy to learn his own name as well as some simple commands from as early as two months old.

3. **Basic training should cover several areas:** housetraining, chew prevention, puppy biting, simple commands like sit, come, stay and familiarizing him with a collar and lead. Adopt a gentle approach when your dog is young. He will lose attention and get frightened if you are too harsh. Start with five to 10 minutes a day and build up. Often the way a dog responds to his or her environment is a result of owner training and management – or lack of it.

4. **Take the time to learn what sort of temperament your dog has** – and train him accordingly. Is he by nature a nervous type or a confident chap? What was he like as a puppy, did he rush forward or hang back? Did he fight to get upright when you turned him on his back or was he happy to lie there? Is he a couch potato or a bundle of energy? Your puppy's temperament will affect his behavior and how he reacts to the world around him. A timid Bulldog will not respond well to being shouted at, whereas a dominant, strong-willed one will need more effort on your part as well as more discipline and exercise.

5. **Socialize your dog with other dogs and people.** Lack of interaction with people and other canines is one of the major causes of bad behavior. Puppy classes or adult dog obedience classes are a great way to start, but make sure you do your homework afterwards. Spend a few minutes each day reinforcing what you have both learned in class. Owners need training as well as Bulldogs!

Socialization does not end at puppyhood. Dogs are social creatures that thrive on seeing, smelling and even licking their fellow canines. While the foundation for good behavior is laid down during the first few months, good owners will reinforce social skills and training throughout a dog's life. Exposing your dog to different kinds of people, animals and environments - from dog obedience classes to visits to the vet and friends' houses, and walks in the park - helps him develop confidence and ease. This goes a long way in helping a dog become a more stable, happy and trustworthy companion and reduces his chances of developing unwanted behavior traits.

6. **Enough exercise and stimulation.** A lack of exercise is another main reason why dogs behave badly. Most Bulldogs do not need great amounts of exercise, but a daily walk out of the yard or garden is a good idea, not only for keeping them from becoming obese, but also for mental and physical stimulation. A lack of these can result in poor behavior, such as chewing, ignoring commands or excessive barking, as the dog becomes bored or frustrated.

7. **Reward your dog for good behavior.** All training should be based on positive reinforcement; praising and rewarding your dog when he does something good, like responding to a command. Generally Bulldogs are quite keen to please their owners, although they will not hang on your every word and jump to attention when you demand it. They are Bulldogs, not Collies! They can, however, resort to bad behavior when the

boundaries are not set. The main aims of training are to build a better relationship between your dog and you, the master, and to make him feel secure. Bulldogs may become stubborn and stop obeying commands when there is not much interaction between them and their owners. Make sure you take the time to train him and tell him what a good boy he is when he behaves well. If he ignores you, stick with it and offer him treats – most Bulldogs will do almost anything for a treat.

8. **Ignore bad behavior**, no matter how hard this may be. If, for example, he is chewing  his or way through your kitchen units, couch or plasterboard walls, remove your Bully from the situation and then ignore him. For some dogs even negative attention, such as shouting, is some attention. The more time you spend praising and rewarding good behavior while ignoring bad behavior, the more likely he is to respond to you. If your pup is a chewer, like most Bulldogs, make sure he has plenty of durable toys to keep him occupied.

9. **Learn to leave your dog.** Just as leaving your dog alone for too long can lead to behavior problems, so can being with him 100% of the time. The dog becomes over-reliant on his owner and then gets stressed when left. This is known as *separation anxiety* and usually results in a Bulldog chewing, whining or barking when separated from his owner.

It is a stressful situation for both owner and dog. When your dog is a puppy, or when he arrives at your house as an adult, start by leaving him for a few minutes every day and gradually build it up so that after a few weeks or months you can leave him for up to four hours. See the section on **Separation Anxiety** later in this chapter.

10. **Love your dog – but don't spoil him,** however difficult that might be. Bulldog pups are adorable and almost impossible not to spoil. Their big head, squashed-in features and husky body resemble that of a plump little baby. But remember that they will grow into large dogs and can be strong-willed. This strength of character can turn to stubbornness, making them hard to control if they are allowed to rule the roost. You also don't do your dog any favors by giving him too many treats for good behavior. Obesity can be a contributory factor to a number of health problems, including diabetes and bladder stones.

Dogs don't just suddenly start behaving badly for no reason. As with humans, there's usually a trigger - often a bad experience or a pattern of poor behavior you and your Bulldog get into. Get to know the temperament of Bulldogs in general and your own dog's individual personality and build up a loving, trusting relationship.

Excessive Barking

Bulldogs, especially youngsters, will push the envelope to see what they can "train" their owners to do. While Bullies are excellent, loving companions, they can have a bit of a stubborn streak and can be challenging to train.

Some puppies start off by being noisy from the outset, while others hardly bark at all until they reach adolescence or adulthood. On our website we get emails from dog owners worried that their young pets are not barking enough. However, we get many more from owners whose dogs are barking too much!

Although not normally noisy dogs, some Bulldogs will bark excessively and the root of it is usually to demand your attention in no uncertain terms. The advice here is very simple: ignore him.

Excessive, habitual barking is a problem which should be corrected early on before it gets out of hand and drives you and your neighbors nuts. The problem often develops during adolescence or early adulthood as the dog becomes more confident.

If your barking dog is an adolescent, he is probably still teething, so get him a good selection of hardy chews, and stuff a Kong Toy with a treat or peanut butter to keep him occupied and gnawing. But give him these when he is quiet, not when he is barking, or he will associate barking with rewards and then you will have a bigger problem on your hands.

Your behavior can also encourage a dog to bark excessively. If your dog barks non-stop for several minutes and then you give him a treat to quieten him, he will associate his barking with getting a nice treat and keep doing it.

A better way to deal with it is to say in a firm voice "Quiet" after he has made a few barks. When he stops, praise him and he will get the idea that what you want him to do is stop. The trick is to nip the bad behavior in the bud before it becomes an ingrained habit.

If ignoring him doesn't work, leave the room and don't allow him to follow you, so you deprive him of your attention. Do this as well if his barking and attention-seeking turns to nipping. Tell him to STOP! in a firm voice (not shouting), remove your hand or leg and, if necessary, vacate the room.

As humans, we can use our voice in many different ways: to express happiness or anger, to scold, to shout a warning, and so on. Dogs are the same; different barks give out different messages. A very high pitched bark may indicate fear. **Listen** to your dog and try and distinguish the different meanings.

A dog does not have different words to express himself, he has to rely on the tone of his bark. Learn to recognize the difference between an alert bark, an excited bark, an aggressive bark or a plain "I'm barking coz I can bark" bark.

Speak and Shush!

Bulldogs are not generally good watch dogs or guard dogs, they couldn't care less if somebody breaks in and walks off with the family silver – they might even approach them for a pat or a treat. But if you do have a problem with excessive barking when somebody visits your home, the Speak and Shush! technique is one way of getting him to quieten down. (If your Bulldog doesn't bark, a slight variation of this method can also be used to get him to bark as a way of alerting you that someone is at the door.)

When your dog barks at an arrival at your house, gently praise him after the first few barks. If he persists, gently tell him that that is enough. Like humans, some dogs can get carried away with the sound of their own voice, so try and discourage too much barking from the outset.

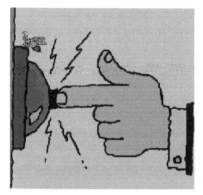

The Speak and Shush technique teaches your dog or puppy to bark and be quiet on command. Get a friend to stand outside your front door and say "Speak" (or "Woof" or "Alert"). This is the cue for your accomplice to knock or ring the bell - you might both feel like fools, but it does work!

When your dog barks, praise him profusely. You can even bark yourself in encouragement! After a few good barks, say "Shush" and then dangle a tasty treat in front of his nose. He will stop barking as soon as he sniffs the treat, because it is physically impossible for a dog to sniff and woof at the same time.

Praise your dog again as he sniffs quietly and then give him the treat. Repeat this routine a few times a day and your dog will learn to bark whenever the doorbell rings and you ask him to speak. Eventually your dog will bark after your request but BEFORE the doorbell rings, meaning he has learned to bark on command. Even better, he will learn to anticipate the likelihood of getting a treat following your "Shush" request and will also be quiet on command.

With Speak and Shush training, progressively increase the length of required shush time before offering a treat - at first just a couple of seconds, then three, five, 10, 20, and so on. By alternating instructions to speak and shush, the dog is praised and rewarded for barking on request and also for stopping barking on request.

To get your Bulldog to bark on command, you need to have some treats at the ready. Wait until he barks, for whatever reason, then say "Speak" and whatever word you want to use, praise him and give him a treat. At this stage, he won't know why he is receiving the treat. Keep praising him every time he barks and give him a treat.

After you've done this for several days, hold a treat in your hand in front of his face and say "Speak." Your Bully will probably still not know what to do, but will eventually get so frustrated at not getting the treat that he will bark. At which point, praise him and give him the treat.

Always use your favorite 'teacher voice' when training, speak softly when instructing your dog to shush, and reinforce the shush with whisper-praise. The more softly you speak, the more your dog will be likely to pay attention.

Aggression

Some breeds are more prone to be aggressive than others. Fortunately, this is a problem not often seen in Bulldogs, as they are generally non-aggressive by nature. However, given a certain set of circumstances, any dog can growl or bite. And if a Bulldog does get involved in a fight – beware. He will NEVER back down.

Although the aggression of the original bull-baiting Bulldogs has been bred out, the breed's determination and tenacity remains. Avoid confrontations with other, potentially aggressive, dogs and do not allow your Bully to get into an eyeballing situation with confrontational canines. Chances are your Bulldog will not start a fight, but he won't back down from one either.

Aggression may be caused by a number of factors: an adolescent dog trying to see how far he can push you - and other canines - a particularly dominant dog, jealousy or even fear, which is one of the most common triggers. This fear often comes from a bad experience the dog has suffered or from lack of proper socialization. Another form of fear-aggression is when a dog becomes over-protective of his owner.

An owner's treatment of a dog can be a further reason. If the owner has been too harsh with the dog, such as shouting, using physical violence or reprimanding the dog too often, this in turn causes poor behavior. Aggression breeds aggression. Dogs can also become aggressive if they are consistently chained, under-fed or under-exercised. A bad experience with another dog or dogs can be a further cause.

Many dogs are more combative on the lead (leash). This is because once on a lead, they cannot run away and escape. They therefore become more aggressive, barking or growling to warn off the other dog or person. The dog knows he can't run off, so tries to make himself as frightening as possible. Socializing your puppy when young is very important. The first six months of a puppy's life is the critical time for socialization and during that early period they should be introduced to as many different situations, people and dogs as possible.

Techniques

Teaching your dog what is unacceptable behavior in the first place is the best preventative measure. Early training, especially during puppyhood and before he or she develops the habit of biting, can save a lot of trouble in the future. Professional dog trainers employ a variety of techniques with a dog which has become aggressive. Firstly they will look at the causes and then they almost always use reward-based methods to try and cure aggressive or fearful dogs.

Counter conditioning is a positive training technique used by many professional trainers to help change a dog's aggressive behavior towards other dogs. A typical example would be a dog which snarls, barks and lunges at other dogs while on the leash. It is the presence of other dogs which is triggering the dog to act in a fearful or anxious manner.

Every time the dog sees another dog, he or she is given a tasty treat to counter the aggression. With enough steady repetition, the dog starts to associate the presence of other dogs with a tasty treat. Properly and patiently done (it won't happen overnight), the final result is a dog which calmly looks to the owner for the treat whenever he or she sees another dog while on the leash.

Whenever you encounter a potentially aggressive situation, divert your Bulldog's attention by turning his head away from the other dog and towards you, so that he cannot make eye contact with the other dog.

Aggression Towards People

In evolutionary terms, it is not that long ago that dogs were wild creatures, living in packs, hunting for food and defending themselves and their territory against potential enemies.

For today's dog, aggression toward people is born out of fear and surfaces as a result of a real or perceived threat. The classic example is of a person who walks straight up to a dog, stares him in the eyes and pats him on top of his head. To the dog, each one of those actions suggests confrontation.

The person might be communicating: "Hey, how are you?" But the dog may read the human behavior as dangerous and an attempt to dominate. It is not the dog's fault, he is reacting instinctively to a given situation. However, it is not acceptable for a dog to attack people, so he must learn to stop this behavior.

If your dog doesn't like people or is afraid of them, you need to find a way to instill confidence. When somebody comes to your house or into the garden or yard, your dog needs to feel that this is a friend, not an enemy. If you have regular delivery person or postman that your dog takes a dislike to, some behaviorists recommend having treats available that the person can give to your dog to try and gain his trust. If your dog is persistently aggressive towards people, this behavior must be dealt with so, if you can afford it, call in a professional dog trainer or behaviorist.

Desensitization is the most common method of treating aggression. It starts by breaking down the triggers for the behavior one small step at a time. The aim is to get the dog to associate pleasant things with the trigger, i.e. people or a specific person which he previously feared or regarded as a threat.

This is done through using positive reinforcement, such as praise or treats. Successful desensitization takes time, patience and knowledge. (A professional behaviorist will give you detailed instructions.) If your dog is starting to growl or snarl at people, there are a couple of techniques you can try to break him of this bad habit before it develops into full-blown biting.

One method is to arrange for some friends to come round, one at a time. When they arrive at your house, get them to scatter kibble on the floor in front of them so that your dog associates the arrival of people with tasty treats. As they move into the house, and your dog eats the kibble, praise your canine for being a good boy. Manage your dog's environment. Don't over-face him. Most Bulldogs love children but if he's at all anxious around them, manage him carefully around them or avoid them altogether. Children typically react to dogs enthusiastically and some dogs may regard this as an invasion of their space.

Some canines are aggressive towards the partner of a dog owner. Several people have written to our website on this topic and it usually involves a male partner or husband! Often the dog is jealous of the attention his owner is giving to the man, or it could be that the dog feels threatened by him. However, this is more common with small breeds rather than Bulldogs, which tend to be pretty friendly with everyone. Bulldogs may have a favorite person, but they are not particularly one-man or one-woman dogs.

If this does arise, the key here is for the partner to gradually gain the trust of the dog. He or she should show that they are not a threat by speaking gently to him and giving treats for good behavior. Avoid eye contact, as the dog may see this as a challenge. If the subject of the aggression lives in the house, then try letting this person give the dog his daily feeds. The way to a Bulldog's heart is often through his stomach!

Coprophagia (Eating Feces)

It is hard for us to understand why a dog would want to eat his or any other animal's feces (poop or poo, call it what you will!), but it does happen. Nobody fully understands why dogs do this, it may simply be an unpleasant behavior trait or there could be an underlying reason.

If your dog eats feces from the cat litter tray (a problem several owners have contacted us about), the first thing to do is to place the litter tray somewhere where the dog can't get to it – but the cat can. Perhaps on a shelf or put a guard around it, small enough for the cat to get through but not your Bulldog.

Our dog sometimes eats cow or horse manure when out in the countryside. He usually stops when we tell him to and he hasn't suffered any after effects – so far.

Vets have found that canine diets with low levels of fiber and high levels of starch increase the likelihood of coprophagia. If your dog is exhibiting this behavior, first check that the diet you are feeding is nutritionally complete. Look at the first ingredient on the dog food packet or tin – is it corn or meat? Does he look underweight? Check that you are feeding him the right amount.

If there is no underlying medical reason, then you will have to modify your dog's behavior. Remove cat litter trays, clean up after your dog and do not allow him to eat his own feces. If it's not there, he can't eat it. Don't reprimand the dog for this behavior. A better technique is to distract him while he is in the act and then remove the offending material.

Coprophagia is usually seen in pups between six months to a year old and often disappears after this age.

Separation Anxiety

It's not just Bulldogs that experience separation anxiety - people do too. About 7% of adults and 4% of children suffer from this disorder. Typical symptoms for humans are:

- ❖ distress at being separated from a loved one
- ❖ fear of being left alone

Our canine companions aren't much different to us. When a dog leaves the litter, his owners become his new family or pack. It's estimated that as many as 10% to 15% of dogs suffer from separation anxiety. Both male and female Bulldogs are susceptible because they are companion dogs and thrive on being with people; they generally do not do well if left alone for long periods. Separation anxiety is an exaggerated fear response caused by separation from their owner.

It is on the increase and recognized by behaviorists as the most common form of stress for dogs. Millions of dogs suffer from separation anxiety.

It can be equally distressing for the owner - I know because our dog, Max, suffers from this. He howls whenever we leave home without him. Fortunately his problem is only a mild one. If we return after only a short while, he's usually quiet. Although if we silently sneak back home and peek in through the letterbox, he's never asleep. Instead he's waiting by the door looking and listening for our return.

It can be embarrassing. Whenever I go to the Post Office, I tie him up outside and even though he can see me through the glass door, he still barks his head off - so loud that the people inside can't make themselves heard. Luckily the lady behind the counter is a dog lover and, despite the large **'GUIDE DOGS ONLY'** sign outside, she lets Max in. He promptly dashes through the door, sits down beside me and stays quiet as a mouse!

Tell-Tale Signs

Does your Bulldog do any of the following -

- ❖ Dig, chew, or scratch at doors and windows trying to join you?
- ❖ Tear up paper or chew cushions, couches and other furniture?
- ❖ Howl, bark or cry in an attempt to get you to return?
- ❖ Grunt or growl when you leave?
- ❖ Foul or urinate inside the house, even though he is housetrained? (This **only** occurs when left alone).
- ❖ Follow you from room to room whenever you're home?
- ❖ Exhibit restlessness - such as licking his coat excessively, pacing or circling?
- ❖ Greet you ecstatically every time you come home – even if you've only been out to empty the trash?
- ❖ Get anxious or stressed when you're getting ready to leave the house?

❖ Dislike spending time outdoors alone?

If so, he or she may suffer from separation anxiety. Fortunately, in many cases, this can be cured.

Canine Separation Anxiety in Puppies

This is fairly common, dogs are pack animals and it is not natural for them to be alone. Puppies need to be patiently taught to get used to isolation slowly and in a structured way if they are to be comfortable with it.

A puppy will emotionally latch on to his new owner who has taken the place of his mother and siblings. He will want to follow you everywhere initially and although you want to shower him with love and attention, it's important to leave your new puppy alone for short periods in the beginning and then later on to avoid him becoming totally dependent on you.

Adopted dogs may be particularly susceptible to separation anxiety. They may have been abandoned once already and fear it happening again.

I was working from home when we got Max. With hindsight, it would have been better if we'd regularly left him alone for a couple of hours more often in the first few months.

Symptoms are not commonly seen in middle-aged dogs, although dogs that develop symptoms when young may be at risk later on. Separation anxiety is, however, common in elderly dogs. Pets age and - like humans - their senses, such as hearing and sight, deteriorate. They become more dependent on their owners and may then become more anxious when they are separated from them - or even out of view.

It may be very flattering and cute that your dog wants to be with you all the time, but it is an insecurity and separation anxiety is a form of panic, which is distressing for your dog. If he shows any signs, help him to become more self-reliant and confident; he will be a happier dog.

So what can you do if your dog is showing signs of canine separation anxiety? Every dog is different, but here are tried and tested techniques which have proved effective for some dogs.

Top 10 Tips to Reduce Separation Anxiety

1. Practice leaving your Bulldog for short periods, starting with a minute or two and gradually lengthening the time you are out of sight.

2. Exercise. Tire your dog out before you leave him alone. Take him for a walk or play a game until he runs out of steam. When you leave the house he'll be too tired to make a big fuss.

3. Keep arrivals and departures low key. Don't make a big fuss when you go out or when you come home. For example when I come home, Max is hysterically happy and runs round whimpering with a toy in his mouth. I make him sit and stay and then let him out into the garden without patting or acknowledging him. I pat him several minutes later.

4. Leave your dog a "security blanket" such as an old piece of clothing you have recently worn which still has your scent on it.

5. Leave a radio on - but not too loud - in the room with the dog so he doesn't feel so alone. Try and avoid a heavy rock station! If it will be dark when you return, leave a lamp on a timer.

6. Associate your departure with something good. As you leave, give your dog a rubber toy like a Kong filled with a tasty treat. This may take his mind off of your departure. (We've tried this with Max, but he "punishes" us by refusing to touch the treat until we return home - and then he wolfs it down.)

7. If your dog is used to a crate, try crating him when you go out. Many dogs feel safe there, and being in a crate can also help to reduce their destructiveness. Always take his collar off first. Pretend to leave the house, but listen for a few minutes. A word of warning: if your dog starts to show major signs of distress, remove him from the crate immediately as he may injure himself.

8. Structure and routine can help to reduce anxiety in your Bulldog. Carry out regular activities such as feeding and exercising at the same time every day.

9. Dogs read body language very well and many Bulldogs are particularly intuitive. They may start to fret when they think you are going to leave them. One technique is to mimic your departure routine when you have no intention of leaving. So put your coat on, grab your car keys, go out of the door and return a few seconds later. Do this randomly and regularly and it may help to reduce your dog's stress levels when you do them for real.

10. Some dogs show anxiety in new places, try exposing him to different environments and people.

In severe cases, the dog may require medication from a qualified vet. Before this happens, the dog needs a thorough history and medical examination to rule out any other behavioral problems or illnesses.

Sit-Stay-Down

Another technique for reducing separation anxiety in dogs is to practice the common "sit-stay" or "down-stay" training exercises using positive reinforcement. The goal is to be able to move briefly out of your dog's sight while he is in the "stay" position. Through this your dog learns that he can remain calmly and happily in one place while you go about your normal daily life.

You have to progress extremely slowly with this and much patience is needed, it may take weeks or even months. Get your dog to sit and stay and then walk away from him for five seconds, then 10, 15 and so on, gradually increase the distance you move away from your dog. Reward your dog with a treat every time he stays calm.

Then move out of sight or out of the room for a few seconds, return and give him the treat if he is calm, gradually lengthen the time you are out of sight. If you're watching TV with the dog by your side and you get up for a snack, tell him to stay and leave the room. When you come back, give him a treat or praise him quietly.

It is a good idea to practice these techniques after exercise or when your dog is sleepy, as he is likely to be more relaxed.

What You Must Never Do

Canine Separation Anxiety is NOT the result of disobedience or lack of training. It's a psychological condition, your dog feels anxious and insecure.

NEVER punish your dog for showing signs of separation anxiety – even if he has chewed your best couch. This will only make him worse.

NEVER leave your dog in a crate if he's frantic to get out, it can cause physical or mental harm.

Important: This chapter provides just a general overview of dog behavior. If your dog exhibits behavior problems, particularly if he or she is aggressive towards people or other dogs, you should seek help from a reputable canine behaviorist.

7. Training a Bulldog

Obedience Training

Training a Bulldog is like bringing up a child. Put in the effort early on and you will be rewarded with a sociable individual who will be a joy to spend time with for years to come. Bulldogs make great companions for us humans, but let your Bully do what he wants, allow him to think he's the boss and you may well finish up with a stubborn, attention-seeking adult.

Too many dogs end up in rescue shelters because they didn't turn out like their owners expected. This is more often than not the owner's fault, and lack of training often played a part in why the dog developed unwanted behavior traits. If you want a Bulldog who will be a perfect companion, rather than a pain in the you-know-what, spend time early on teaching him some good manners and your rules.

Bulldogs are placid by nature, but underneath that mellow and often comical exterior lies a streak of stubbornness. You are not going to click your fingers and have your Bully jump to attention every time. Nope. He might or he might not, but he will want to weigh everything up first before he decides IF he is going to do what you ask.

Some of this might be down to his nature, some of it may be that he can't be bothered and some if it is down to the breed itself.

Psychologist and canine expert Dr Stanley Coren has written a book called ***The Intelligence of Dogs"*** in which he ranks 80 breeds of dog. He used "understanding of new commands" and "obey first command" as his standards of intelligence, surveying dog trainers to compile the list. He says there are three types of dog intelligence:

- ❖ Adaptive Intelligence (learning and problem-solving ability). This is specific to the individual animal and is measured by canine IQ tests.
- ❖ Instinctive Intelligence. This is specific to the individual animal and is measured by canine IQ tests.
- ❖ Working/Obedience Intelligence. This is breed-dependent.

Bulldoggers will be horrified to hear that their beloved breed was listed 78th out of 80 breeds, with only the Basenji and Afghan Hound lower down the list. They were all in the section headed Lowest Degree of Working/Obedience Intelligence:

- ❖ Understanding of new commands: 80 to 100 repetitions or more.
- ❖ Obey first command: 25% of the time or worse.

So you see, you have your work cut out! To be fair, the Bulldog is not a breed which is particularly unintelligent, this is far from the truth - Bulldogs can be particularly empathetic, picking up on your mood. Indeed, the list did not take account of genetic intelligence, which can be measured by ingenuity and a dog's understanding of a common situation.

The drawback of this rating scale, by the author's own admission, is that it is heavily weighted towards obedience-related behavioral traits (e.g. working or guard dogs), rather than understanding or creativity (e.g. hunting dogs).

As a result, some breeds appear lower on the list due to their stubborn or independent nature, but this nature does not make them unintelligent or impossible to train. And the Bulldog falls firmly into this category. (Incidentally, the top dogs were, in order, Border Collie, Poodle and German Shepherd.)

OK, so we all know that the Bulldog is not a Border Collie, nor would we want him to be, so how do we go about training him? Well, for a start, training should always be positive, not punitive, and most Bulldogs are highly motivated by treats.

You might also consider enlisting the help of a professional trainer, but that option may not be practical or within the budget of some new owners. One excellent option is to join a puppy training/ behavior class in your town. This way the pup or adolescent learns with his peers and is socialized with other dogs at the same time. You could also think about getting a dog training DVD - the beauty of this is that it brings training techniques right into your home – but it should not replace classes with other dogs.

When you train your Bulldog remember the golden rule: training should **always** be based on rewards and not punishment. It is not a battle of wills between you and your dog, it should be a positive learning experience for both. Bulldogs can be sensitive critters, and bawling at the top of your voice or smacking should play no part in training.

Dogs are pack animals and very hierarchical. They - and you – need to learn their place in the pack - and yours is as pack leader (alpha). This is not something forced on a dog through shouting and hitting, it is the establishment of the natural order of things by mutual consent and brought about by good training. If not made aware of their place in the household and the rules to abide by, Bullies may end up bullying you and your family.

Bulldogs, like most dogs, respect the pecking order and are happy when they know and are comfortable with their place in it. They may push the boundaries, especially as lively adolescents, but stick to your guns and establish yourself - or a family member - as pack leader and the household will run much smoother. Again, this is done with positive techniques, not threats.

Bulldogs are not fierce by nature. The vast majority do not show aggression towards other dogs or humans or bark incessantly. If they do, then you need to nip it in the bud with a bout of firm but fair training. The first two to three years are your Bulldog's formative years and the most important time for the development of his character and behavior.

It's your house, you set the rules and with proper training, your Bulldog will learn to follow them. Be firm, but **never** aggressive with your dog. You will either frighten him or teach him to be aggressive back.

Sometimes your dog's concentration will lapse during training, particularly with a pup or young dog. Keep training short and fun, especially at the beginning. If you have adopted an older dog, you can still train him, but it will take a little longer to get rid of bad habits and instill good manners. Patience and persistence are the keys here.

Some Common Training Questions:

1. **At what age can I start training my Bulldog puppy?**
   As soon as he arrives home. Begin with a couple of minutes a day. Your Bully will grow to be 40lb to 55lb, and some cute puppy habits are not so appealing with a big, heavy dog. Some Bulldogs may try to establish dominance over their human housemates, so lay down the household rules from the beginning. Bulldogs make companions second-to-none when they are relaxed and know their place in the household.

2. **How important is socialization for Bulldogs?**
   Extremely. It should begin as soon as your dog is safe to go out after his vaccinations. Your puppy's breeder will begin this process for you with the litter and then it's up to you to keep it going when your new pup arrives home. A critical time for your puppy's learning is before he is 16 weeks old. During this time, puppies can absorb a great deal of information, but they are also vulnerable to bad experiences.

   Pups who are not properly exposed to different people and other animals can find them very frightening when they do finally encounter them at an older age. They may react by growling, cowering, or even biting. But if they have positive experiences with people and animals before they turn 16 weeks of age, they are less likely to be afraid later. Don't leave your dog at home, take him out with you, get him used to new people and places and noises. Bulldog puppies that miss out on being socialized can become aggressive, over-protective or jealous. A puppy class  is a great place to help develop these socialization skills.

3. **What challenges does Bulldog training involve?**
   Chewing can be a big issue with Bulldogs, especially when they are young. Train your Bulldog only to chew the things you give him – so don't give him your footwear, an old piece of carpet nor anything that resembles anything you don't want him to chew! Instead get purpose-made long-lasting chew toys. You will also need patience, as Bulldogs can be stubborn and it may take much repetition of a command (in short doses) before your Bully obeys naturally.

Socialization

Socialization means learning to be part of society. When we talk about socializing puppies, it means helping them learn to be comfortable within a human society that includes many different types of people, environments, buildings, sights, noises, smells, animals and other dogs.

Most young animals, including dogs, are naturally able to get used to the everyday things they encounter in their environment—until they reach a certain age. When they reach that age, they naturally become much more suspicious of things they haven't yet experienced. Mother Nature is smart!

This age-specific natural development lets a young puppy get comfortable with the everyday sights, sounds, people and animals that will be a part of his life. It ensures that he doesn't spend his life jumping in fright at every blowing leaf or bird song. The suspicion they develop in later puppyhood also ensures that he does react with a healthy dose of caution to new things that could truly be dangerous.

Developing the Well-Rounded Adult Dog

Well-socialized puppies usually develop into safer, more relaxed and enjoyable adult dogs. This is because they're more comfortable in a wider variety of situations than poorly socialized canines. This means they're less likely to behave fearfully or aggressively when faced with something new. Dogs which have not been properly socialized are much more likely to react with fear or aggression to unfamiliar people, dogs and experiences.

Dogs who are relaxed about other dogs, honking horns, cats, cyclists, veterinary examinations, crowds and long stairwells are easier and safer to live with than dogs who find these situations threatening. Well socialized dogs also live much more relaxed, peaceful and happy lives than canines which are constantly stressed by their environment.

Socialization isn't an "all or nothing" project. You can socialize a puppy a bit, a lot, or a whole lot. The wider the range of experiences you expose him to, the better his chances are of being comfortable in a wide variety of situations as an adult. The importance of socializing your Bulldog from an early age is vitally important. But it's not just for pups, socialization should continue throughout your dog's life.

Don't over-face your Bulldog in the beginning, socialization should never be forced, but approached systematically and in a manner that builds confidence and curious interaction. If your pup finds a new experience frightening, take a step back, introduce your puppy to the scary situation much more gradually, and to make a big effort to do something he loves during the situation or right afterwards.

For example, if your puppy seems to be frightened by traffic at a busy intersection, take him further away from the action and offer him a treat each time a huge noisy truck goes past. Another solution is to go to a much quieter road, use praise and treats to help convince him it's a great place to be, and then over days or even weeks, gradually approach the busy intersection again once he's started to get used to the sound of noisy traffic.

Meeting Other Dogs

When you take your gorgeous and vulnerable little Bulldog pup out with other dogs for the first few times, you are bound to be a little nervous. To start with, introduce your puppy to just one other dog – one which you know to be friendly, rather than taking him straight to the park where there are lots of dogs of all sizes, which may frighten more timid dogs. Always make the initial introductions on neutral ground, so as not to trigger territorial behavior. You want your Bully to approach other dogs with confidence, not fear. Fear can turn to aggression.

From the first meeting, help both dogs experience "good things" when they're in each other's presence. Let them sniff each other briefly, which is normal canine greeting behavior. As they do, talk to them in a happy, friendly tone of voice; never use a threatening tone. (Don't allow them to investigate and sniff each other for too long, however, as this may escalate to an aggressive response.) After a short time, get the attention of both dogs and give each a treat in return for obeying a simple command, such as "sit" or "stay." Continue with the "happy talk," food rewards, and simple commands.

So here are some signs of fear to look out for when your dog interacts with other canines.

- ❖ Running away
- ❖ Freezing on the spot
- ❖ Frantic/nervous behavior, such as excessive sniffing, drinking or playing with a toy frenetically
- ❖ A lowered body stance or crouching
- ❖ Lying on his back with his paws in the air – this is a submissive gesture
- ❖ Lowering of the head, or turning the head away
- ❖ Ears flattened right back against the head
- ❖ Lips pulled back baring teeth and/or growling
- ❖ Hair raised on his back (hackles)

Some of these responses are normal. A pup may well crouch on the ground or roll on to his back to show other dogs he is not a threat to them. Try not to be over-protective, your Bully has to learn how to interact with other dogs, but if the situation looks like escalating into something more aggressive, calmly distract the dogs or remove your puppy – don't shout or shriek. The dogs will pick up on your fear and this in itself could trigger an unpleasant situation.

Another sign to look out for with Bulldogs is eyeballing - or staring at other dogs. In the canine world, staring a dog in the eyes is a challenge and may trigger an aggressive response in the other dog. This is more relevant to adult Bullies, as a young pup will soon be put in his place by bigger or older dogs; it is how they learn.

The rule of thumb with puppy socialization is to keep a close eye on your pup's reaction to whatever you expose him to so that you can tone things down if he seems at all frightened. Always follow up a socialization experience with praise, petting, a fun game or a special treat.

A typical Bulldog posture when things are going well is a "play-bow" - your Bully will crouch with his front legs on the ground and his rear end in the air. This is an invitation to play, and a posture that usually gets a friendly response from the other dog.

Puppy Classes

One great way to help socialize a young Bulldog is to attend puppy kindergarten classes. These are classes designed especially for puppy training and early socialization. In a typical puppy class, off-leash play and play-fighting helps socialize puppies with each other, teaches them to be gentle with their mouthing and biting, and gets them used to being handled by a variety of people.

Some classes even include exposure to odd sights and sounds using props, CDs of sounds, and

theatrics with costumes. Puppy classes also teach some basic obedience skills, so as well as socialization, you'll learn how to give your pup commands in the correct manner, enabling him to behave according to your expectations.

Socialization is essential for helping your puppy develop into a happy, fun and safe companion. Most owners find it easier and more enjoyable to live with a Bulldog who's relaxed with strangers, gets along well with dogs and adapts easily to new experiences. Most dogs are very impressionable when young and can learn to take everything in stride. Socializing your puppy gives him the greatest chance possible to develop into a dog that's comfortable in his environment and a joy to be with.

Top 14 Tips for Training Your Bulldog

1. **Start training and socializing early.** Like babies, puppies learn quickly and it's this learned behavior which stays with them through adult life. Old dogs can be taught new tricks, but it's a lot harder to unlearn bad habits. It's best to start training with a clean slate. Puppy training should start with a few minutes a day from Day One when you bring him home, even if he's only a few weeks old.

2. **Your voice is your most important training tool.** Your dog has to learn to understand your language and you have to understand him. Your voice and the tone you employ are very important. Commands should be issued in a calm, authoritative voice - not shouted. Praise should be given in a happy, encouraging voice, accompanied by stroking or patting. If your dog has done something wrong, use a firm, stern voice, not a harsh shriek. This applies even if your Bulldog is unresponsive at the beginning.

3. **Avoid giving your dog commands you know you can't enforce.** Every time you give a command that you don't enforce, he learns that commands are optional.

4. **Train your dog gently and humanely.** Bulldogs can be sensitive dogs and do not respond well to being shouted at or hit. Do not get into a battle of wills with your Bulldog,

instead teach him using friendly, motivational methods. Keep training sessions short and upbeat so the whole experience is enjoyable for you and him. If obedience training is a bit of a bore, pep things up a bit by "play training". Use constructive, non-adversarial games such as Go Find, Hide and Seek or Fetch. The game Tug Of War is not recommended for young Bulldogs as they have extremely strong jaws and will likely win, thus promoting dominance and aggression. The dog may also – either accidentally or on purpose – grip your hand in his jaws in an attempt to get the toy. It's OK to play with an older, well-trained Bully who has already learned your house rules and knows his boundaries so will stop or let go when you tell him to do so.

5. **Begin your training around the house and garden or yard**. How well your dog responds to you at home affects his behavior away from the home as well. If he doesn't respond well at home, he certainly won't respond any better when he's out and about where there are 101 distractions, such as food scraps, other dogs, people, cats, interesting scents, etc.

6. **One command equals one response.** Give your dog only one command - twice maximum - then gently enforce it. Repeating commands or nagging will make your Bulldog tune out. They also teach him that the first few commands are a bluff. Telling your dog to **"SIT, SIT, SIT, SIT!!!"** is neither efficient nor effective. Give your dog a single "SIT" command, gently place him in the sitting position and then praise him.

7. **It's all about good communication**. It's NOT about getting even with the dog. If you're taking an "it's-me-against-the-dog, I'll soon whip him into shape" approach, you will build a relationship based on fear. It will undermine your relationship with him and you'll miss out on all the fun that a positive training approach can offer.

8. **Use your Bulldog's name often and in a positive manner.** When you bring your pup or new dog home, start using his name often so he gets used to the sound of it. He won't know what it means in the beginning, but it won't take him long to realize you're talking to him.

When training, DON'T use his name when you are reprimanding, warning or punishing him. He should trust that when he hears his name, good things happen. His name should always be a word he responds to with enthusiasm, never hesitancy or fear. Use the words "NO" or "BAD BOY/GIRL" in a stern (not shouted) voice instead. Some people, especially those with children, prefer not to use the word "NO" with their Bulldog, as it is a word they use often around the human kids and is likely to confuse the canine youngster! You can make a sound like "ACK!" instead. Say it sharply and the dog should stop whatever it is he is doing wrong – it works for us.

9. **Don't give your dog lots of attention (even negative attention) when he misbehaves.** Bulldogs love attention. If he gets lots of attention when he jumps up on you, his bad behavior is being reinforced. If he jumps up, push him away, use the command "NO" or "DOWN" and then ignore him.

10. **Timing is critical to successful training.** When your puppy does something right, praise him immediately. Similarly, when he does something wrong, correct him straight away. If you don't praise or scold your puppy immediately for something he has done, you cannot do it at all, as he will have no idea what he has done right or wrong.

11. **Have a 'NO' sound.** When a puppy is corrected by his mother – for example if he bites her with his sharp baby teeth – she growls at him to warn him not to do it again. When your puppy makes a mistake, make a short sharp sound like **"ACK!"** to tell the puppy not to do that again. This works surprisingly well.

12. **Be patient.** Rome wasn't built in a day and a Bulldog won't be trained in a week either. But you'll reap the rewards of a few weeks of regular training sessions for the rest of the dog's life when you have a happy, well-behaved friend and loving companion for life.

13. **Give your dog attention when YOU want to** – not when he wants it. Bulldogs are sociable creatures, they love being with you and around the family. When you are training, give your puppy lots of positive attention when he is good. But if he starts jumping up, nudging you constantly or barking to demand your attention, ignore him. If you give in to his every demand, he will start to think he is the boss and become more demanding. Wait a while and pat him when you want and when he has stopped demanding your attention.

14. **Start as you mean to go on.** In other words, in terms of rules and training, treat your cute little Bully as though he were fully grown: make him abide by the rules you want him to live by as an adult. If you don't want him to take over your couch or jump up at people when he is big, don't allow him to do it when he is small. You can't have one set of rules for a pup and one set for an adult dog, he won't understand.

This simple phrase holds the key to successful Bulldog training: TREATS, NOT THREATS.

Starting Off on the Right Foot

Despite what you may think, training a Bulldog can be a pleasure of toil. Properly done it is a rewarding experience, a learning curve and a lot of fun - for both you and your dog. No matter how placid or laid back your Bulldog is, obedience training is an absolute must. As he grows and gets more confident in his new surroundings, he may try to push the boundaries and jump up at people, ignore your call or sit in your favorite chair - if you'll let him.

These things may happen around adolescence - between a few months and two or so years old. If you decide to allow your Bulldog up onto the sofa or bed, that is your decision. But what you can't do is allow him up there as a puppy and then tell him it's out of bounds when he's bigger, older, noisier and gassier!

If you allow your dog to get away with bad habits, the poor behavior will soon become ingrained - Bullies soon figure out what they can and can't get away with. If you don't want yours to become a pest, start your training early and stick with it.

Bulldogs love to be at the centre of family life with their humans, many are attention seekers. Praise for a job well done has a powerful effect on them during training. Like most dogs, they don't respond well to negative reinforcement, which only increases stress and anxiety.

Without discipline and guidelines, stubbornness can become a problem. Some dogs, just like children, will act up in order to get attention – or treats. However hard it might be, ignore your dog and even leave him alone in the room, deprived of your company, if he is behaving badly and refuses to stop. Don't shout, or he will soon realize that shouting means he gets attention, which makes his behavior even worse. Or he will become frightened.

Many Bullies have short attention spans. When training he may be tempted to wander off to sniff or follow something more interesting than you, or simply switch off and ignore you. The key to successful training is **variety**, keep training interesting, short and fun.

Training your Bulldog is a must-do. A well-behaved dog that you can take anywhere without worrying is a marvelous companion. Try and do a little bit every day, starting with a daily few minutes with a new puppy, and once your dog has learned good behavior, reinforce it every now and again, rewarding him with an occasional treat. Training doesn't stop because a dog grows up, he continues to learn throughout his life. Dogs, like humans, can get into bad habits as they get older and more set in their ways!

If you start your training early enough, and then take a few minutes in your normal daily routine to reinforce what your dog has learned, you'll end up with a wonderful companion that is not only a pleasure to be with, but also the envy of all your friends.

Teaching Basic Commands

Sit

Teaching the Sit command to your Bully is relatively easy. Teaching a young pup to sit still is a bit more difficult! In the beginning you may want to put your protégé on a lead (leash) to hold his attention.

1. Stand facing each other and hold a treat between your thumb and fingers just an inch or so above his head. Don't let your fingers and the treat get any farther away or you might have trouble getting him to move his body into a sitting position. In fact, if your dog jumps up when you try to guide him into the Sit, you're probably holding your hand too far away from his nose. If your dog backs up, you can practice with a wall behind him.

   NOTE: It's rather pointless paying for a high quality, possibly hypoallergenic dog food and then filling him with trashy treats. Buy premium treats with natural ingredients which won't cause allergies, or use natural meat, fish or poultry tidbits.

2. As he reaches up to sniff it, move the treat upwards and back over the dog towards his tail at the same time as saying "Sit". Most dogs will track the treat with their eyes and follow it with their noses, causing their snouts to point straight up.

3. As his head moves up toward the treat, his rear end should automatically go down towards the floor. TaDa! (drum roll!)

4. As soon as he sits, say "Yes!" give him the treat and tell your dog (s)he's a good boy/girl. Stroke and praise him for as long as he stays in the sitting position. If he jumps up on his back legs and paws you while you are moving the treat, be patient and start all over again. Another method is to put one hand on his chest and with your other hand, gently push down on his rear end until he is sitting, while saying "Sit". Give him a treat and praise, even though you have made him do it, he will eventually associate the position with the word 'sit'.

5. Once your dog catches on, leave the treat in your pocket (or have it in your other hand). Repeat the sequence, but this time your dog will just follow your empty hand. Say "Sit" and bring your empty hand in front of your dog's nose, holding your fingers as if you had a treat. Move your hand exactly as you did when you held the treat.

6. When your dog sits, say "Yes!" and then give him a treat from your other hand or your pocket.

7. Gradually lessen the amount of movement with your hand. First, say "Sit" then hold your hand eight to 10 inches above your dog's face and wait a moment. Most likely, he will sit. If he doesn't, help him by moving your hand back over his head, like you did before, but make a smaller movement this time. Then try again. Your goal is to eventually just say "Sit" without having to move or extend your hand at all.

Once your dog reliably sits on cue, you can ask him to sit whenever you meet and talk to people. The key to this is anticipation. Give your Bulldog the cue before he gets too excited to hear you and before he starts jumping up on the person just arrived. Generously reward your dog the instant he sits. Say "Yes" and give him treats every few seconds while he holds the Sit.

Whenever possible, ask the person you're greeting to help you out by walking away if your dog gets up from the sit and lunges or jumps towards him or her. With many consistent repetitions of this exercise, your Bully will learn that lunging or jumping makes people go away, and polite sitting makes them stay and give him attention.

'Sit' is a useful command and can be used in a number of different situations. For example when you are putting his lead on, while you are preparing his meal, when he returned the ball you have just thrown, when he is demanding attention or getting over-excited.

Come

This is another basic command which you can teach right from the beginning. Teaching your dog to come to you when you call (also known as the recall) is the most important lesson. A dog who responds quickly and consistently can enjoy freedoms that other dogs cannot. Although you might spend more time teaching this command to your Bully than any other, the benefits make it well worth the investment.

No matter how much effort you put into training, no dog is ever going to be 100% reliable at coming when called. Dogs are not machines. They're like people in that they have their good days and their bad days. Sometimes they don't hear you call, sometimes they're paying attention to something else, sometimes they misunderstand what you want, and sometimes a Bulldog simply decides that he would rather do something else.

Whether you're teaching a young puppy or an older Bully, the first step is always to establish that coming to you is the best thing he can do. Any time your dog comes to you whether you've called him or not, acknowledge that you appreciate it. You can do this with smiles, praise, affection, play or treats. This consistent reinforcement ensures that your dog will continue to "check in" with you frequently.

1. Say your puppy's (or adult dog's) name followed by the command **"Come!"** in an enthusiastic voice. You'll usually be more successful if you walk or run away from him while you call. Dogs find it hard to resist chasing after a running person, especially their pet parent.

2. He should run towards you. NOTE: Dogs tend to tune us out if we talk to them all the time. Whether you're training or out for an off-leash walk, refrain from constantly chattering to your dog. If you're quiet much of the time, he is more likely to pay attention when you call him.

3. When he does, praise him and give him a treat.

4. Often, especially outdoors, a dog will start off running towards you, but then get distracted and head off in another direction. Pre-empt this situation by praising your dog and cheering him on when he starts to come to you and before he has a chance to get distracted. Your praise will keep him focused so that he'll be more likely to come all the way to you. If he stops or turns away, you can give him feedback by saying "Uh-uh!" or "Hey!" in a different tone of voice (displeased or unpleasantly surprised). When he looks at you again, smile, call him and praise him as he approaches you.

Progress your dog's training in baby steps. If he's learned to come when called in your kitchen, you can't expect him to be able to do it straight away at the dog park when he's surrounded by a pack of buddies.

When you try this outdoors, make sure there's no one around to distract your dog when you first test his recall. It's a good idea to consider using a long training leash - or to do the training within a safe, fenced area. Only when your dog has mastered the recall in a number of locations and in the face of numerous distractions can you expect that he'll come to you.

At home, you can repeat the Come! command before you go for a walk, to train him to come to you for the collar and leash. You can also call him for mealtimes, when his bowl of food is the reward.

Down

There are a number of different ways to teach this command. It is one which does not come naturally to a young pup, so it may take a little while for him to master. Don't make it a battle of wills and, although you may gently push him down, don't physically force him down against his will. This will be seen as you asserting dominance in an aggressive manner and your dog will not respond well.

1. Give the **Sit** command.

2. When your dog sits, don't give him the treat immediately, but keep it in your closed hand. Slowly move your hand straight down toward the floor, between his front legs. As your dog's nose follows the treat, just like a magnet, his head will bend all the way down to the floor.

3.   When the treat is on the floor between your dog's paws, start to move it away from him, like you're drawing a line along the floor. (The entire luring motion forms an L-shape).

4.   At the same time say "Down!" in a firm manner.

5.   To continue to follow the treat, your dog will probably ease himself into the Down position. The instant his elbows touch the floor, say "Yes!" and immediately let him eat the treat. If your dog doesn't automatically stand up after eating the treat, just move a step or two away to encourage him to move out of the Down position. Then repeat the sequence above several times. Aim for two short sessions of five to 10 minutes per day.

If it doesn't work, try using a different treat. And if your dog's back end pops up when you try to lure him into a Down, quickly snatch the treat away. Then immediately ask your dog to sit and try again. It may help to let your dog nibble on the treat as you move it toward the floor. If you've tried to lure your dog into a Down but he still seems confused or reluctant, try this trick:

   ❖   Sit down on the floor with your legs straight out in front of you. Your dog should be at your side. Keeping your legs together and your feet on the floor, bend your knees to make a "tent" shape.
   ❖   Hold a treat right in front of your dog's nose. As he licks and sniffs the treat, slowly move it down to the floor and then underneath your legs. Continue to lure him until he has to crouch down to keep following the treat.
   ❖   The instant his belly touches the floor, say "Yes!" and let him eat the treat. If your dog seems nervous about following the treat under your legs, make a trail of treats for him to eat along the way.

Some dogs find it easier to follow a treat into the Down from a standing position.

   ❖   Hold the treat right in front of your dog's nose, and then slowly move it straight down to the floor, right between his front paws. His nose will follow the treat.
   ❖   If you let him lick the treat as you continue to hold it still on the floor, your dog will probably plop into the Down position.
   ❖   The moment he does, say "Yes!" and let him eat the treat.

(Many dogs are reluctant to lie on a cold floor. It may be easier to teach yours to lie down on a carpet.) The next step is to introduce a hand signal. You'll still reward him with treats, though, so keep them nearby or hidden behind your back.

   ❖   Start with your dog in a Sit.
   ❖   Say "Down!"
   ❖   Without a treat in your fingers, use the same hand motion you did before.
   ❖   As soon as your dog's elbows touch the floor, say "Yes!" and immediately get a treat to give him. Important: Even though you're not using a treat to lure your dog into position, you must still give him a reward when he lies down. You want your dog to learn that he doesn't have to see a treat to get one!

Clap your hands or take a few steps away to encourage him to stand up. Then repeat the sequence from the beginning several times for a week or two. When your dog readily lies down as soon as you say the cue and then use your new hand signal, you're ready for the next step.

You probably don't want to keep bending all the way down to the floor to make your Bulldog lie down. To make things more convenient, you can gradually shrink the signal so that it becomes a

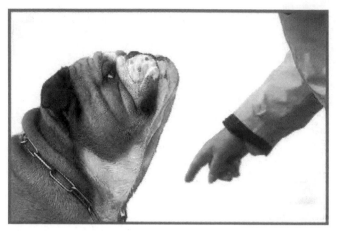

smaller movement. To make sure your dog continues to understand what you want him to do, you'll need to progress slowly.

Repeat the hand signal, but instead of guiding your dog into the Down by moving your hand all the way to the floor, move it almost all the way down. Stop moving your hand when it's an inch or two above the floor. Practice the Down exercise for a day or two, using this slightly smaller hand signal. Then you can make your movement an inch or two smaller, stopping your hand three or four inches above the floor.

After practicing for another couple of days, you can shrink the signal again. As you continue to gradually stop your hand signal farther and farther away from the floor, you'll bend over less and less. Eventually, you won't have to bend over at all. You'll be able to stand up straight, say "Down," and then just point to the floor.

Your next job is to practice your dog's new skill in many different situations and locations so that he can lie down whenever and wherever you ask him to. Slowly increase the level of distraction, for example, first practice in calm places like different rooms in your house or in your backyard when there's no one else around. Then increase the distractions, practice at home when family members are moving around, on walks and then at friends' houses, too.

Stay

This is a very useful command, but it's not so easy to teach a lively young Bulldog pup to stay still for any length of time. Here is a simple method to get your dog to stay, but if you are training a young dog, don't ask him to stay for more than a few seconds at the beginning.

1. As this requires some concentration from your dog, pick a time when he's relaxed and well exercised, especially if training a youngster.

2. Start with your dog in the position you want him to hold, either the Sit or the Down position.

3. Command your dog to sit or lie down, but instead of giving a treat as soon as he hits the floor, hold off for one second. Then say "Yes!" in an enthusiastic voice and give him a treat. If your dog tends to bounce up again instantly, have two treats ready. Feed one right away, before he has time to move; then say "Yes!" and feed the second treat.

4. You need a release word or phrase. It might be "Free!" or "Here!" or a word which you only use to release your dog from this command. Once you've given the treat, immediately give your release cue and encourage your dog to get up. Then repeat the exercise, perhaps up to a dozen times in one training session, gradually wait a tiny bit longer before releasing the treat. (You can delay the first treat for a moment if your dog bounces up.)

5. A common mistake is to hold the treat high up and then give the reward slowly. As your dog doesn't know the command yet, he sees the treat coming and gets up to meet the food. Solve this problem by bringing the treat toward your dog quickly - the best place to

deliver it is right between his front paws. If you're working on a Sit-Stay, give the treat at chest height.

6. When your dog can stay for several seconds, start to add a little distance. At first, you'll walk backwards, because your Bulldog is more likely to get up to follow you if you turn away from him. Take one single step away, then step back towards your dog and say "Yes!" and give the treat. Give him the signal to get up immediately, even if five seconds haven't passed.

The stay gets harder for your dog depending on how long it is, how far away you are, and what else is going on around him. Trainer shorthand is "distance, duration, distraction." For best success in teaching a stay, work on one factor at a time. Whenever you make one factor more difficult, such as distance, ease up on the others at first, then build them back up. That's why, when you take that first step back from your dog, adding **distance,** you should cut the **duration** of the stay.

7. Now your dog has mastered the Stay with you alone, move the training on so that he learns to do the same with distractions. Have someone walk into the room, or squeak a toy or bounce a ball once. A rock-solid stay is mostly a matter of working slowly and patiently to start with. Don't go too fast, the ideal scenario is that your Bully never breaks out of the Stay position until you release him. If he does get up, take a breather and then give him a short refresher, starting at a point easier than whatever you were working on when he cracked. If you think he's tired or had enough, leave it for the day and come back later – just finish off on a positive note by giving one very easy command you know he will obey, followed by a treat reward.

Don't use the "Stay" command in situations where it is unpleasant for your Bulldog. For instance, avoid telling him to stay as you close the door behind you on your way to work. Finally, don't use Stay to keep a dog in a scary situation.

Clicker Training

Clicker training is a method of animal training that uses a sound (a click) to tell an animal when he does something right. The clicker is a tiny plastic box held in the palm of your hand, with a metal tongue that you push quickly to make the sound.

The clicker creates an efficient language between a human trainer and a trainee. First, a trainer teaches a dog that every time he hears the clicking sound, he gets a treat. Once the dog understands that clicks are always followed by treats, the click becomes a powerful reward.

When this happens, the trainer can use the click to mark the instant the animal performs the right behavior. For example, if a trainer wants to teach a dog to sit, she'll click the instant his rump hits the floor and then deliver a tasty treat. With repetition, the dog learns that sitting earns rewards.

So the 'click' takes on huge meaning. To the animal it means: "What I was doing the moment my trainer clicked, **that's** what she wants me to do!" The clicker in animal training is like the winning buzzer on a game show that tells a contestant she's just won the money! Through the clicker, the trainer communicates precisely with the dog, and that speeds up training.

Although the clicker is ideal because it makes a unique, consistent sound, you do need a spare hand to hold it. For that reason, some trainers prefer to keep both hands free and instead use a one-syllable word like "Yes!" or "Good!" to mark the desired behavior. In the steps below, you can substitute the word in place of the click to teach your pet what the sound means.

It's easy to introduce the clicker to your Bully. Spend half and hour or so teaching him that the sound of the click means "Treat!" Here's how:

1. Sit and watch TV or read a book with your dog in the room. Have a container of treats within reach.

2. Place one treat in your hand and the clicker in the other. (If your dog smells the treat and tries to get it by pawing, sniffing, mouthing or barking at you, just close your hand around the treat and wait until he gives up and leaves you alone.)

3. Click once and immediately open your hand to give your dog the treat. Put another treat in your closed hand and resume watching TV or reading. Ignore your dog.

4. Several minutes later, click again and offer another treat.

5. Continue to repeat the click-and-treat combination at varying intervals, sometimes after one minute, sometimes after five minutes. Make sure you vary the time so that your dog doesn't know exactly when the next click is coming. Eventually, he'll start to turn toward you and look expectant when he hears the click—which means he understands that the sound of the clicker means a treat is coming his way.

If your pet runs away when he hears the click, you can make the sound softer by putting it in your pocket or wrapping a towel around your hand that's holding the clicker. You can also try using a different sound, like the click of a retractable pen or the word "Yes."

Clicker Training Basics

Once your dog seems to understand the connection between the click and the treat, you're ready to get started.

1. Click just once, right when your pet does what you want him to do. Think of it like pressing the shutter of a camera to take a picture of the behavior.

2. Remember to follow every click with a treat. After you click, deliver the treat to your pet's mouth **as quickly as possible.**

3. It's fine to switch between practicing two or three behaviors within a session, but work on one behavior at a time. For example, say you're teaching a dog to sit, lie down and raise his paw. You can do 10 repetitions of sit and take a quick play break. Then do 10

repetitions of down, and take another quick break. Then do 10 repetitions of stay, and so on. Keep training sessions short and stop before you or your pet gets tired of the game.

4. End training sessions on a good note, when your pet has succeeded with what you're working on. If necessary, ask him to do something you know he can do well at the end of a session.

Collar and Leash Training

Your Bulldog has to be trained to get used to a collar and leash – and then he has to be taught to walk nicely on the leash. Teaching leash manners can be challenging because Bulldogs are strong and they don't necessarily want to walk at the same pace as you.

Firstly, you have to get him used to the collar and leash – some dogs don't mind them and others will resist. You need to be patient and calm and proceed at a pace comfortable to your dog, don't fight him and force the collar on.

1. The secret to getting a collar is to buy one that fits your puppy now (not one he is going to grow into), so choose a small lightweight one that he will hardly notice. A big collar will be too heavy and frightening for him. You can buy one with clips to start with, just put it on and clip it together, rather than fiddling with buckles, which can be scary when he's wearing a collar for the first time.

   Stick to the principle of positive reward-based training (treats not threats) and give him a treat once the collar is on. Give the treat while the collar is on, not after you have taken it off. Then gradually increase the length of time you leave the collar on.

   IMPORTANT: If you leave your Bulldog in a crate, or leave him alone in the house, take off the collar. He is not used to it and it may get caught on something, causing panic or injury to your dog.

   So put the collar on when there are other things that will occupy him, like when he is going outside to be with you, or in the home when you are interacting with him. Or put it on at mealtimes or when you are doing some basic training. Don't put the collar on too tight, you want him to forget it's there. If he scratches the collar, get his attention by encouraging him to follow you or play with a toy, so he forgets the irritation.

2. Once your puppy is happy wearing the collar, introduce the leash. An extending or retractable one is not really suitable for a Bulldog, they are not strong enough and also no good for training him to walk close. Buy a fixed-length, strong leash. Start off in the house, don't try to go out and about straight away. Think of the leash as a safety device to stop him running off, not something to drag him around with. You want a Bulldog that doesn't pull on the leash, so don't start by pulling him around. You definitely don't want to get into a tug of war contest.

3. Attach the leash to the collar and give him a treat while you put it on. The minute the leash is attached, use the treats (instead of pulling on the leash) to lure him beside you, so that he gets used to walking with a collar and leash. As well as using treats you can also make good use of toys to do exactly the same thing - especially if your dog has a favorite. Walk around the house with the leash on and lure him forwards with the toy.

It might feel a bit odd but it's a good way for your pup to develop a positive relationship with the collar and leash with the minimum of fuss. Act as though it's the most natural thing in the world for you to walk around the house or apartment with your dog on a leash – and just hope that the neighbors aren't watching!

Some dogs react the moment you attach the leash and he feels some tension on it – a bit like when a horse is being broken in for the first time. Drop the leash and allow him to run round the house or yard, dragging it after him, but be careful he doesn't get tangled and hurt himself. Try to make him forget about the leash by playing with him or starting a short fun training routine with treats. Treats are a huge distraction for most Bulldogs! While he is concentrating on the new task, occasionally pick up the leash and call him to you. Do it gently and in an encouraging tone.

4. The most important thing is to never pull on the leash. If it is gets tight, just lure him back beside you with a treat or a toy while walking. All you're doing is getting him to move around beside you with the leash and collar on. Remember to keep your hand down (the one holding the treat or toy) so your dog doesn't get the habit of jumping up at you. If you feel he is getting stressed when walking outside on a leash, try putting treats along the route you'll be taking to turn this into a rewarding game: good times are ahead! That way he learns to focus on what's ahead of him with curiosity and not fear.

Take collar and leash training slowly, give your Bulldog time to process all this new information about what the leash is and does. Let him gain confidence in you, and then in the leash and himself. Some dogs can sit and decide not to move. If this happens, walk a few steps away, go down on one knee and encourage him to come to you using a treat, then walk off again.

For some pups, the collar and leash can be restricting and they will react with resistance. Some dogs are perfectly happy to walk alongside you off-leash, but behave differently when they have a leash on. Patience and repetition are the keys. Proceed in tiny steps if that is what your puppy is happy with, don't over face him, but stick at it if you are met with resistance. Your puppy **will** learn to walk nicely on a leash, it is just a question of time.

Walking on a Leash

Bulldogs are extremely powerful dogs. If you don't want to get dragged round your neighborhood by 40lb or 50lb of pure strength, it is essential yours is trained to walk nicely on a leash - the sooner the better. If you live in an apartment, you may have to put your dog on a leash every time he leaves home.

Firstly, you have to get your Bully used to the whole idea of a collar and leash and, as already stated, some take to it much quicker than others. Some dogs hate the idea of being constrained, so progress at a pace your dog is happy with. When you are both ready, pick up the leash, but don't try and get him to walk to heel straight away – it's one step at a time, literally!

There are different methods, but we have found the following one to be successful for quick results. Initially the leash should be kept fairly loose. Have a treat in your hand as you walk, it will encourage your dog to sniff the treat as he walks alongside. He will not pull ahead, as he will want to remain near the treat. Give him the command **Walk** or **Heel** and then proceed with the treat in your hand, keep giving him a treat every few steps initially, then gradually extend the time between treats. Eventually, you should be able to walk with your hand comfortably at your side, periodically (every minute or so) reaching into your pocket to grab a treat to reward your dog.

We have found that a training collar is very useful in getting a dog to walk to heel on the leash in a short space of time. The training collar is half chain, half leather or nylon, so that when you pull the leash sharply, it tightens around the dog's neck, but only to a point. It is much less severe than a choke collar.

If your dog starts pulling ahead, first give him a warning, by saying **No** or **Easy,** or a similar command. If he slows down, give him a treat. But if he continues to pull ahead so that your arm becomes fully extended, give the leash a sharp jerk by pulling swiftly backwards and upwards. You need to move your arm forward a few inches to give yourself the slack on the leash to jerk back. (Make sure your action is a sharp jab and not a slower pull.) You may need to do this a couple of times before the dog slows down.

Your dog will not like the sensation of the tightened training collar, but soon realizes that this is what happens when he pulls ahead. How much pressure you apply depends on the individual dog. If your Bully is sensitive, you will need only slight force, if he's a bit more single minded or stubborn, he'll need a sharper jab. Be sure to quickly reward him with treats and praise any time he doesn't pull and walks with you with the leash slack. If you have a lively young Bully who is dashing all over the place on the leash, try starting training when he is already tired - after playing or running round.

Many Bulldog owners have a body harness instead of a collar, but these are not suitable for training, as they actually encourage the dog to pull in the beginning. Before you progress to a body harness, train your Bully with a collar and leash. Similarly, extendable leashes are not suitable for training a dog to walk to heel.

Puppy Biting

Bulldog puppies spend a great deal of time chewing, playing, and investigating objects. All of these normal activities involve them using their mouths and their needle-sharp teeth. When puppies play with people, they often bite, chew and mouth on people's hands, limbs and clothing. Play biting is normal for puppies, they do it all the time with their littermates. They bite moving targets with their sharp teeth; it's a great game. But when they arrive in your home, they have to be taught that human skin is sensitive and body parts are not suitable material for biting.

Try not to encourage play-biting. As a puppy grows and feels more confident in his surroundings, he may become slightly more aggressive and his bites may hurt someone – especially if you have children or elderly people at home. Make sure every time you have a play session, you have a soft toy nearby and when he starts to chew your hand or feet, clench your fingers (or toes!) to make it more difficult and distract him with a soft toy in your other hand.

Keep the game interesting by moving the toy around or rolling it around in front of him. (He may be too young to fetch it back if you throw it.) He may continue to chew you, but will eventually realize that the toy is far more interesting and lively than your boring hand.

If he becomes over-excited and too aggressive with the toy, if he growls a lot, stop playing with him and **walk away**. Although it might be quite cute and funny now, you don't want your Bulldog doing this as an adult 50-pounder with one of the most powerful jaws in the canine world. Remember, if not checked, any unwanted behavior traits will continue into adulthood, when you certainly don't want him to bite your children's hands – even accidentally.

When you walk away, don't say anything or make eye or physical contact with your puppy. Simply ignore him, this is extremely effective and often works within a few days. If your pup is more persistent and tries to bite your legs as you walk away, thinking this is another fantastic game, stand still and ignore him. If he still persists, tell him **"No!"** in a very stern voice, then praise him when he lets go. If you have to physically remove him from your trouser leg or shoe, leave him alone in the room for a while and ignore his demands for attention if he starts barking.

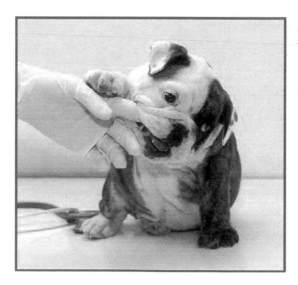

Many Bulldogs are very sensitive and another method which can be very successful is to make a sharp cry of **"Ouch!"** when your pup bites your hand – even when it doesn't hurt. This worked very well for us. Your pup may well jump back in amazement, surprised that he has hurt you.

Divert your attention from your puppy to your hand. He will probably try to get your attention or lick you as a way of saying sorry. Praise him for stopping biting and continue with the game. If he bites you again, repeat the process. A sensitive Bulldog will soon stop biting you. You may also think about keeping the toys you use to play with your puppy separate from other toys he may have. That way he will associate certain toys with having fun with you and will work harder to please you.

CREDIT: With thanks to the American Society for the Prevention of Cruelty to Animals for assistance with parts of this chapter. The ASPCA has a ton of good advice and training tips on its website at: http://www.aspca.org/pet-care/virtual-pet-behaviorist/dog-behavior/training-your-dog

Top 10 Tips for Housetraining (Potty Training)

The good news is that a dog's instinct is not to soil his own den. From about the age of three weeks, a puppy will leave his sleeping area to go to the toilet. The bad news is that when you bring your little pup home, he doesn't realize that the whole house or apartment is his den. Therefore you need to teach him that it is unacceptable to make a mess anywhere inside the house. How long this takes depends on how quickly your Bulldog learns and how persistent and patient you are. It could take from a few days to several months if neither of you are vigilant. Follow these tips to speed up the process:

1. **Constant supervision** for the first week or two is essential if you are to housetrain your puppy quickly. This is why it is important to book the week off work when you bring a new puppy home. Making sure you are there to take him outside regularly is very important. If nobody is there, he will learn to urinate or poo(p) inside the house.

2. **Take your pup outside at the following times:**
   - ❖ As soon as he wakes – every time
   - ❖ Shortly after each feed
   - ❖ After a drink
   - ❖ When he gets excited
   - ❖ After exercise or play
   - ❖ Last thing at night
   - ❖ Initially every hour – whether or not he looks like he wants to go.

You may think that the above list is an exaggeration, but it isn't. Housetraining a pup is almost a full-time job for the first few days. If you are serious about housetraining your puppy quickly, then clear your diary for a few days and keep your eyes firmly glued on your pup! Most puppies learn quickly once they know what is expected of them.

3. Take your puppy to **the same place** every time, you may need to use a leash in the beginning - or tempt him there with a treat if he is not yet leash-trained. Only pick him up and dump him there in an emergency, it is better if he learns to take himself to the chosen toilet spot. Dogs naturally develop a preference for going in the same spot or on the same surface - often grass. Take him to the same patch every time so he learns this is his bathroom - preferably an area in a far corner of your yard or garden.

4. **No pressure – be patient** You must allow your distracted little Bully time to wander around and have a good sniff before performing his duties – but do not leave him, stay around a short distance away. Sadly, puppies are not known for their powers of concentration, it may take a while for them to select that perfect spot to pee on!

5. **Housetraining is reward-based.** Praise him or give him a treat immediately when he performs his duties in the chosen spot. Bulldogs love treats as well as pleasing their owners. Reward-based training is the most successful method and treats are particularly effective with Bulldogs.

6. **Share the responsibility.** It doesn't have to be the same person that takes the dog outside all the time. In fact it's easier if there are a couple of you, as housetraining a pup is a very time-consuming business. Just make sure you stick to the same routines and patch of ground.

7. **Stick to the same routine.** Dogs understand and like routine. Sticking to the same one for mealtimes, short exercise sessions, play time, sleeping and toilet breaks will help to not only housetrain him quicker, but help him settle into his new home.

8. **Use your voice if you catch him in the act indoors.** A short sharp negative sound is best - **NO! ACK! EH!** - it doesn't matter so long as it is loud enough to make him stop. Then start running enthusiastically towards your door, calling him into the garden and the chosen spot and patiently wait until he has finished what he started indoors.

9. **No punishment.** Accidents will happen at the beginning, do not punish your dog for them. He is a baby with a tiny bladder and bowels, and housetraining takes time - it is perfectly natural to have accidents early on. (Even adult Bulldogs do not have large bladders and need to be allowed to urinate regularly.)

Remain calm and clean up the mess with a good strong-smelling cleaner to remove the odor, so he won't be tempted to use that spot again. Dogs have a very strong sense of smell and to make 100% sure there is no trace of what they left behind, you can use a special spray from your vet or a hot solution of washing powder to completely eliminate the odor. Smacking or rubbing his nose in it can have the opposite effect: he will become afraid to do his business in your presence and may start going behind the couch or under the bed, rather than outside. Only shout if you catch him in the act, never afterwards.

10. **Look for the signs.** These may be sniffing the floor in a determined manner, circling looking for a place to go or walking uncomfortably, particularly at the rear end! Take him outside straight away. **Do not pick him up**, he has to learn to walk to the door himself when he needs to go outside.

Apartment Living

If you live on the 21st floor of an apartment in downtown New York or Los Angeles - where the Bulldog is the most popular breed of dog - housetraining can be a little trickier, as you don't have easy access to the outdoors. One suggestion is to indoor housetrain your puppy.

Luckily, most indoor dogs can be housetrained fairly easily, especially if you start early. Stick to the same principles already outlined, the only difference is that you will be placing your pet on training pads or newspaper instead of taking him outdoors.

Start by blocking off a section of the apartment for your pup, you can use a baby gate or make your own barrier. Despite their strength, most Bulldogs will not generally attempt to breach a barrier. (Pick a chew-proof material!) You will be able to keep a better eye on him than if he has free run of the whole place. It will also be easier to monitor his "accidents."

Select a corner away from his eating and sleeping area that will become his permanent bathroom area – a carpeted area is to be avoided if at all possible. At first, cover a larger area than is actually needed - about three to four square feet - with training pads. You can reduce the area as training progresses. Take your puppy there as indicated in the Housebreaking Tips on the pervious pages.

Praise him enthusiastically when he eliminates on the training pad or newspaper. If you catch him doing his business out of the toilet area pick him up and take him back there. Correct with a firm voice - never a hand. With positive reinforcement and a strict schedule, he will soon be walking to the area on his own.

Owners attempting indoor housetraining should be aware that it will generally take longer than outdoor training. Some dogs will resist. Also, once a dog learns to go indoors, it can be difficult to train them to go outdoors on their walks.

Any laziness on your part by not monitoring your puppy carefully enough - especially in the beginning – will make indoor housetraining a lot longer and more difficult process. The first week is crucial to your puppy learning what is expected of him.

GENERAL HOUSETRAINING TIP: You may also want to use a trigger to encourage your dog to perform his duties; this can be very effective. Some people use a clicker or a bell, we used a word, well two actually. In a relatively short space of time, we trained our dog to urinate on the command of "wee wee." Think carefully before choosing the word or phrase, as I often feel an idiot wandering around our garden last thing at night shouting "Max, wee wee!" in an encouraging manner (although I'm not sure that "Go potty" sounds much better!).

8. Exercising Your Bulldog

Bulldogs have, somewhat unfairly, got themselves a reputation as couch potatoes. Many people have confused the placid temperament and the Bulldog's love of being indoors alongside his family as meaning he doesn't want or need any exercise.

This is far from the truth. All dogs require exercise – even Bulldogs, particularly as the breed is prone to put on weight.

But let's be realistic, most Bulldogs are not athletic and are quite happy sitting at home, snoozing in a comfortable chair surrounded by their human family. Although young Bullies are often playful and full of energy, most slow down as they mature and are regarded as a breed which does well indoors with medium to low exercise requirements. Indeed, this may have been a major reason why you chose one.

The Bulldog is primarily a companion dog. If you have an active lifestyle and are looking for a canine jogging or cycling partner, then the Bulldog will not be suitable. You should choose a more athletic breed with more stamina.

Don't expect your Bully to go swimming with you either - or plunge into lakes and the ocean to retrieve that ball or stick. Some Bulldogs are OK around water, but most swim like stones and drowning is a major cause of death within the breed. Some Bulldoggers who regularly visit water buy a lifejacket for their dog. Neither is the Bulldog suited to very hot or very cold conditions, so if you live in a warm climate, exercise him in the cool of the morning or evening.

This chapter will outline why daily exercise – even in small doses – is good for your dog and then what a good exercise regime is for a Bulldog.

Benefits of Regular Exercise

One thing all dogs – including every Bulldog ever born - have in common is that they need daily exercise and the best way to give them this is by regular walks. Daily exercise away from the home helps to keep you and your dog healthy, happy and free from disease. It:

- ❖ Strengthens respiratory and circulatory systems
- ❖ Helps get oxygen to tissue cells
- ❖ Wards off obesity
- ❖ Keeps muscles toned and joints flexible
- ❖ Helps digestion
- ❖ Keeps your dog mentally stimulated (regularly exercised dogs are less likely to have behavior problems)

Dogs, unlike humans, do not suffer from hardening of the arteries, but Bulldogs can be susceptible to heart problems. One way of staving off the ill effects is a daily walk or two which keeps the heart muscles exercised. Bulldogs are not known for their longevity, but regular exercise which raises the heartbeat can help to prolong your Bully's short life.

Whether you live in an apartment or on a farm, start regular exercise and feeding patterns early so the dog gets used and adapts to his and your daily routine. When you are out on a walk, keep your Bulldog within sight. The breed tends to want to suit itself, not you, and may wander off with a stranger.

How Much Exercise?

Bulldogs are regarded as having low to medium exercise requirements. There is no one-rule-fits-all solution, the amount of exercise that each individual dog needs varies tremendously. It depends on a number of issues, including temperament, natural energy levels, whether he is kept with other dogs, your living conditions and, importantly, what he gets used to.

Veterinarians advise that you take your Bulldog out for at least one walk every day, even if you have a large garden or yard. For some Bulldogs 15 or 20 minutes a day is enough, while others will enjoy longer daily walks more often. A walk is a stimulating experience for a dog. As well as the physical exercise, there are new scents, people, places, sounds, dogs and experiences, all of which help to keep him mentally stimulated. Boredom is one of the main causes of poor behavior – and chewing - in dogs.

Despite originally being a very athletic breed, since bull-baiting was banned some 180 years ago, the Bulldog has been bred to accentuate certain features, such as the distinctive massive head, short nose and wrinkles, extremely broad shoulders and shorter legs. The knock-on effect of this is that the pushed-in face and short necks mean that the Bulldog's air passages are very small for its size, restricting the flow of oxygen. Excessive exercise, or exercising in heat, can lead to serious respiratory problems and even death - see the section on **Overheating** in **Chapter 9. Health** for signs of distress.

A fenced garden or yard is an advantage, but should not be seen as a replacement for daily walks. You shouldn't think about getting a Bulldog - or any other type of dog - if you cannot commit to at least one short walk every day. Exercise also plays an important role in socializing your dog, giving him new experiences away from the cozy home environment.

It's good practice to establish an exercise regime early in your dog's life. Dogs like routine, but remember there are strict guidelines to stick to with puppies – see our section later in this chapter. It is important not to over-exercise them, their bones and joints are developing and cannot tolerate a great deal of stress, so playing Frisbee for hours on end with your adolescent or Bulldog puppy is not a good option. You'll end up with a damaged dog and a pile of vets' bills.

Establish a Routine

What is a good idea, however, is to get your dog used to exercise at the same time every day at a time that fits in with your daily routine - and stick to it. If you begin by taking your Bully out once or twice a day and then suddenly stop, he may start chewing, become attention-seeking or simply switch off because he has been used to having more exercise. Conversely, don't expect a Bulldog used to very little exercise to suddenly go on long walks, he will probably struggle.

Test your dog's temperament, show him his leash and see how he reacts. Is he is excited at the prospect of leaving the home and going for a walk or would he rather snooze on the sofa? Adjust the level of exercise to suit your dog – but one short daily walk should be the minimum.

If your Bulldog's behavior deteriorates or he suddenly starts chewing things he's not supposed to, the first question you should ask yourself is: "Is he getting enough exercise?" Boredom through lack of exercise or stimulation (such being alone or staring at four walls all day) leads to bad behavior and it's why some Bullies end up in rescue centers through no fault of their own. On the other hand, a Bulldog at the heart of the family getting daily exercise and mental stimulation is a happy dog and a wonderful companion.

Don't think that as your dog gets older, he won't need exercising. Senior dogs need gentle exercise to keep their bodies, organs, joints and systems functioning properly. They need a less strenuous regime than younger dogs, but still enough to keep them alert and healthy as well as mentally stimulated.

Exercising Puppies

We are often asked how much to exercise a pup. It does, of course, vary depending on the factors already discussed. Bulldog puppies, like babies, have different temperaments and some will be livelier and need more exercise than others.

All puppies require much less exercise than fully-grown dogs. If you over-exercise a growing puppy you can overtire him and damage his developing joints, especially causing early arthritis or other issues. The golden rule is to start slowly and build it up. The worst danger is a combination of over exercise and overweight when the puppy is growing.

Do not take him out of the yard or garden until he has completed his vaccinations and it is safe to do so. Then start with short walks on the leash every day. A good guideline is a maximum of *five minutes exercise per month of age* until the puppy is fully grown. That means a total of 15 minutes when he is three months (13 weeks old), 20 minutes when four months (17 weeks) old, and so on, although Bulldogs are on the low side of this scale in terms of minutes per day. Slowly increase the time as he gets used to being exercised and this will gradually build up his muscles and stamina. Once he is fully grown, he can go out for longer.

Remember, a long, healthy life is best started slowly.

Puppies have enquiring minds. They should be allowed out for exercise every day in a safe and secure area, such an enclosed garden or yard, or they may become frustrated and develop bad habits. If you live in an apartment, make the effort to take him out at least once a day once he has had all his vaccinations. There is no substitute for exploring new environments and socializing with other dogs and people. Get your pup used to being outside the home environment and experiencing new situations as soon as possible.

If you have two dogs, they will naturally get more exercise than a single dog living with humans. If you are thinking of getting two Bulldogs, it is a good idea to wait until the first pup has grown so it can teach the new arrival some good manners. Another point to consider is that if you keep two puppies from the same litter, their first loyalty may be the one with them since birth – i.e. their loyalty to each other, rather than to you as their owner. They may also be harder to train.

Under no circumstances leave a puppy imprisoned in a crate for hours on end.

Exercise Tips

❖ Never exercise your dog on a full stomach as this can cause bloat. Your dog should not be allowed strenuous exercise within an hour before or after eating. Canine bloat causes gases to build up quickly, blowing up the stomach like a balloon. This cuts off normal blood circulation to and from the heart and the dog can go into shock and then cardiac arrest within hours. If you suspect this is happening, get him to a vet immediately. See our **Chapter 9. Health** for more information.

❖ Do not throw a ball or toy repeatedly for a puppy, as he may run and run to fetch it in order to please you - or because he thinks it is a great game. He may become over-tired, damage his joints, pull a muscle, strain his heart or otherwise damage himself.

❖ Some Bulldogs have a stubborn streak, particularly adolescent ones who are pushing the boundaries. If your Bulldog stares at you and tries to pull or lead you in another direction, ignore him. Do not return his stare as he is challenging you. Just continue along the way YOU want to go, not him!

❖ Bulldogs overheat easily, don't exercise them in hot or humid conditions – wait until it's cooler

❖ On hot days, always carry water on your walks, dogs can't sweat

❖ Bulldogs do not have much stamina – don't over-exert your dog. Keep play sessions and walks fairly short

❖ Be vigilant near water

❖ Vary your exercise route – it will be more interesting for you and the dog

❖ If your Bulldog seems to be panting excessively, foaming or struggling for breath, stop the exercise immediately.

Daily exercise helps you to bond with your dog, it helps keep both of you fit and healthy, you'll experience new scenery and socialize with other companions – both canine and human. Trust me, it will enhance both your lives.

9. Bulldog Health

The Bulldog has many endearing qualities, but being a naturally healthy breed is sadly not one of them. While some owners enjoy a decade or more of genuine happiness with their wonderful Bulldogs and would not consider any other breed, many others have to deal with expensive veterinary bills or a shortened lifespan for their beloved pet.

In a recent survey carried out by a large pet insurance company, Bulldogs were one of the five dog breeds in the list of the 10 most expensive pets. The others were French Bulldog, Bernese Mountain Dog, Great Dane and Rottweiler and the rest were cats.

When one reads about so-called "designer dogs," one usually thinks of crossbreeds such as Cockapoos, Labradoodles or Goldendoodles. However, the Bulldog can be considered the original designer dog, as it has been specifically bred over many decades to look a certain way in order to appeal to humans, rather than for any other purpose.

A modern Bulldog looks very different from a Bulldog of 50 years ago. He has a larger head, shorter nose, shorter legs, heavier body and more wrinkled skin.

Bulldogs, along with other breeds, including Boxers, Boston Terriers, Cavalier King Charles Spaniels, Pekingese, Chinese Pugs, Lhasa Apsos, Shih Tzus and Bull Mastiffs, are all regarded as **brachycephalic** breeds of dog. "Brachy" means shortened and "cephalic" means head.

Over the years, successive breeding has led to the skull bones of brachycephalic dogs being shortened to give the face and nose a "pushed in" appearance. This skull shape gives the dogs the characteristic flattened face and short nose. Although this makes them appear extremely appealing - a feature which matches the Bulldog's big personality - it can also cause some major health issues. The oversized shortened head coupled with short legs have led to breathing, skin, eye, mating and birthing problems and an intolerance to heat.

The Media on Bulldog Health

The Bulldog was one of the breeds highlighted in the BBC documentary **Pedigree Dogs Exposed** which investigated health and welfare issues caused by the breeding of some purebred dogs. It was aired on TV in the UK in 2008 and caused a stir around the world.

In it the Kennel Club (the UK's governing body for pedigree dogs which runs the prestigious dog show Crufts) was criticized for allowing breed standards, judging standards and breeding practices to compromise the health of pedigree (purebred) dogs.

The BBC had previously broadcast the highly popular Crufts show for 42 years, but withdrew its coverage and has still not renewed it in an effort to persuade breeders to place more emphasis on the health of their puppies, rather than just physical appearance.

The Kennel Club lodged a complaint with broadcasting regulator, claiming unfair treatment and editing. However, due to strong public opinion, the KC later rolled out new health plans and reviewed standards for every breed. Three separate health reports were commissioned as a result of the program.

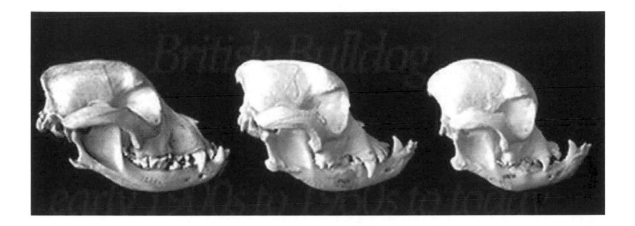

The change in the skull shape of the British Bulldog over the last fifty years.

Image courtesy of Natural History Museum, Bern

They concluded that current breeding practices were detrimental to the welfare of pedigree dogs and made various recommendations to the KC and UK breeders to improve pedigree dog health. Bulldogs were noted in all three reports as a breed in need of an intervention.

In November 2011 the New York Times Magazine ran a feature entitled 'Can the Bulldog be Saved?' in which it claimed that the Bulldog had more health issues than any other single breed.

A few months before the article, the UK Kennel Club announced that it was revising the Bulldog breed standard in an effort to make Bulldogs sleeker and healthier. The new UK breed standard calls for a "relatively" short face, a slightly smaller head and less-pronounced facial wrinkling.

According to the New York Times, The Bulldog Club of America (BCA), which owns the copyright to the American breed standard, says it has no plans to follow suit. The American standard still calls for the breed to have a "massive, short-faced head," a "heavy, thick-set, low-swung body," a "very short" face and muzzle, and a "massive" and "undershot" jaw.

Bulldogs are no longer used for the cruel sport of baiting bulls, yet their trademark features have been accentuated over the years, rather than reduced. Some scientists say that this look has been created to '***anthropomorphize***' Bulldogs or, in plain speak, to make them look more like us.

James Serpell, director of the Center for the Interaction of Animals and Society at the University of Pennsylvania said that those physical handicaps can be easily masked by an outgoing, playful personality: "Bulldog breeders will insist that their dogs are happy and have a very good life," he said.

"But a dog can love its owner and be happy at times, but that doesn't mean his life isn't needlessly compromised. In many ways, dogs are their own worst enemy. They don't complain. They just kind of plod along, trying to make the best of things."

"That's how I see many bulldogs. They are severely handicapped because of what we have done to them, but they still have these amazing personalities that shine through despite it all."

When bull-baiting was outlawed in England way back in 1835, the Bulldog was regarded as a vicious killing machine. Over the decades breeders have worked to successfully eliminate this trait until today, when Bulldogs are regarded as one of the most gentle and loving breeds around.

The steps being taken in the UK to reduce some of the physical exaggerations of the breed will reduce physical suffering. How far these will go we do not yet know.

Many Bulldog owners argue that to change the look of the Bulldog would mean that the dog is no longer a Bulldog. You will have to make up your own mind. All this book is recommending is that, if the Bulldog is definitely the dog for you, that you do your darndest to choose a healthy one bred from healthy stock for the sake of you and your dog.

Three Golden Tips for New Bulldog Owners

There are three golden tips for anybody thinking of getting a Bulldog which will in all likelihood save you thousands of dollars (or pounds).

Tip Number 1: Buy a well-bred puppy.

Scientists have come to realize the important role that genetics play in determining a person's long-term health. Well, the same is true of dogs. This means ensuring you get your puppy from a reputable breeder who selects the parent dogs based on a number of factors, the main ones of which are health and temperament.

A good breeder selects their breeding stock based on:

- **health history**
- **bloodline**
- **conformation**
- **temperament**

If you talk to owners who have healthy, happy Bulldogs, the one factor that most of them have in common is that they did their homework, spent a lot of time researching the breed and, specifically, breeders before taking the plunge.

Although Bulldog puppies are expensive, many good and responsible breeders will make little or no money on the sale of their puppies. Breeding Bulldogs is a specialized art and the main concern of a good breeder is to improve the breed through producing healthy puppies with good temperaments.

Far better to spend time beforehand choosing a puppy which has been properly bred than to spend a great deal of time and money later as your wonderful pet develops health problems due to poor breeding, not to mention the heartache that causes. As the English upper classes say (in a very posh accent): *"There is no substitute for good breeding, darling!"*

So spend some time to find a reputable breeder and read **Chapter 4. Puppies** for information on finding a good breeder and knowing the right questions to ask.

- Don't buy a puppy from a pet shop. No reputable breeder allows their pups to end up in pet shops. You will, in all probability, be buying a Bulldog with questionable heritage and breeding – and you will be extremely lucky if this does not result in problems at some point in the dog's life.

- Never buy a puppy from a small ad on the internet unless you can personally visit the owners and get the full details of the pup's background, parents and health history.

- Never buy a pup or adult Bulldog unseen with a credit card deposit – you are storing up trouble and expense for yourself.

Tip Number 2: Get pet insurance as soon as you get your Bulldog.

Don't wait until he or she has a health issue and needs to see a veterinarian. Most insurers will exclude all pre-existing conditions on their policies.

For example, if your dog has soft palate surgery (see the section on 'Elongated Soft Palate' later in this chapter) this could cost you anything from US$750 to around $2,500 (£500 to £1,600 in the UK).

Surgery to correct breathing problems can be even more expensive. Make sure you remember to take out annual pet insurance while your dog still has a clean bill of health.

With any luck you won't need it, although the likelihood is that you will be glad of it at some point in your Bulldog's relatively short life. There are various pet insurance comparison websites on the internet. Shop around for the best deal, but also check the small print to make sure that any condition which might occur is covered, and that if the problem is a chronic or recurring one, then it will continue to be covered year after year.

When you are working out costs for getting a Bulldog, make sure you factor in the annual cost of good pet insurance and trips to a vet for regular check-ups.

Tip Number 3: Find a veterinarian that knows and understands the Bulldog. This is a breed which requires specialist care. You could waste a lot of time and money by visiting a vet who is not familiar with the breed and its specialist healthcare requirements. If you already have a vet, check if he or she is experienced with Bulldogs, if not you'd be advised to find one who is.

Firstly, how can you tell if your dog is in good health? Well, our **Top Ten Signs** are a good start. Here are some positive things to look for in a healthy Bulldog.

The 13 Signs of a Healthy Bulldog

1. **Breathing** – most Bulldogs snore, but they should not pant excessively, nor should their breathing be excessively noisy or labored when excited or exercising. Regular, quiet breathing is a good sign.

2. **Eyes** – a healthy Bulldog's eyes are shiny and bright with no yellowish tint. The area around the eyeball (the conjunctiva) should be a healthy pink; paleness could be a sign of underlying problems. A red swelling in the corner of one or both eyes could by a sign of Cherry Eye, an ailment which some Bulldogs are prone to. There should be no thick, green or yellow discharge from the eyes. A cloudy eye could well be a sign of cataracts.

3. **Coats** – these are easy-to-monitor indicators of a healthy dog. A Bulldog has a short, smooth coat which should be glossy. It sheds a little right throughout the year. A dull, lifeless coat, a discolored one or a coat which loses excessive hair can be a sign that something is amiss.

4. **Skin** – This should be smooth without redness. (Normal skin pigment can vary according to the color of the Bulldog.) Some Bulldogs are prone to skin conditions, such as hot spots and inter-digital cysts (between the toes of his paws). If your dog is scratching, licking or biting himself a lot, he may have a skin problem which needs addressing before he makes it worse. Open sores, scales, scabs or growths can be a sign of a problem. Signs of fleas, ticks and other external parasites should be treated immediately.

5. **Ears** – ear infections can be a particular problem with many breeds of dog, including Bulldogs. The warm place under the ear flap is an ideal breeding ground for mites and infections. The ears should smell normal and not be hot. A bad smell, a hot ear or one full of brown wax is often a sign of infection, so get him to the vet or it could ultimately lead to a burst eardrum or even deafness.

   Ear problems may be caused by a number of factors, including bacteria, ear mites, allergies, hypothyroidism, the shape of the ear (anatomy) or even excessive cleaning. Your dog's ears should be clean with no dark or bloody discharge, redness, swelling or unpleasant odors. The key to healthy ears is to keep them clean and dry, checking them regularly.

6. **Mouth** – Gums should be a healthy pink or pigmented with black. A change in color can be an indicator of a health issue. Paleness or whiteness can be a sign of anemia or lack of oxygen due to heart or breathing problems. Blue gums or tongue are a sign that your Bulldog is not breathing properly. Red, inflamed gums can be a sign of gingivitis or other tooth disease. Again, your Bulldog's breath should smell OK. Young dogs will have sparkling white teeth, whereas older dogs will have darker teeth, but they should not have any hard white, yellow, green or brown bits.

7. **Weight** –Bulldogs are known for their heavy-set bodies, and should tip the scales at around 40lb to 55lb, with males generally being heavier than females. But the fact that this is a sturdy breed does not excuse obesity, which is bad for any dog as it causes strain on joints and organs. Dogs may have weight problems due to factors such as diet, lack of exercise, allergies, diabetes, thyroid or other problems. A Bulldog has a deep chest and a general rule of thumb is that your Bulldog's stomach should be above or, at worse, in a line with his rib cage when standing. If his stomach hangs below, he is overweight or he may have a pot belly, which can also be a symptom of other conditions.

8. **Nose** – a dog's nose is an indicator of health symptoms. All Bulldog puppies are born with pink noses, but these should turn to jet black. The Kennel Clubs state that a Bulldog's nose must be black for showing, but in reality some have mottled pink and black noses. With all the breeding of new colors (many of which do not conform to KC standards), other nose colors such as liver are appearing. The nose should normally be moist and cold to the touch. The moistness should be free from clear, watery secretions. Any yellow, green or foul smelling discharge is not normal. In younger dogs this can be a sign of canine distemper.

9. **Temperature** – The normal temperature of a dog is 101°F. Excited or exercising dogs may run a slightly higher temperature. Anything above 103°F or below 100°F should be checked out. The exceptions are female dogs about to give birth that will often have a temperature of 99°F. If you take your dog's temperature, make sure he or she is relaxed and *always* use a purpose-made thermometer.

10. **Attitude** – a generally positive attitude and personality is the sign of good health. Symptoms of illness may be not eating food, a general lack of interest in his or her surroundings, lethargy and sleeping a lot – although these last two traits are fairly typical of many Bulldogs! The important thing is to look out for any behavior which is out of the ordinary for your dog.

11. **Energy** – The Bulldog is generally regarded as a dog with low to medium energy levels, although some may be more active – especially puppies and adolescent Bullies. Your dog should have good energy levels with fluid and pain-free movements. Lethargy or lack of energy – if it is not the dog's normal character – could be a sign of an underlying problem.

12. **Stools** –poop, poo, business, feces – call it what you will! - it's the stuff that comes out of the less appealing end of your dog on a daily basis! It should be firm, not runny, with no signs of worms or parasites. Watery stools or a dog not pooping regularly are both signs of an upset stomach or other ailments. If it continues for a day or two, consult your veterinarian. If puppies have diarrhea they need checking out much quicker as they can quickly dehydrate.

13. **Smell** – your Bulldog should have a pleasant "doggie" smell. If there is a musty, "off" or generally unpleasant odor coming from his body, it could be a sign of yeast infection. There can be a number of reasons for this, such as his facial wrinkles not being cleaned properly or an allergy to a certain type of food. You need to get to the root of the problem.

So now you know some of the signs of a healthy dog – what are the signs of an unhealthy one? There are many different symptoms that can indicate that your beloved canine companion isn't feeling great. If you don't know your dog, then we recommend you spend some time getting to do so.

What are his normal character and temperament? Lively or sedate, playful or serious, happy to be alone or loves to be with people, a keen appetite or a fussy eater? How often does he empty his bowels, does he ever vomit? (Dogs will often eat grass to make themselves sick, this is perfectly normal and a canine's natural way of cleansing his digestive system.)

You may think your Bulldog can't talk, **but he can!** If you really know your dog, his character and habits, then he CAN tell you when he's not well. He does this by changing his patterns. Some symptoms are physical, some emotional and others are behavioral. It's important for you to be able to recognize these changes as soon as possible. Early treatment can be the key to keeping a simple problem from snowballing into a serious illness.

If you think your Bulldog is unwell, it is useful to keep an accurate and detailed account of his symptoms to give to the vet. This will help him or her correctly diagnose and effectively treat your dog. Most canine illnesses are detected through a combination of signs and symptoms.

Five Vital Signs of Illness

1. Temperature

A newborn puppy will have a temperature of 94-97ºF. This will reach the normal adult body temperature of 101ºF at about four weeks old. Anything between 100ºF and 102ºF to 103ºF is normal. Like all dogs, a Bulldog's temperature is normally taken via his rectum. If you do this, be very careful. It's easier to get someone to hold your dog while you do this. Digital thermometers are a good choice, but **only use one specifically made for rectal use,** as normal glass thermometers can easily break off in the rectum.

Ear Thermometer

Ear thermometers are now available, making the task much easier, although they can be expensive and don't suit all dogs' ears. (Walmart has started stocking them). Remember that exercise or excitement can cause the temperature to rise by 2ºF to 3ºF when your dog is actually in good health, so better to wait until he is relaxed and calm before taking his temperature. If it is above or below the norms, give your veterinarian a call.

2. Respiratory Rate

Another symptom of canine illness is a change in breathing patterns. This varies a lot depending on the size and weight of the dog. An adult dog will have a respiratory rate of 15-25 breaths per minute when resting. You can easily check this by counting your dog's breaths for a minute with a stopwatch handy. Don't do this if the dog is panting – it doesn't count.

3. Heart Rate

You can feel for your Bulldog's heartbeat by placing your hand on his lower ribcage – just behind the elbow. Don't be alarmed if the heartbeat seems irregular compared to a human. It IS irregular in some dogs. Your Bulldog will probably love the attention, so it should be quite easy to check his heartbeat. Just lay him on his side and bend his left front leg at the elbow, bring the elbow in to his chest and place your fingers or a stethoscope on this area and count the beats.

* Big dogs have a normal rate of 70 to 120 beats per minute

* Medium-sized dogs have a normal rate of 80 to 120 beats per minute

* Small dogs have a normal rate of 90 to 140 beats per minute

* A young puppy has a heartbeat of around 220 beats per minute

* An older dog has a slower heartbeat

4. Behavior Changes

Classic symptoms of illness are any inexplicable behavior changes. If there has NOT been a change in the household atmosphere, such as another new pet, a new baby, moving home or the absence of a family member, then the following symptoms may well be a sign that all is not well with your Bulldog:

- ❖ **Depression**
- ❖ **Anxiety**
- ❖ **Tiredness**
- ❖ **Trembling**
- ❖ **Falling or stumbling**
- ❖ **Loss of appetite**
- ❖ **Walking in circles**

5. Breathing Patterns

Bulldogs are particularly susceptible to breathing problems due to their anatomy. If your dog has difficulty breathing, here are some signs to look out for:

- ❖ **The belly and chest move when breathing**
- ❖ **Nostrils may flare open when breathing**
- ❖ **Breathing with an open mouth**

- ❖ **Breathing with the elbows sticking out from the body**
- ❖ **Neck and head are held low and out in front of the body**
- ❖ **Noisy breathing**
- ❖ **Fast breathing and shallow breaths**
- ❖ **Excessive panting**

Your Bulldog may normally show some of these signs, but if any of them appear for the first time or worse than usual, you need to keep your Bully under close watch for a few hours or even days. Quite often he will return to normal of his own accord. Like humans, dogs have off-days too.

If he is showing any of the above symptoms, then don't over-exercise him, and avoid stressful situations and hot places. Make sure he has access to clean water. There are many other signals of ill health, but these are five of the most important. Keep a record for your vet. If your dog does need professional medical attention, most vets will want   to   know:

WHEN the symptoms first appeared in your dog

WHETHER they are getting better or worse, and

HOW FREQUENT the symptoms are. Are they intermittent, continuous or increasing in frequency?

This section has highlighted some of the indicators of good and poor health to help you monitor your dog's wellbeing. Getting to know your dog's character, habits and temperament will go a long way towards being able to spot the early signs of ill health.

The next section looks in detail at some of the most common ailments which affect Bulldogs, with much of the complicated medical terminology explained in simple terms. We also cover the symptoms and treatments of various conditions.

Brachycephalic Upper Airway Obstruction Syndrome (BUAOS)

Brachycephalic breeds include Bulldogs, Boxers, Boston Terriers, Pekingese, Chinese Pugs, Lhasa Apsos, Shih Tzus and Bull Mastiffs.

"Brachy" means shortened and "cephalic" means of the head. The shortened skull bones give the dog's face and nose a pushed-in appearance, which is often very appealing. However, it can also cause breathing problems.

Although the Bulldog head has been getting smaller over time, the amount of soft tissue inside it has remained the same. This includes the soft palate, cartilage inside the nose and the tongue, which are all now crammed into a small space. There is also a lack of nasal bone which causes the nostrils to become very narrow, like small slits instead of open holes.

The term BUAOS - also called Brachycephalic Airway Syndrome - is used to describe the range of abnormalities which result from this and includes an elongated soft palate, stenotic nares, a hypoplastic trachea and everted laryngeal saccules. A dog with this syndrome may have one or a combination of these conditions, with variable effects on his respiration.

An elongated soft palate (the soft part of the roof of the mouth) is too long for the short mouth and so partially blocks the entrance to the trachea (windpipe) at the back of the throat. Dogs with **stenotic nares** have nostrils which are too narrow, restricting the amount of air that can be inhaled. A **hypoplastic trachea** means that the windpipe is narrower than normal.

The knock-on effect of a dog struggling to breathe can create another problem. Unfortunately the increased effort creates a suction effect in the back of the throat at the opening to the windpipe. This opening into the windpipe is called the larynx (or voice box in people) and it has a tough cartilage frame which keeps it open wide.

However, constant suction in this area over a period of months or years can cause it to fold inwards which narrows the airway even further and really does cause serious breathing difficulty. This secondary problem is called **laryngeal collapse**. The **laryngeal saccules** are small pouches just inside the larynx. They evert (turn outwards) causing a further obstruction of the airways.

Symptoms of BUOAS

- ❖ **Loud snoring**
- ❖ **Noisy breathing – especially during excitement or exercise**
- ❖ **Panting**
- ❖ **Poor ability to exercise**
- ❖ **Intolerance to heat**
- ❖ **Choking on food**
- ❖ **Regurgitating**
- ❖ **Labored breathing**
- ❖ **Blue gums or tongue**
- ❖ **Fainting**

Affected dogs may also suffer from:

- ❖ **Difficulty swallowing**
- ❖ **Strange body posture as he tries to breathe more efficiently**
- ❖ **Tooth or gum disease**
- ❖ **Increased eye problems**
- ❖ **Infections in the facial skin folds**

The problem is that a large number of brachycephalic dogs may show a mild form of some of these symptoms in their daily lives. Some veterinarians believe that our tolerance of what is acceptable in Bulldogs has shifted to think that the above signs are normal, which they are not.

They are, however, all signs that the respiratory system is not functioning efficiently. Another problem for the stoic Bulldog is that he has an extremely high tolerance to pain which may hide the fact that he is in distress.

Veterinarians are keen to get the message out that **these symptoms are not normal** and if your Bulldog is displaying some of them then he needs help. If you are thinking of getting a puppy, do not choose one exhibiting any of the above symptoms.

Treatment

Fortunately there are things that can be done to reduce the breathing problems associated with this syndrome. Various forms of **surgery** can be carried out to help Bulldogs breathe. Although these treatments will not produce a normal airway, they will improve the flow of air, helping the dog to breathe more easily and improving his quality of life and ability to exercise. Exercise is important to avoid obesity, which makes things much worse.

One of the most important factors in deciding outcomes is how early the problem(s) are diagnosed. Tackling breathing issues early in the Bulldog's life helps to reduce the amount of suction at the back of the throat and to prevent or delay the development of the dreaded laryngeal (voice box) collapse, for which there are only limited options.

The veterinarian may have a good idea that BUAOS is the problem, based on symptoms, age and the fact that your dog is a Bulldog, a breed prone to the condition. But before he or she can make a proper diagnosis, the dog will have to be examiner under general anesthetic – which is also not without risk for brachycephalic breeds. The vet may also take a biopsy (small tissue sample) and blood sample to check carbon dioxide and alkaline levels.

A small flexible camera called an **endoscope** (left) may be used to examine the throat, larynx and possibly the windpipe. Many vets prefer to perform corrective surgery to remodel some of the soft tissue at the same time, so that the dog is only knocked out once. Dogs which still have excessive soft tissue have a higher risk of problems due to anesthesia. Your vet will discuss all of this with you.

Here are some of the options your vet may discuss with you:

Stenotic nares (pinched or narrow nostrils) can be surgically opened by removing a wedge of tissue from the nares allowing better airflow through the nose.

An **elongated soft-palate** can be surgically shortened so it no longer protrudes into the back of the throat.

Everted laryngeal saccules can be surgically removed to increase the size of the laryngeal airway.

With today's laser technology some of these procedures can be performed with a minimal amount of bleeding and no need for stitches. The level of success depends on the age of the animal and when these procedures are performed. The earlier BUAOS is diagnosed and treated, the better, as the condition can worsen with time and cause other abnormalities.

Everted laryngeal saccules and a weakening of the windpipe can result when the Bulldog has to breathe through a restrictive airway for a long time. If the veterinary surgeon can increase the size of the airway and decrease the inspiratory (breathing in) pressure before the airway is damaged, then the dog can breathe much easier.

The key here is to keep a lookout for the tell-tale signs and if you are at all worried that your dog is showing one or several of the symptoms, then consult a veterinarian. The earlier BUOAS is diagnosed and treated, the better the outlook for your dog.

Hip Dysplasia

Canine Hip Dysplasia (CHD) is the most common cause of hind leg lameness in dogs. It is a hereditary condition which occurs mainly in large breeds.

Several factors contribute to the development of the disease and some breeds are genetically predisposed to the disease, including Labrador Retrievers, Golden Retrievers, German Shepherds, Rottweilers and Giant Schnauzers. Smaller breeds may also suffer, but the effects are not as obvious.

In tests carried out by the Orthopedic Foundation for Animals (OFA) between 1974 and 2013, the Bulldog had the worst score of all breeds tested. Of the 564 Bulldogs tested, 71.6% were found to be dysplastic, while only 0.4% were rated as excellent.

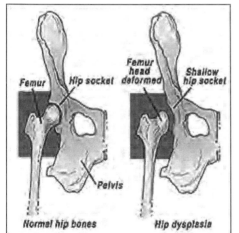

Of the 98 Bulldogs born between 2006 and 2010 which were tested, 61.2% were found to be dysplastic and only one dog was rated as excellent.

Currently the strongest link to contributing factors - other than genetic predisposition - appears to be to rapid growth and weight gain. The hip is a ball and socket joint. Hip dysplasia is caused when the head of the femur (thigh bone) fits loosely into a shallow and poorly-developed socket in the pelvis.

The right hand side of the diagram shows a shallow hip socket and a deformed femur head, causing hip dysplasia. The healthy joint is on the left.

Most dogs with dysplasia are born with normal hips, but due to their genetic make-up – and possibly other factors such as diet – the soft tissues that surround the joint develop abnormally.

The joint carrying the weight of the dog becomes loose and unstable, muscle growth lags behind normal development and is often followed by degenerative joint disease or osteoarthritis, which is the body's attempt to stabilize the loose hip joint. Early diagnosis gives your vet the best chance to tackle the problem as soon as possible, minimizing the chance of arthritis developing.

Symptoms range from mild discomfort to extreme pain. A puppy with canine hip dysplasia usually starts to show signs between five and 13 months old.

Symptoms

- ❖ Lameness in the hind legs, particularly after exercise
- ❖ Difficulty or stiffness when getting up or climbing uphill
- ❖ A 'bunny hop' gait
- ❖ Dragging the rear end when getting up
- ❖ Waddling rear leg gait
- ❖ A painful reaction to stretching the hind legs, resulting in a short stride
- ❖ A side-to-side sway of the croup (area above the tail) with a tendency to tilt the hips down if you push down on the croup
- ❖ A reluctance to jump, exercise or climb stairs
- ❖ Sitting like a frog with legs splayed behind (although this can be normal for some dogs)

Hip evaluations should not be delayed until two years of age (especially in susceptible breeds), but should be performed as young as five to six months old. Using a technique called palpation and hip manipulation, veterinarians can often detect hip dysplasia before symptoms become evident and when radiographs fail to identify malformations. Moving the knee towards the center causes the hip to fall out of its socket and moving the knee away from the center causes the hip to return to the socket.

Causes and Triggers

Canine hip dysplasia is usually an inherited condition. But there are also factors which can trigger or worsen the condition, including:

1. Overfeeding, especially on a diet high in protein and calories
2. Excess calcium, also usually due to overfeeding
3. Extended periods without exercise – or too much vigorous exercise – especially when your young dog and his bones are growing
4. Obesity

Advances in nutritional research have shown that diet plays an important role in the development of hip dysplasia. The Bulldog is also a breed prone to putting on weight, and it's important for owners to realize that, no matter how cutely he stares at you pleading for food with those beautiful big brown eyes, excess pounds will place a strain on your dog and eventually take their toll.

Feeding a high-calorie or high calcium diet to growing dogs can trigger a predisposition to hip dysplasia, as the rapid weight gain places increased stress on the hips. During their first year of life, Bulldog puppies should be fed a special diet which will contain the correct amount of calories, minerals and protein, thereby reducing the risk of hip dysplasia.

When you take your puppy to the vet's for his injections, ask for advice on the best diet. Also speak to your breeder, a good breeder will remain at the end of a phone line to give advice throughout your Bully's life.

Exercise may be another risk factor. Dogs that have a predisposition to hip dysplasia may have an increased chance of getting it if they are over-exercised at a young age. On the other hand, dogs with large leg muscle mass are likely to cope better with hip dysplasia than dogs with small muscle mass.

The key here is moderate, low impact exercise for fast-growing young dogs. High impact activities which apply a lot of force to the joint, such and jumping and catching Frisbees, is not recommended with young Bulldogs.

Treatment

As with most conditions, early detection leads to a better outcome. Your vet will take X-rays to make a diagnosis. Treatment is geared towards preventing the hip joint getting worse and decreasing pain. Various medical and surgical treatments are now available to ease the dog's discomfort and restore some mobility.

Treatment depends upon several factors, such as the dog's age, how bad the problem is and, sadly, how much money you can afford to spend on treatment. Management of the condition usually consists of restricting exercise, keeping body weight down and then managing pain with analgesics and anti-inflammatory drugs.

As with humans, cortisone injections may sometimes be used to reduce inflammation and swelling. Cortisone can be injected directly into the affected hip to provide almost immediate relief for a tender, swollen joint. In severe cases, surgery may be an option, especially with older dogs.

Hip Testing

The Penn Hip system was developed to provide a reliable method for predicting the development of Canine Hip Dysplasia and can be used on dogs as young as 16 weeks old. The Penn Hip method uses three separate radiographs taken under deep sedation or general anesthesia.

Thirty years ago the British Veterinary Association (BVA) and Kennel Club in the UK set up a hip screening program for dogs, which tests them using radiology and gives them a rating or 'hip score'. The KC is responsible for publishing hip dysplasia results for all pedigree dogs in the Kennel Club Breed Records.

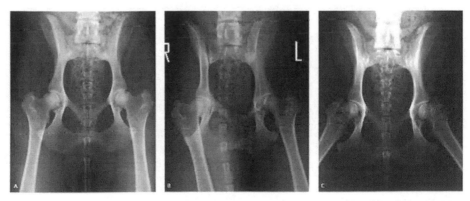

Figure A is the healthy hip, B shows lateral tilting, C shows outward rotation

Veterinary MRI and radiology specialist Ruth Dennis, of the Animal Health Trust, states: *"For dogs intended for breeding, it is essential that the hips are assessed before mating to ensure that they are free of dysplastic changes or only minimally affected."*

Elbow Dysplasia

Elbow dysplasia is more commonly seen in fast-growing large puppies and is not a simple condition to understand nor easy to explain. It is really a syndrome in which one or more conditions are present.

The exact cause is unknown, but it is probably due to a combination of genetic factors, over-nutrition with rapid growth, trauma and hormonal factors. Affected dogs include: Labrador Retrievers, Golden Retrievers, Rottweilers, Bernese Mountain Dogs, Newfoundlands, German Shepherds and Chow Chows. Signs usually begin between four to 12 months of age. The Bulldog is not listed among the breeds most at risk of developing elbow dysplasia, but some do develop the condition.

Many bones in a newborn puppy are not just one piece of bone, but several different pieces of bone with cartilage in between. This is especially true of long bones of the limbs.

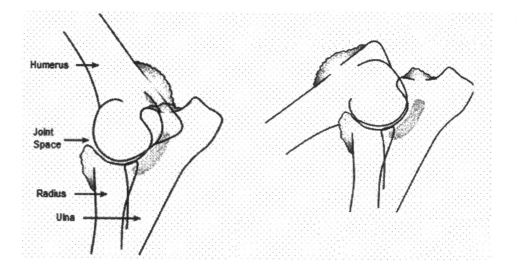

Figure 4a   **Figure 4b**
Figures 4a and 4b. Osteoarthritic changes to the shape and structure of the elbow joint. The shaded areas on figure 4a (extended elbow) and 4b (flexed elbow) represent the changes to bone and cartilage as a result of UAP and other forms of elbow dysplasia.

Images courtesy of the British Veterinary Association.

As the puppy grows, the cartilage changes into bone and several pieces of bone fuse together forming one entire bone. For instance, the ulna, a bone in the forearm, starts out as four pieces of bone that eventually fuse into one. Elbow dysplasia occurs when certain parts of the elbow joint develop abnormally as a dog grows. Some parts of the joint may have abnormal development, resulting in an uneven joint surface, inflammation, lameness and arthritis. It eventually results in elbow arthritis which may be associated with joint stiffness (reduced range of motion) and lameness.

Symptoms and Diagnosis

The most notable symptom is an obvious limp. Your Bulldog may hold his leg out from the body while walking, or even lift the front leg completely, putting no weight on it at all.

Signs may be noted as early as four months old and many affected dogs will go through a period between six months and a year old when the symptoms will be at their worst. After this, most will show some signs occasionally, but they will be less severe. As the affected adolescent continues to mature, there will probably be permanent arthritic changes causing problems.

Many dogs will have more than one of the conditions that contribute to elbow dysplasia. One or both elbows may be affected. The symptoms of front leg lameness and pain in the elbow are typical.

However, there are other conditions that can affect the front leg of a young dog that closely mimic the signs of elbow dysplasia. Your vet will have to take X-rays of the affected joint or joints for a proper diagnosis.

Treatment

Treatment varies, depending on the exact cause of the condition. The young dog is usually placed on a regular, low-impact exercise programme - swimming can be a good exercise. Owners must carefully manage their dog's diet and weight.

Oral or injected medication such as nonsteroidal anti-inflammatory drugs (NSAIDS) may be necessary to make the dog more comfortable. These are prescribed to decrease pain and inflammation.

After the age of 12 or 18 months, the dog's lameness becomes less severe and some dogs function very well. Elbow dysplasia is, however, a lifelong problem, although some can be very effectively helped with surgery. In most cases degenerative joint disease (arthritis) will occur as the dog gets older, regardless of the type of treatment.

Luxating Patella

Luxating patella, also called 'floating kneecap' or 'slipped stifle' is a painful condition akin to a dislocated knee cap. It is often congenital (present from birth) and more typically affects small and miniature breeds. However Bulldogs are also listed as a breed susceptible to luxating patella.

Symptoms

A typical sign would be if your dog is running across the park when he suddenly pulls up short and yelps with pain. He might limp on three legs and then after a period of about 10 minutes, drop the affected leg and start to walk normally again.

If the condition is severe, he may hold up the affected leg up for a few days. Dogs that have a luxating patella on both hind legs may change their gait completely, dropping their hindquarters and holding the rear legs further out from the body as they walk.

In the most extreme cases they might not even use their rear legs, but walk like a circus act by balancing on their front legs so their hindquarters don't touch the ground.

Genetics, injury and malformation during development can all cause this problem. Because the most common cause is genetics, a dog with this ailment should never be used for breeding. If you are buying a puppy, ask if there is any history in either parent. Typically most sufferers are middle-aged dogs with a history of intermittent lameness in the affected rear leg or legs, although the condition may become apparent as early as four to six months old.

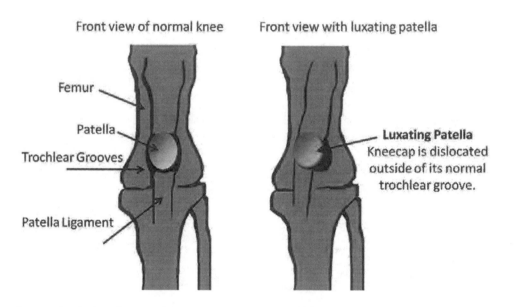

A groove in the end of the femur (thigh bone) allows the knee cap to glide up and down when the knee joint is bent, while keeping it in place at the same time. If this groove is too shallow, the knee cap may luxate – or dislocate. It can only return to its natural position when the quadriceps muscle relaxes and increases in length, which is why the dog may have to hold his leg up for some time after the dislocation. Sometimes the problem can be caused by obesity, the excess weight putting too much strain on the joint – another good reason to keep your Bulldog's weight in check.

Treatment

There are four grades of patellar luxation, ranging from Grade I, which causes a temporary lameness in the joint, to Grade IV, in which the patella cannot be realigned manually. This gives the dog a bow-legged appearance. If left untreated, the groove will become even shallower and the dog will become progressively lamer, with arthritis prematurely affecting the joint. This will cause a permanently swollen knee and reduce your Bulldog's mobility. It is therefore important to get your Bulldog in for a veterinary check-up ASAP if you suspect he may have a luxating patella.

In severe cases one option is surgery, although this should not be undertaken lightly with Bulldogs, due to potential breathing problems under anesthetic. The groove at the base of the femur may be surgically deepened to better hold the knee cap in place. This operation is known as a **trochlear modification**. The good news is that dogs generally respond well, whatever the type of surgery, and are usually completely recovered within one to two months.

Cherry Eye

Humans have two eyelids, but dogs have a third eyelid, called a nictating membrane. This third eyelid is a thin, opaque tissue with a tear gland which rests in the inner corner of the eye. Its purpose is to provide additional protection for the eye and to spread tears over the eyeball.

Usually it is retracted and therefore you can't see it, although you may notice it when your dog is relaxed and falling asleep. When the third eyelid becomes visible it may be a sign of illness or a painful eye.

Cherry Eye is a medical condition, officially known as nictitans gland prolapse, or prolapse of the gland of the third eyelid. Bulldogs are prone to this, although it is not known whether the condition is inherited.

Other susceptible breeds include the Beagle, Bloodhound, Boston Terrier, Bull Terrier, Cocker Spaniel, Lhasa Apso, Saint Bernard and Shar-Pei.

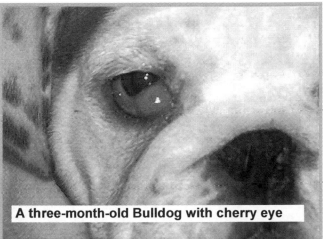

A three-month-old Bulldog with cherry eye

Causes

The exact cause of cherry eye is not known, but it is thought to be due to a weakness of the fibrous tissue which attaches the gland to the surrounding eye. This weakness allows the gland to fall down, or prolapse. Once this has happened and the gland is exposed to the dry air and irritants, it can become infected and/or begin to swell. The gland often becomes irritated, red and swollen. There is sometimes a mucous discharge and if the dog rubs or scratches it, he can further damage the gland and even possibly create an ulcer on the surface of the eye.

Symptoms

The main visible symptom in a red, often swollen, mass in the corner of one or both eyes, which is often first seen in young dogs up to the age of two years. It can occur in one or both eyes and may be accompanied by swelling and/or irritation. Although it may look sore, it is not a painful condition for your dog.

Treatment

At one time, it was popular to surgically remove the gland to correct this condition. While this was often effective, it could create problems later on. The gland of the third eyelid is very important for producing tears, without which dogs could suffer from 'dry eye', also known as keratoconjunctivitis sicca (KCS). These days, removing the gland is not considered a good idea.

A far better and straightforward option is to surgically reposition the gland by tacking it back into place with a single stitch that attaches the gland to the deeper structures of the eye socket. There is also another type of operation during which the wedge of tissue is removed from directly over the gland. Tiny dissolving stitches are used to close the gap so that the gland is pushed back into place. After surgery the dog may be placed on antibiotic ointment for a few days.

Healthy Bulldog eyes

Mostly, surgery is performed quickly and few dogs experience complications. However, some dogs do have a recurrence of cherry eye. The eye should return to normal after about seven days, during which time there may be some redness or swelling. If the affected eye suddenly seems uncomfortable or painful for your dog, or you can see protruding stitches, then take him back to the veterinarian to get checked out. Other options include anti-inflammatory eye drops to reduce the swelling and manually manipulating the gland back into place.

Tip

Sometimes a Bulldog will develop cherry eye in one eye and then the condition will also appear some time later in the other eye. If you have a young dog diagnosed with cherry eye, discuss waiting a few weeks or months before having any surgery to see if the second eye is affected. This will save the dog being anesthetized twice and will also save you money. Discuss this with your veterinarian.

Eyelid Problems

The Bulldog is susceptible to both ectropion and entropion.

Entropion is a condition in which the edge of the lower eyelid rolls inward, causing the dog's fur to rub the surface of the eyeball, or cornea. In rare cases the upper lid can also be affected, and one or both eyes may be involved. This painful condition is thought to be hereditary and is more commonly found in dog breeds with a wrinkled face, such as the Bulldog.

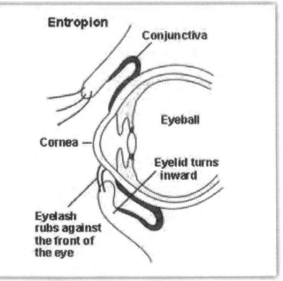

Other affected breeds include the Chow Chow, Bloodhound, Pug, Bull Mastiff, Great Dane, Rottweiler, Akita, Shar Pei, Spaniel, Poodle, and Labrador.

The affected dog will scratch at his painful eye with his paws and this can lead to further injury. If your Bulldog is to suffer from entropion, he will usually show signs at or before his first birthday. You will notice that his eyes are red and inflamed and they will produce tears. He will probably squint.

The tears typically start off clear and can progress to a thick yellow or green mucus. If the entropion causes corneal ulcers, you might also notice a milky-white color develop. This is caused by increased fluid which affects the clarity of the cornea.

For your poor dog, the irritation is constant. Imagine how painful and uncomfortable it would be if you had permanent hairs touching your eyes. It makes my eyes water just thinking about it.

It's important to get your dog to the vet as soon as you suspect entropion before your dog scratches his cornea and worsens the problem. Entropion can cause scarring around the eyes or other issues which can jeopardize a dog's vision if left untreated.

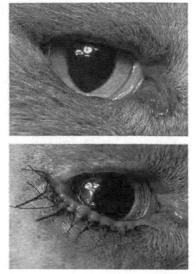

A veterinarian will make the diagnosis after a painless and relatively simple inspection of your dog's eyes. Before your vet can diagnose entropion, he or she will have to rule out other issues, such as allergies, which might also be making your Bulldog's eyes red and itchy. That's another reason why it is a good idea to find a vet who is familiar with Bulldogs and their associated health issues.

In young Bulldogs, some vets may delay surgery and treat the condition with medication until the dog's face is fully formed to avoid having to repeat the procedure at a later date.

In mild cases, the veterinarian may successfully prescribe eye drops, ointment or other medication. However, the most common treatment for more severe cases is a fairly straightforward surgical procedure to pin back the lower eyelid. Discuss the severity of the condition and all possible options with your vet before proceeding to surgery, anesthetic is not without risk for Bulldogs.

Ectropion is a condition where the lower lids turn outwards. This causes the eyelids to appear droopy, and one or both eyes may be involved. It can occur in any breed, but certain breeds, including Bulldogs, have a higher incidence of the condition. Other breeds affected are Cocker Spaniels, Saint Bernards, Mastiffs, Bassett Hounds, Newfoundlands, and Bloodhounds.

'Acquired ectropion' can occur in any dog at any age and it means that a reason other than genetics has caused the eyelid to sag. These include:

- ❖ Facial nerve paralysis
- ❖ Hypothyroidism
- ❖ Scarring secondary to injury
- ❖ Chronic inflammation and infection of the tissues surrounding the eyes
- ❖ Surgical overcorrection of ectropion
- ❖ Neuromuscular disease

Ectropion causes the lower lid to droop, thereby exposing the conjunctiva and forming a pouch or pocket where pollens, grasses and dust can collect and rub against the sensitive conjunctiva. This is a consistent source of irritation to the dog, and leads to increased redness of the conjunctiva and the production of tears which flow over the lower lid and face, often causing a brownish staining of the fur below the eyes. A thick mucus discharge may appear along the eyelid margin and the dog may rub or scratch his eyes if it becomes uncomfortable.

Diagnosis is usually made on physical examination. If the dog is older, blood and urine tests may be performed to search for an underlying cause. Your vet may also perform corneal staining to see if any ulcers are present.

Many dogs live normal lives with ectropion. However, some develop repeated eye infections due to the collection of dirt and dust within the eye. Therefore, the risks are minor except in severe cases, where secondary eye infections may develop.

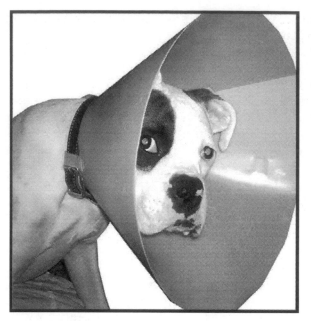

Some dogs require no treatment. But if eye irritations develop, you should see your veterinarian. Mild cases can be treated with lubricating eye drops and ointments to prevent the cornea and conjunctiva from drying out. Special eye (ophthalmic) antibiotics will be used to combat any corneal ulcers. These medications will alleviate irritations and/or infections when they occur.

In severe cases, surgery is undertaken to remove excess tissue to tighten the lids and remove the abnormal pocket which is trapping the dirt, etc. Surgical correction is usually successful. In some cases, your vet may recommend performing two separate operations in order to avoid over-correction, which would cause an entropion to develop. As always, the risks of anesthesia and surgery for Bulldogs have to be weighed against any potential benefits for your dog.

Eye Care for Bulldogs

Some eye conditions affecting Bulldogs may be inherited, but there are other issues, such as dirt or pollen in the eye, which are environmental. Bulldogs love to root around in all sorts of places and can easily finish up with irritating material in their eyes, which will cause them to rub or scratch. Also, some Bulldogs may suffer from allergies which will also cause their eyes to become irritated.

Whatever the reason, it is a good idea to get into the habit of cleaning your Bulldog's eyes and the surrounding skin folds (wrinkles) at least once a week – preferably even more often. This also enables you to monitor any changes in the eyes and, if a problem such as infection, cherry eye or entropion/ectropion does occur, to get on top of it right away.

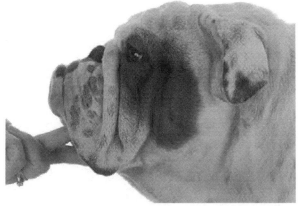

Distichiasis is another condition to look out for. It occurs when small eyelashes grow on the inner surface or very edge of the eyelids, causing the eye to become red and inflamed and the dog to blink a lot. This problem can be treated with electrolysis.

Tear staining is a common problem with Bulldogs, especially with lighter colored ones. These brownish, wet stains are also a breeding ground for bacteria and yeast. The most common is Red Yeast, which is usually associated with reddish-brown facial stains, and which may emit an odor.

Tear staining can be related to health and diet as well as genetics. Most vets agree that face staining results from excessive tear production and a damp face. In addition, the wrinkles or folds around the eyes and nose attract dirt, so keeping them clean should be a regular part of your Bulldog maintenance program!

Despite the fact that your Bulldog looks extremely robust, as far as his health is concerned, he is a rather delicately balanced creature which needs to be lavished with a great deal of care and attention to remain in tip top condition - rather like a very expensive and finely tuned sports car.

Cleaning your dog's tear stains will also help to avoid infection. To do this, wet a cotton ball with a sterile eye wash, or use eye wipes, to gently rub the folds around your Bulldog's eyes, clearing them of any dried discharge. Repeat the action with clean cotton balls or wipes until the area is clean. There are videos on YouTube which demonstrate how to clean your Bulldog's eyes and facial skin folds. Remember to dry the wrinkles after cleaning to deter yeast infections.

There are many canine tear stain removers on the market. One product which some owners have found useful is Angel Eyes for Dogs. It's quite expensive, but if is saves you having to visit the vet's with eye infections, it will be worth it in the long run. Other owners have tried home remedies with some success, but be extremely careful of the substances you put near to your Bulldog's sensitive eyes. If in any doubt at all about a product or remedy, check with your vet.

Be on the lookout for **dry eye,** a condition which occurs when the eyes are not producing enough tears. A green discharge is usually present, and a hazy blue film can appear on the eyeball. Your vet can carry out a simple test to diagnose the problem, and may prescribe artificial tears which you should apply daily. (Humans can get the same problem, particularly when they get older.)

Head Tremors

It is well documented that some Bulldogs develop head tremors. These are also referred to as **idiopathic head tremors,** which means that the cause is unknown. Other breeds affected include Pit Bulls, Dachshunds, Boxers, Doberman Pinchers and Chinooks and medical research is continuing into the condition.

It can be very distressing for the owner to witness their beloved Bully experiencing head tremors, but vets believe that the dog is not in pain or unduly distressed during the tremors.

Head tremors are different from seizures, see the next section on **Epilepsy** to read about

seizures and their symptoms. Typically, a Bulldog suffering from head tremors will bob his head up and down or side to side. To see what this looks like, go to YouTube on the internet, type in 'Bulldog Head Tremors', and you will find numerous videos of the episodes.

If your dog has head tremors, the best piece of advice is: REMAIN CALM. Panicking will only make things worse for your dog. If you can, record the episode with a mobile phone or video recorder which you can show to your veterinarian later on. Notice whether your dog is alert and responsive or in a trance, how long and how often the head tremors occur and any other details you think may be relevant.

Many owners say that their Bulldogs are entirely aware during episodes. Their ears stay up as if alert, they respond to calls and commands as usual, and their appetites aren't affected. There is anecdotal evidence to suggest that sometimes the head tremors may be triggered either by excitement or by low blood sugars. Sometimes a Bulldog may start to exhibit head tremors some time after having surgery, when previously he had none.

If your dog has a tremor episode, get his attention by calling him over to you and making him sit still so he can focus. Some owners give their dogs honey, frozen yoghurts, ice pops or other treats to help release them from the tremors. Veterinarians do not recommend giving seizure medication to treat head tremors.

The following are extracts from the article **'Head Tremors in the Bulldog - Partial/ Focal Seizures, Paroxysmal Dyskinesia'** by Kathy Jacobsen, of Rely-A-Bull Bulldogs.

"What qualifies me to discuss such a topic, you might ask? My answer to you would be good old experience. I have been in bulldogs for close to 25+ years, had seven litters and of those seven litters have had five dogs/bitches who have exhibited one or more of these behaviors.

In my experience, head tremor activity in the Bulldog usually starts around the age of two years old. The motion you will see will almost always be a fast side to side rocking motion (ear to shoulder, ear to shoulder) occurring in rapid succession. Occasionally I have seen an up and down motion (like they are shaking their heads to say yes), but for the most part it is the same fast rocking. The way it was defined to me was that the neuron cluster that controls a certain motor function (in this case head movement) begins to fire continuously. The reason for this rapid fire is truly unknown.

I have not experienced any drooling or other body part involvement. It has always been isolated to the head. When you call the dog's name they can stop the bobbing motion for a few seconds and will look at you, then it will kick in again. They can move their heads and watch you move from place to place, they can even walk around etc.

Scenario I: The bully will be sleeping very soundly and all of a sudden the head will start rocking usually from side to side very quickly - occasionally you might experience one bobbing up and down. This sudden head motion will cause the bully to awaken suddenly. An episode will last from 15 to 30 seconds, sometimes longer. It may stop on its own and then as the dog lies down to go back to sleep the head tremor will reoccur.

Scenario II: A bitch will be pre-season or just come into season and can show head tremor activity due to the increase in hormones. In addition you may witness your males/stud dogs show head bobbing activity. The female hormones can trigger the tremors in the male also due to the excitement from the scent of a girl in season/extra hormonal activity.

Scenario III: A bitch is post whelp, in the milk let-down phase of lactation, and trying to nurse a litter of hungry pups. In this case the bitch has had surgical trauma as the result of a C section, is in pain, is not eating and is trying to make milk. This, in my opinion is different than the head tremors described in Scenario I and II. When you see this what do you do? The first time we experienced this phenomena was a scenario III post-whelp and I panicked. I grabbed the puppies off the bitch and almost caused one to aspirate.

When I gained a little composure I called a breeder friend of mine and explained what I was seeing. She told me that it was not uncommon and I should try to get some sugar, honey, Karo corn syrup into her. The thought is that the blood sugar had experienced a sharp drop at that point in time thus stimulating this type of a response. We gave the girl the Karo and lo and behold the tremors stopped within a couple of seconds.

The next time we witnessed this behavior was a little different. The bitch was not post whelp. However, she was three days prior to coming into season. She had been sleeping on the couch. We gave her honey. It stopped. Started up 15 minutes later we repeated this time with Karo syrup. Same result.

We gave her frozen yogurt, same result. This went on for almost 24 hours with the length of time between episodes varying from 10-15 minutes to as long as a half hour. Needless to say we packed her up and went off to the vet who said: "This is not unusual in this breed. Normally we don't do anything. Epilepsy meds have proven to be ineffective for the most part; phenobarb has too many side effects."

The veterinarian stated that they suspect it has something to do with the growth activity at this age or stress, which can cause a sudden drop in glucose levels in the blood. There can be different things or circumstances that can trigger an episode, such as a traumatic experience, an injury, hormones, etc. In this girl's case we have determined that it is a hormone trigger, specifically at the time of a progesterone spike associated with ovulation.

The vet recommended calcium and taurine supplementation twice daily. As you know, calcium is one of the minerals needed for healthy nerve growth and electrical conductivity, Taurine is an amino acid that works with calcium. The vet said she might grow out of it. So we took that information and we asked for a referral to a neurologist.

The specialist did all of the neurological tests and determined she was fine. She ordered ionized calcium levels along with several other specific blood tests. The results all came back normal. She recommended an MRI to determine if there was an injury or tumor. We declined this step at the time due to finances, but decided if she showed any other neurological symptoms such as falling down or aggression (which could be indicative of an injury or tumor) that we would come back to do the MRI.

Six months went by on the calcium and taurine supplementation to which we added a heaped tablespoon of ricotta cheese every morning, and every couple of days a bowl of frozen vanilla yogurt with honey in the evening. No incidents. The day we bred her (at the time of the progesterone spike indicating ovulation that we were waiting for) she had one mild episode, then nothing for the entire pregnancy. The episodes started up the second week of lactation when the calcium bolus given at the time of the C-section was gone and six hungry puppies were pulling on her calcium/glucose levels. Five months have since passed and she has been just fine, with no episodes. My recommendations:

1. If your dog exhibits this head bobbing behavior a. DON'T PANIC!!! This could only worsen the situation by adding additional stress on the dog. Give them a bowl of ice cream or frozen vanilla yogurt with honey to get the situation under control. If you don't have any of those then Ensure, Pediasure, Karo syrup all work because of the sugar and or calcium content. Liquids work quicker because they are absorbed into the mucosa of the mouth.

2. Call your veterinarian and advise of the situation. Schedule an appointment for a visit and have your vet do a health screening with blood work. Odds are the blood work for calcium and sugar will be fine.

3. Keep a record of each episode, every time one occurs describe it in great detail, time it occurred how long, how frequent. Give this info to the vet when you see him.

4. IF they do not get any worse than the head bobs don't do anything else but observe and document. If the behavior changes in any way, call the vet, you may need additional assistance at this point. Two other behaviors I would like to mention briefly are the fly chasing and the circling behaviors. Fly chasing is just that, the dog seems to be chasing and trying to catch imaginary flies.

Again, if you call the dog by name he will stop and look at you then resume the behavior. The other is circling. This looks like VERY slow motion tail-chasing, usually in the same direction each time. If you call the dog they will stop to acknowledge you then start up again. In this case, I go over and give my girl a nudge and she stops and resumes whatever she had started to go outside to do.

5. Distraction helps. Take the dog outside to run around. Throw a ball and play fetch or whatever their favorite game is. The distraction sometimes help to cut the duration of the tremor down because the dogs focus is elsewhere

6. Lastly the other thing you can do is nothing. While this is very difficult on the owner, the tremors will stop on their own. They seem to last only as long as the nerve has acetylcholine to cause it to fire. Once it depletes the stores, the tremor or bobbing motion will stop on its own.

2014 update: There is a study currently in progress on this subject. Hopefully a report with some significant findings will be produced. Up until recently it was not studied as it is not a life-threatening syndrome. Yet it is being seen more and more in the Bulldog as well as other breeds."

With thanks to Kathy Jacobsen for kind permission to reproduce these extracts.

Epilepsy

Thanks to **www.canineepilepsy.co.uk** for assistance with this article. If your Bulldog has epilepsy, we recommend reading this excellent website to gain a greater understanding of the illness.

If you have witnessed your dog having a seizure (convulsion), you will know how frightening it can be. Seizures are not uncommon in dogs, but many dogs have only a single seizure. If your dog has had more than one seizure it may be that he or she is epileptic. Just as in people, there are medications for dogs to control seizures, allowing your dog to live a more normal life.

Epilepsy means repeated seizures due to abnormal activity in the brain and is caused by an abnormality in the brain itself.

If seizures happen because of a problem somewhere else in the body, such as heart disease (which stops oxygen reaching the brain), this is not epilepsy.

Your vet may do tests to try to find the reason for the epilepsy but in many cases no cause can be identified. Epilepsy affects around four or five in every 100 dogs and in some breeds it can be hereditary. The Bulldog is not listed as one of the breeds more susceptible to epilepsy, although some do suffer from head tremors, which can be mistaken for epilepsy, but are entirely different.

Symptoms

Some dogs seem to know when they are about to have a seizure and may behave in a certain way. You will come to recognize these signs as meaning that a seizure is likely. Often dogs just seek out their owner's company and come to sit beside them when a seizure is about to start.

Once the seizure starts, the dog is unconscious – he cannot hear or respond to you (unlike with head tremors). Most dogs become stiff, fall onto their side and make running movements with their legs. Sometimes they will cry out and may lose control of their bowels or bladder.

Most seizures last between one and three minutes - **it is worth making a note of the time the seizure starts and ends** because it often seems that a seizure goes on for a lot longer than it actually does.

After a seizure, dogs behave in different ways. Some dogs just get up and carry on with what they were doing, while others appear dazed and confused for up to 24 hours afterwards.

Most commonly, dogs will be disoriented for only 10 to 15 minutes before returning to their old self. They often have a set pattern of behavior that they follow - for example going for a drink of water or asking to go outside to the toilet. If your dog has had more than one seizure, you may well start to notice a pattern of behavior which is typically repeated.

Most seizures occur while the dog is relaxed and resting quietly. It is very rare for a seizure to occur while exercising. Often seizures occur in the evening or at night. In a few dogs, seizures seem to be triggered by particular events or stress. It is common for a pattern to develop and, should your dog suffer from epilepsy, you will gradually recognize this as specific to your dog.

What Should I Do?

The most important thing is to **stay calm**. Remember that your dog is unconscious during the seizure and is not in pain or distressed. It is likely to be more distressing for you than for him.

Make sure that he is not in a position to injure himself, for example by falling down the stairs, but otherwise do not try to interfere with him. Never try to put your hand inside his mouth during a seizure or you are very likely to get bitten.

Seizures can cause damage to the brain and if your dog has repeated occurrences, it is likely that further seizures will occur in the future. The damage caused is cumulative and after a lot of seizures there may be enough brain damage to cause early senility (with loss of learned behavior and house-training or behavioral changes).

It is very rare for dogs to injure themselves during a seizure. Occasionally they may bite their tongue and there may appear to be a lot of blood, but is unlikely to be serious; your dog will not swallow his tongue.

If a seizure goes on for a very long time (more than 10 minutes), his body temperature will rise and this can cause damage to other organs such as the liver and kidneys as well as the brain. In very extreme cases, some dogs may be left in a coma after severe seizures.

If you are able to record your dog's seizure on a mobile phone or video recorder, this will be most useful to show the veterinarian.

When Should I Contact the Vet?

Generally, if your dog has a seizure lasting more than five minutes, or is having more than two or three a day, you should contact your vet.

When your dog starts a seizure, make a note of the time. If he comes out of it within five minutes, allow him time to recover quietly before contacting your vet. It is far better for him to recover quietly at home rather than be bundled into the car and carted off to the vet right away.

However, if your dog does not come out of the seizure within five minutes, or has repeated seizures close together, contact your vet immediately, as he or she will want to see your dog as soon as possible. If this is his first seizure, your vet may ask you to bring him in for a check and some routine blood tests. Always call your vet's practice before setting off to be sure that there is someone there who can help your dog.

There are many things other than epilepsy which cause seizures in dogs. When your vet first examines your dog, he or she will not know whether your dog has epilepsy or another illness.

It's unlikely that the vet will see your dog during a seizure, so it is **vital** that you're able to describe in some detail just what happens. You might want to make notes or take a video on your mobile phone. Epilepsy usually starts when the dog is aged between one and five. So if your dog is older or younger, it's more likely he has a different problem.

Your vet may need to run a range of tests to ensure that there is no other cause of the seizures. These may include blood tests, possibly X-rays, and maybe even a scan (MRI) of your dog's brain. If no other cause can be found, then a diagnosis of epilepsy may be made. If your Bulldog already has epilepsy, remember these key points:

- ❖ ***Don't change or stop any medication without consulting your vet.**
- ❖ ***See your vet at least once a year for follow-up visits.**
- ❖ ***Be sceptical of "magic cure" treatments.**

Remember, live **with** epilepsy not **for** epilepsy. With the proper medical treatment, most epileptic dogs have far more good days than bad ones. Enjoy all those good days.

Treatment

It is not usually possible to remove the cause of the seizures, so your vet will use medication to control them. Treatment will not cure the disease, but it will manage the signs – even a well-controlled epileptic will have occasional seizures. Sadly, as yet there is no miracle cure for epilepsy, so don't be tempted with "instant cures" from the internet.

There are many drugs used in the control of epilepsy in people, but very few of these are suitable for long-term use in a dog. Two of the most common are Phenobarbital and Potassium Bromide. Many epileptic dogs require a combination of one or more types of drug to achieve the most effective control of their seizures. Treatment is decided on an individual basis and it may take some time to find the best combination and dose of drugs for your pet. You need patience when managing an epileptic pet.

It is important that medication is given at the same time each day. Once your dog has been on treatment for a while, he will become dependent on the levels of drug in his blood at all times to control seizures. If you miss a dose of treatment, blood levels can drop and this may be enough to trigger a seizure. Each epileptic dog is an individual and a treatment plan will be designed specifically for him. It will be based on the severity and frequency of the seizures and how they respond to different medications.

Keep a record of events in your dog's life, note down dates and times of seizures and record when you have given medication. Each time you visit your vet, take this diary along with you so he or she can see how your dog has been since his last check-up.

If seizures are becoming more frequent, it may be necessary to change the medication. The success or otherwise of treatment may depend on you keeping a close eye on your Bulldog to see if there are any physical or behavioral changes.

It is rare for epileptic dogs to stop having seizures altogether. However, provided your dog is checked regularly by your vet to make sure that the drugs are not causing any side-effects, there is a good chance that he will live a full and happy life. Visit **www.canineepilepsy.co.uk** for more information.

Hypothyroidism

Hypothyroidism is a common hormonal disorder in dogs and is due to an under-active thyroid gland. This gland (located on either side of the windpipe in the dog's throat) does not produce enough of the hormone thyroid, which controls the speed of the metabolism. Dogs with very low thyroid levels have a slow metabolic rate. It occurs mainly in dogs over the age of five. Bulldogs may be more prone to hypothyroidism than some other breeds.

Generally, hypothyroidism occurs most frequently in large, middle-aged dogs of either gender. The symptoms are often non-specific and quite gradual in onset, and they may vary depending on breed and age. Most forms of hypothyroidism are diagnosed with a blood test.

Common Symptoms

The following symptoms have been listed in order, with the most common ones being at the top of the list:

- ❖ **High blood cholesterol**

- ❖ **Lethargy**

- ❖ **Hair Loss**

- ❖ **Weight gain or obesity**

- ❖ **Dry coat or excessive shedding**

- ❖ **Hyper pigmentation** or darkening of the skin, seen in 25% of cases

- ❖ **Intolerance to cold,** seen in 15% of dogs with the condition

Treatment

Although hypothyroidism is a type of auto-immune disease and cannot be prevented, the good news is that symptoms can usually be easily diagnosed and treated. Most dogs suffering from hypothyroidism can be well-managed on oral thyroid hormone replacement therapy (tablets).

The dog is normally placed on a daily dose of a synthetic thyroid hormone called thyroxine (levothyroxine). The dose and frequency of administration of the drug varies depending on the severity of the disease and the response of the individual dog to the drug.

A dog is usually given a standard dose for his weight and then blood samples are taken periodically to check his response and the dose is adjusted accordingly. Depending upon your dog's preferences and needs, the medication can be given in different forms, such as a solid tablet, in liquid form, or a gel that can be rubbed into your Bulldog's ears. Once treatment has started, he will have to be on it for the rest of his life.

In some less common situations, surgery may be required to remove part or all of the thyroid gland. Another treatment is radioiodine, where radioactive iodine is used to kill the overactive cells of the thyroid. While this is considered one of the most effective treatments, not all animals are suitable for the procedure and a lengthy hospitalization is often required. Happily, once the diagnosis has been made and treatment has started, whichever treatment your dog undergoes, the majority of symptoms disappear.

NOTE: **Hyper**thyroidism (as opposed to **hypo**thyroidism) is caused by the thyroid gland producing too much thyroid hormone. It is quite rare in dogs, but more often seen in cats. A common symptom is the dog being ravenously hungry all the time while actually losing weight.

Canine Bloat

Canine bloat is a serious medical condition which requires urgent medical attention. Without it, the dog can die. In fact, it is one of the leading killers of dogs after cancer.

Bloat is known by several different names: twisted stomach, gastric torsion or, to give the ailment its medical term: Gastric Dilitation-Volvulus (GDV). It occurs when the dog's body becomes overstretched with too much gas.

The reasons for it are not fully understood, but there are some well-known risk factors. Bloat occurs mainly in larger breeds, particularly those with deep chests like Great Danes, Doberman Pinschers and Setters, but these are not the only breeds affected and it can happen to smaller dogs. It also happens more - but not exclusively- to dogs over seven years of age and it is more common in males than in females. The risks increase if the stomach is very full, either with food or with water.

A dog which is fed once daily and eats very quickly, or gets access to the food store and gorges itself, could be at higher risk. Exercising after eating or after a big drink increases the risk, and stress can also act as a trigger.

Bloat occurs when gas is taken in as the dog eats or drinks. It can occur with or without the stomach twisting (volvulus). As the stomach swells with gas, it can rotate 90° to 360°.

The twisting stomach traps air, food, and water inside and the bloated organ stops blood flowing properly to veins in the abdomen, leading to low blood pressure, shock and even damage to internal organs.

Bloat can kill a dog in less than one hour. If you suspect your Bulldog has bloat, get him into the car and off to the vet **IMMEDIATELY**. Even with treatment, mortality rates range from 10% to 60%. With surgery, this drops to 15% to 33%.

Causes

The causes are not completely clear, despite research being carried out into the condition. However, the following conditions are generally thought to be contributory factors:

❖ Air is gulped down as the dog eats or drinks. This is thought more likely to cause a problem when the dog's bowls are on the floor. Some owners buy or construct a frame for the bowls so they are at chest height. However, some experts believe that this may actually increase the risk of bloat. Discuss the situation with your vet. Another option is to moisten your dog's food to slow him down.

❖ A large meal eaten once a day. For this reason, many owners feed their Bulldog two smaller feeds every day.

❖ Diet may be a factor: avoid dog food with high fats or which use citric acid as a preservative, also avoid food with tiny pieces of kibble. Don't overfeed your dog, try and prevent him from eating too fast and avoid feeding scraps as these may upset his stomach and lead to bloat.

❖ Drinking too much water just before, during or after eating. Remove the water bowl just before mealtimes, but be sure to return it soon after.

❖ Vigorous exercise before or after eating. Allow one hour either side of mealtimes before allowing your dog strenuous exercise.

❖ Age, temperament and breeds: older dogs are more susceptible and more males suffer than females. Deep-chested dogs are most at risk and some breeds, such as Doberman Pinschers, Great Danes and Giant Schnauzers, have a hereditary disposition for bloat.

❖ Stress can possibly be a trigger, with nervous and aggressive dogs being more prone to the illness. Try and maintain a peaceful environment for your dog.

Symptoms

Bloat is extremely painful and the dog will show signs of distress, although it may be difficult to distinguish them from other types of stress. He may stand uncomfortably or seem to be anxious for no apparent reason. Another symptom is dry retching: a dog with bloat will often attempt to vomit every five to 30 minutes, but nothing is fetched up, except perhaps foam.

Other signs include swelling of the abdomen – this will usually feel firm like a drum – general weakness, difficulty breathing or rapid panting, drooling or excessive drinking. His behavior will change and he may do some of the following: whine, pace up and down, look for a hiding place or lick the air.

Treatment

Bloat is an emergency condition. Get your dog to a veterinary surgery immediately.

Heart Problems

Heart failure, or congestive heart failure (CHF), occurs when the heart is not able to pump enough blood around the dog's body. The heart is a mechanical pump. It receives blood in one half and forces it through the lungs, then the other half pumps the blood through the entire body.

The two most common forms of heart failure in dogs are Degenerative Valvular Disease (DVD) and Dilated Cardiomyopathy (DCM), also known as an enlarged heart. In people, heart disease usually involves the arteries that supply blood to the heart muscle becoming hardened over time, causing the heart muscles to receive less blood than they need. Starved of oxygen, the result is often a heart attack.

In dogs, hardening of the arteries (arteriosclerosis) and heart attacks are very rare. However, heart disease is very common. In dogs, heart disease is often seen as heart failure, which means that the muscles 'give out.' This is usually caused by one chamber or side of the heart being required to do more than it is physically able to do. It may be that excessive force is required to pump the blood through an area and, over time, the muscles fail.

Unlike a heart attack in humans, heart failure in the dog is a slow insidious process that occurs over months or years. In these cases, once symptoms are noted, they will usually worsen over time until the animal is placed on treatment.

Heart failure in older dogs is usually due to problems with the mitral valve of the heart, and occurs most commonly in smaller breeds, such as Poodles, Yorkies, Pugs, Lhasa Apsos and Pomeranians.

Symptoms

- ❖ The dog becomes tired

- ❖ His activity levels decrease

- ❖ He is restless, pacing around instead of settling down to sleep.

- ❖ Intermittent coughing, especially during exertion or excitement. This tends to occur at night, sometimes about two hours after the dog goes to bed or when he wakes up in the morning. This coughing is an attempt to clear fluid in the lungs and is often the first clinical sign of a mitral valve disorder.

As the condition worsens, other symptoms may appear:

- ❖ Lack of appetite

- ❖ Rapid breathing

- ❖ Abdominal swelling (due to fluid)

- ❖ Noticeable loss of weight

❖ Fainting (syncope)

❖ Paleness

Diagnosis

If your dog is exhibiting a range of the above symptoms, the veterinarian may suspect congestive heart failure. He will carry out tests to make sure. These may include listening to the heart, chest X-rays, blood tests, electrocardiogram (a record of your dog's heartbeat) or an echocardiogram (ultrasound of the heart).

Treatment

If the heart problem is due to an enlarged heart (DCM) or valve disease, the condition cannot be reversed. Instead, treatment focuses on managing the symptoms with various medications. These may change over time as the condition worsens. The veterinarian may also prescribe a special low salt diet for your dog, as sodium (found in salt) determines the amount of water in the blood, and the amount of exercise your dog has will have to be controlled.

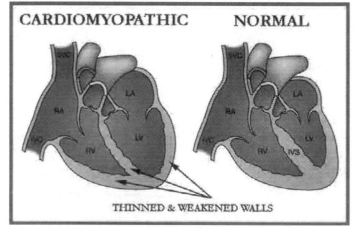

There is some evidence that vitamin and other supplements may be beneficial. Discuss this with your veterinarian.

The prognosis (outlook) for dogs with congestive heart failure depends on the cause and severity, as well as their response to treatment. Sadly, CHF is progressive, so your dog can never recover from the condition. But once diagnosed, he can live a longer, more comfortable life with the right medication and regular check-ups.

Heart Murmurs

Heart murmurs are not uncommon in dogs. Our dog was diagnosed with one a couple of years ago and, of course, your heart sinks when you get that terrible news from the vet. But once the shock is over, it's important to realize that there are several different severities of the condition and, at its mildest, it is no great cause for concern.

Literally, a heart murmur is a specific sound heard through a stethoscope, it results from the blood flowing faster than normal within the heart itself or in one of the two major arteries. Instead of the normal 'lubb dupp' noise, an additional sound can be heard that can vary from a mild 'pshhh' to a loud 'whoosh'. The different grades of heart murmurs are:

- **Grade 1**—barely audible
- **Grade 2**—soft, but easily heard with a stethoscope
- **Grade 3**—intermediate loudness; most murmurs which are related to the mechanics of blood circulation are at least grade III
- **Grade 4**—loud murmur that radiates widely, often including opposite side of chest
- **Grade 5 and Grade 6**—very loud, audible with stethoscope barely touching the chest; the vibration is also strong enough to be felt through the animal's chest wall

Murmurs are caused by a number of factors; it may be a problem with the heart valves or could be due to some other condition, such as hyperthyroidism (see the previous section on this), anemia, or heartworm.

In puppies, there are two major types of heart murmurs, and they will probably be detected by your vet at the first or second vaccinations. The most common type is called an innocent "flow murmur". This type of murmur is soft (typically Grade II or less) and is not caused by underlying heart disease. An innocent flow murmur typically disappears by four to five months of age.

However if a puppy has a loud murmur (Grade III or louder), or if the heart murmur is still easily heard with a stethoscope after four or five months of age, the likelihood of the puppy having an underlying congenital (from birth) heart problem becomes much higher.

The thought of a puppy having congenital heart disease is extremely worrying, but it is important to remember that the disease will not affect all puppies' life expectancy or quality of life.

A heart murmur can also develop suddenly in an adult dog with no prior history of the problem. This is typically due to heart disease that develops with age. In toy and small breeds, a heart murmur may develop in middle-aged to older dogs due to an age-related thickening and degeneration of one of the valves in the heart, the mitral valve.

This thickening of the valve prevents it from closing properly and as a result it starts to leak, this is known as mitral valve disease. The more common type of heart disease affecting larger dog breeds in middle age is Dilated Cardiomyopathy (DCM)

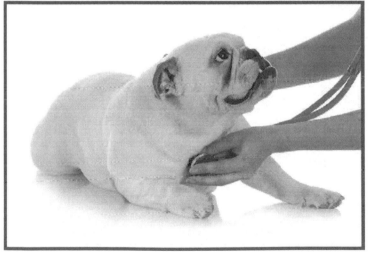

The best way to investigate the cause of the heart murmur is with an ultrasound examination of the heart (an echocardiogram).

By the way, our Max was diagnosed with a Grade II heart murmur and we have taken the vet's advice and ignored it – although we are always on alert for a dry, racking cough, which is a sign of fluid in the lungs (so far, it hasn't happened). The good news is that Max, now nine years old, seems just as fit and active as he was several years ago.

Overheating Bulldogs

It's a fact, Bulldogs overheat more easily than any other breed. They certainly do not cope well with warm temperatures and are prone to heatstroke or hyperthermia. (They can also suffer from **hypo**thermia if they get too cold).

It's also a fact that dogs can't sweat. Well, only a tiny bit through the pads of their paws. Instead of being able to cool down by sweating all over their body like humans, they have the far less efficient mechanism of panting, which circulates cooling air around their body. Couple this inefficient cooling system with the shortened head of the Bulldog and you have a potential recipe for disaster. Make no mistake, heat is a killer for Bulldogs.

Bulldogs have been bred to have shortened facial bone structures to give a pushed-in look. However, the soft tissue inside has stayed the same size, which means that there isn't much room for air to circulate inside the Bulldog's mouth and throat.

Some Bulldogs have elongated palates and extremely narrow nostrils (stenotic nares), which makes breathing difficult, and especially so when they are hot and need to pant. When they try to pant quickly, foam can be produced, which in turn blocks the throat and causes labored breathing. Eventually they will begin to roar as they try to breathe through the blockage. A dog's normal body temperature is around 100-102.5°F, (a puppy's normal rectal temperature is 96-100°F), if this rises to over 106°F, the dog is suffering from severe heatstroke and can die.

Symptoms

❖ He will pant rapidly and 'heave'

❖ This will develop into a roar

❖ His tongue will be bright red and floppy

❖ His gums may be discolored

❖ He will look tired and distressed, perhaps becoming dizzy

❖ He will produce a thick, sticky saliva or foam as his airways become blocked

❖ He may have diarrhea or begin vomiting - sometimes with blood

❖ Shock

❖ Coma

Action

STAY CALM! Your dog will pick up on your fear if you panic, causing him more stress. Remove the dog from the hot area immediately. Lower his temperature by wetting him thoroughly with **cool** water then increase air movement around him with a fan. Part his fur with your fingers to let the cooling air get to his body.

CAUTION: Using very cold water can actually be counterproductive. Cooling too quickly and especially allowing the dog's body temperature to become too low can cause other life-threatening medical conditions. Similarly, some Bulldog owners recommend using ice on the body to cool the dog, but many veterinarians advise against this, as it closes the skin pores and could potentially make the situation worse.

Other suggestions from owners include getting your Bulldog used to eating ice cubes, ice pops or frozen yoghurts from an early age so that if he does start to overheat, you can feed him these and he will readily take them. Another suggestion is that if your dog has started foaming, squirt lemon juice from a plastic lemon into the back of his throat – he will hate it, but the lemon juice will help to break down the foam and clear the throat. Many owners who live in warm climates have found the use of certain products such as cooling or ice collars, cooling jackets and blankets, to be most helpful.

The rectal temperature of an overheated dog should be checked every five minutes. Do this very carefully, preferably with somebody holding him steady. Use a special rectal thermometer and hold on to it, Bulldogs have been known to "suck in" the thermometer.

Once the body temperature is down to 103ºF, the cooling measures should be stopped and the dog should be dried thoroughly and covered so he does not continue to lose heat. Even if the dog appears to be recovering, take him to your vet as soon as possible. He should still be examined as he may be dehydrated or have other complications. Allow him access to water or an electrolyte rehydrating solution if he can drink on his own. Do not try to force-feed cold water as he may inhale it or choke.

Once the temperature is 103ºF or below, take him to the vet who will lower your dog's body temperature to a safe range, if you have not already done so, and continue to monitor his temperature. He or she may administer fluids, and possibly oxygen and may take blood samples to test for clotting. The dog will be monitored for shock, respiratory distress, kidney failure, heart abnormalities and other complications, and treated accordingly.

Dogs with moderate heatstroke often recover without complicated health problems. However, severe heatstroke can cause organ damage that might need ongoing care, such as a special diet prescribed by the vet. Dogs who suffer from heatstroke once have an increased risk of getting it again and steps must be taken to prevent it.

Top 14 Tips to Prevent a Bulldog Overheating

The main factor in determining whether your Bulldog gets heatstroke is YOU. Being aware of your dog's susceptibility to heat is the first step, taking action to prevent it is the second essential step. Bulldogs can overheat alarmingly quickly, here are some preventative measures:

1. Make sure your Bulldog has a cool place indoors and shade outdoors at all times

2. Reduce exercise in warm weather. Only take your dog outside for short periods – early in the morning and in the evening when temperatures are lower are the best times. Ten minutes is enough for some, while others may enjoy a longer walk, get to know what your dog likes. For some Bulldogs, anything in the 70s is hot, while others may be fine outdoors for short periods at temperatures up to 80ºF

3. Make sure your dog has access to water 24/7

4. If your dog does not want to go outside, do not force him

5. Have a shady toilet area in your yard or garden for your Bulldog

6. Always take water with you on your walks in warm weather. Watch your dog carefully for indications that he is over-heating, such as heavy panting, loss of energy, and any weakness or stumbling. If he shows signs, stop in a shady spot and give him some water. If symptoms don't subside, take him home and ring the vet

7. NEVER muzzle your dog

8. NEVER leave your pet in a parked car, even if you're in the shade or will only be gone a short time. The temperature inside a parked car can quickly reach up to 140ºF. Also, there is a high incidence of Bulldog theft, especially in the USA

9. Avoid places like the beach and especially concrete or asphalt areas, where heat is reflected and there is no access to shade

10. Put your dog in a cool area of the house. Air conditioning is one of the best ways to keep a dog cool, but is not always reliable. You can freeze water in soda bottles, or place ice and a small amount of water in several resealable food storage bags, wrap them in a towel or tube sock and put them on the floor for your dog to lie on

11. Do not let your dog become over-excited in warm weather, avoid strenuous games or exercise

12. Don't go jogging with a Bulldog. Most dogs will try to keep up with their owners and this can put stress on the heart or cause Bulldogs to overheat

13. By the time your Bulldog starts to feel hot, he is probably already overheating. Keep an eye on your dog, especially puppies and young dogs who may want to run and play for hours. Monitor his exercise and play time.

14. Do not allow your Bulldog to become obese. An obese dog is more likely to suffer from heatstroke.

Bulldog Tails

There is a slight difference in the definitions laid down by the Kennel Clubs which set the breed standards for the Bulldog and its tail.

In the UK, The Kennel Club says that the tail must be straight and stick out, like this little pup in the photo: "Tail - Set on low, jutting out rather straight and then turning downwards. Round, smooth and devoid of fringe or coarse hair. Moderate in length – rather short than long – thick at root, tapering quickly to a fine point. Downward carriage (not having a decided upward curve at end) and never carried above back. Lack of tail, inverted or extremely tight tails are undesirable."

However, the American Kennel Club has a slightly different definition, which also allows the tail to be "screwed". I'm not sure how a tail can be screwed without being curly or curved, but here is its definition:

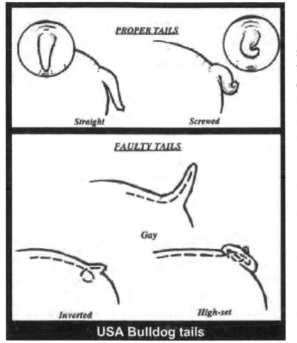

USA Bulldog tails

"The tail may be either straight or "screwed" (but never curved or curly), and in any case must be short, hung low, with decided downward carriage, thick root and fine tip. If straight, the tail should be cylindrical and of uniform taper. If "screwed," the bends or kinks should be well defined, and they may be abrupt and even knotty, but no portion of the member should be elevated above the base or root."

If a Bulldog's tail is screwed too tight, less air can circulate and this causes infections. In extreme cases, some Bulldogs have had a screw or corkscrew tail removed.

A tail pocket is a tiny hidden chamber under a Bulldog's tail. Owners should check for the presence of one - a puppy may not have a tail pocket the first few months but could develop one as it grows. Due to the lack of air circulation, these pockets are ideal breeding grounds for bacteria and yeast infections.

Feel at the base of the tail and see if there is any hidden dark space there. If there is, you should lift the tail, clean, rinse it and dry it well regularly – no matter how unpleasant you find the task. When you decide to become a Bulldogger, you have to take on all that goes with it! Do not leave the tail pocket moist as this will encourage infection.

Urinary Tract Infections

UTIs are very common in Bulldogs, especially females and are almost always caused by bacteria. It has been estimated that 14% of dogs of all breeds will have a urinary tract infection at some time in their lives.

The infection may be picked up from the environment or from the dog's own feces. It usually enters through the urethra and works its way up into the bladder. Sometimes the bacteria pass from the bladder through the ureters to the kidneys. There are a few other causes of urinary tract infections in dogs, but they are much less common than bacterial infection, which is also referred to as "bacterial cystitis."

The urinary system is responsible for filtering wastes from the blood and for forming and getting rid of urine. These functions help the body to maintain the right balance and volume of fluids. Although it has far-reaching effects, the urinary tract is relatively simple and consists of: the kidneys, ureters (tubes carrying urine from the kidney to the bladder), the bladder and the urethra (the tube carrying urine from the bladder to the outside of the dog).

Symptoms

Some dogs with a urinary tract infection may not show any signs of disease, while others may show one or more of the following:

❖ Frequently urinating small amounts (poillakiuria)

❖ Painful urination (dysuria)

❖ Blood in the urine (hematuria)

❖ 'Accidents'

Your vet will carry out a urine analysis to confirm the diagnosis of UTI.

Treatment

This is usually provided in the form of antibiotics. If the infection does not respond, it may be for a number of reasons, including the fact that the bacterial strain may be resistant to a particular antibiotic, or there may be another underlying cause, such as bladder stones, diabetes mellitus, or a suppressed immune system.

It is important that owners ensure that their Bulldog completes the full course of antibiotic treatment to get rid of the infection. Stopping part way through because your dog seems to be OK may cause the infection to return.

Other things owners should do is to make sure their dog drinks plenty of water to help flush out the bacteria, as with any infection. You could also add a spoonful of live yoghurt to one or both meals to replace the good bacteria in your dog's system and consider adding a urinary tract supplement to her feed. It's a good idea to have your dog retested as soon as the antibiotics have finished, as UTIs are notoriously stubborn - and expensive - to shift. Better to ensure you get rid of it properly the first time it occurs.

---

von Willebrand's Disease

Von Willebrand's Disease (vWD) is an inherited bleeding disorder similar to hemophilia in humans. Bulldogs are not at high risk of contracting it, but may have a slightly higher risk than some other breeds. With vWD, the dog lacks a substance which helps to form blood clots.

Technically speaking this substance (called 'von Willebrand's factor ') forms clots and stabilises something called Factor VIII in the normal clotting process. Dogs with von Willebrand's Disease bleed excessively as their blood does not clot properly. Humans can also suffer from vWD. This disease is named after Erik Adolf von Willebrand, a Finnish doctor who documented and studied a rare bleeding disorder in an isolated group of people in 1924. He showed that the disease was inherited, rather than caught by infection.

Symptoms

The main symptom is excessive bleeding, which usually occurs after an injury or surgery. In these cases the blood simply does not clot in the normal time and bleeding is profuse. Dogs with Von Willebrand's disease can also develop nosebleeds or bleeding from the gums.

Bleeding can also occur in the stomach or intestine. If this is the case, you may notice something unusual in your dog's feces; his stools may have blood in them or be black and tarry. Some dogs will have blood in their urine, while others may have bleeding in their joints. In this last case, the symptoms are similar to those of arthritis. The diagnosis is made through a test to check the levels of von Willebrand's factor in the blood.

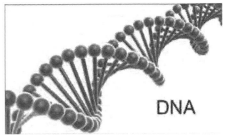

DNA

Treatment

Sadly, as yet, there is no cure for this disease. The only way to stop the spread of vWD is to have dogs tested and to prevent breeding from affected animals. Without treatment, a dog can bleed to death after surgery or what otherwise might normally be considered a less than life-threatening injury. The only proven way to treat vWD is with transfusions of blood collected from healthy dogs.

Some dogs with Von Willebrand's Disease also are **hypothyroid**, meaning they have lower than normal levels of thyroid hormone. These dogs benefit from thyroid hormone replacement therapy. A drug called DDAVP may help dogs with bleeding episodes. It can be administered into the nose to increase clotting, but opinion is still divided as to whether this treatment is effective.

Canine Diabetes

This is not an issue which particularly affects Bulldogs any more than any other type of dog, but can affect dogs of all breeds, sizes and both genders. It does, however, affect obese dogs more than ones of a normal weight and the Bulldog's love of food makes him a candidate for obesity, if his diet is not strictly controlled.

There are two types: **diabetes mellitus** and **diabetes insipidus**. Diabetes mellitus is the most common form and affects one in 500 dogs. Bulldogs are regarded as having a moderate risk of contracting this. Thanks to modern veterinary medicine, the condition is now treatable and need not shorten your Bulldog's lifespan or interfere with his quality of life. Diabetic dogs undergoing treatment now have the same life expectancy as non-diabetic dogs of the same age and gender.

However, if left untreated, the disease can lead to cataracts, increasing weakness in the legs (neuropathy), other ailments and even death. In dogs, diabetes is typically seen anywhere between the ages of four to 14, with a peak at seven to nine years. Both males and females can develop it; unspayed females have a slightly higher risk.

The typical canine diabetes sufferer is middle-aged, female and overweight, but there are also juvenile cases.

What is Diabetes?

Diabetes insipidus is caused by a lack of vasopressin, a hormone which controls the kidneys' absorption of water.

Diabetes mellitus occurs when the dog's body does not produce enough insulin and cannot successfully process sugars.

Dogs, like us, get their energy by converting the food they eat into sugars, mainly glucose. This glucose travels in the dog's bloodstream and individual cells then remove some of that glucose from the blood to use for energy. The substance that allows the cells to take glucose from the blood is a protein called **insulin.**

Insulin is created by beta cells that are located in the pancreas, which is next to the stomach. Almost all diabetic dogs have Type 1 diabetes: their pancreas does not produce any insulin. Without it, the cells have no way to use the glucose that is in the bloodstream, so the cells 'starve' while the glucose level in the blood rises. Your vet will use blood samples and urine samples to check glucose concentrations in order to diagnose diabetes. Early treatment helps to prevent further complications developing.

Symptoms

The most common symptoms of diabetes in dogs include:

- ❖ Extreme thirst

- ❖ Excessive urination

- ❖ Weight loss

- ❖ Increased appetite

- ❖ Coat in poor condition

- ❖ Lethargy

- ❖ Vision problems due to cataracts

Cataracts and Diabetes

Some diabetic dogs do go blind. Cataracts may develop due to high blood glucose levels causing water to build up in the eyes' lenses. This leads to swelling, rupture of the lens fibers and the development of cataracts. In many cases, the cataracts can be surgically removed to bring sight back to the dog. Vision is restored in 75% to 80% of diabetic dogs that undergo cataract removal.

However, some dogs may stay blind even after the cataracts are gone, and some cataracts simply cannot be removed. Blind dogs are often able to get around surprisingly well, particularly in a familiar home.

Treatment

Treatment starts with the right diet. Your vet will prescribe meals low in fat and sugars. He will also recommend medication. Many cases of canine diabetes can be successfully treated with diet and medication. More severe cases may require insulin injections. In the newly-diagnosed dog, insulin therapy begins at home.

Normally, after a week of treatment, you return to the vet who will do a series of blood sugar tests over a 12-14 hour period to see when the blood glucose peaks and when it hits its lows. Adjustments are then made to the dosage and timing of the injections. Your vet will explain how to prepare and inject the insulin. You may be asked to collect urine samples using a test strip (a small piece of paper that indicates the glucose levels in urine).

If your dog is already having insulin injections, beware of a 'miracle cure' offered on some internet sites. It does not exist. There is no diet or vitamin supplement which can reduce your dog's dependence on insulin injections because vitamins and minerals cannot do what insulin does in the dog's body. If you think that your dog needs a supplement, discuss it with your vet first to make sure that it does not interfere with any other medication.

Exercise

Managing your dog's diabetes also means managing his activity level. Exercise burns up blood glucose the same way that insulin does. If your dog is on insulin, any active exercise on top of the insulin might cause him to have a severe low blood glucose episode, called **'hypoglycaemia'**.

Keep your dog on a reasonably consistent exercise routine. Your usual insulin dose will take that amount of exercise into account. If you plan to take your dog out for some extra demanding exercise, such as running round with other dogs, give him only half of his usual insulin dose.

Tips

"I DON'T SEE TABLE SCRAPS."

❖ You can usually buy specially formulated diabetes dog food from your veterinarian

❖ You should feed the same type and amount of food at the same time every day

❖ Most vets recommend twice-a-day feeding for diabetic pets. It is OK if your dog prefers to eat more often

❖ If you have other pets in the home, they should also be placed on a twice-a-day feeding schedule, so that the diabetic dog cannot eat from their bowls. Help your dog to achieve the best possible blood glucose control by not feeding him table scraps or treats between meals

❖ Watch for signs that your dog is starting to drink more water than usual. Call the vet if you see this happening, as it may mean that the insulin dose needs adjusting.

Remember these simple points:

Food raises blood glucose

Insulin and exercise lower blood glucose

Keep them in balance

For more information on canine diabetes visit **www.caninediabetes.org**

Canine Cancer

This is the biggest single killer of dogs of whatever breed and will claim the lives of one in four dogs. It is the cause of nearly half the deaths of all dogs aged 10 years and older, according to the American Veterinary Medical Association.

Symptoms

Early detection is critical. Some things to look out for are:

❖ Swellings anywhere on the body

❖ Lumps in a dog's armpit or under his jaw

❖ Sores that don't heal

❖ Bad breath

❖ Weight loss

❖ Poor appetite, difficulty swallowing or excessive drooling

❖ Changes in exercise or stamina level

❖ Labored breathing

❖ Change in bowel or bladder habits

If your dog has been spayed or neutered, the risk of certain cancers decreases. These cancers include uterine and breast/mammary cancer in females, and testicular cancer in males (if the dog was neutered before he was six months old).

Along with controlling the pet population, spaying is especially important because mammary cancer in female dogs is fatal in about 50% of all cases.

Diagnosis

Just because your dog has a skin growth doesn't mean that it's cancerous. As with humans, tumors may be benign (harmless) or malignant (harmful). Your vet will probably confirm the tumor using X-rays, blood tests and possibly ultrasounds. He or she will then decide whether it is benign or malignant via a biopsy in which a tissue sample is taken from your dog and examined under a microscope.

If your dog is diagnosed with cancer, there is hope. Advances in veterinary medicine and technology offer various treatment options, including chemotherapy, radiation and surgery. Unlike with humans, a dog's hair will not fall out with chemotherapy.

Treatment

Canine cancer is growing at an ever-increasing rate. One of the difficulties is that your pet cannot tell you when a cancer is developing, but if cancers can be detected early enough through a physical or behavioural change, they often respond well to treatment.

Over recent years, we have all become more aware of the risk factors for human cancer. Responding to these by changing our habits is having a significant impact on human health. For example, stopping smoking, protecting ourselves from over-exposure to strong sunlight and eating a healthy, balanced diet all help to reduce cancer rates.

We know to keep a close eye on ourselves, go for regular health checks and report any lumps and bumps to our doctors as soon as they appear. Increased cancer awareness is definitely improving human health.

The same is true with your dog. While it is impossible to completely prevent cancer, a healthy lifestyle with a balanced diet and regular exercise can help to reduce the risk. Also, be aware of any new lumps and bumps on your dog's body and any changes in his behavior.

The success of treatment will depend on the type of cancer, the treatment used and on how early the tumor is found. The sooner treatment begins, the greater the chances of success. One of the best things you can do for your dog is to keep a close eye on him for any tell-tale signs.

This shouldn't be too difficult and can be done as part of your regular handling and grooming. If you notice any new bumps, for example, monitor them over a period of days to see if there is a change in their appearance or size. If there is, then make an appointment to see your vet as soon as possible. It might only be a cyst, but better to be safe than sorry.

The Future

Research into earlier diagnosis and improved treatments is being conducted at veterinary schools and companies all over the world.

Advances in biology are producing a steady flow of new tests and treatments which are now becoming available to improve survival rates and canine cancer care. If your dog is diagnosed with cancer, do not despair, there are many options and new, improved treatments are constantly being introduced.

Our Happy Ending

We know from personal experience that canine cancer can be successfully treated if it is diagnosed early enough. Our dog was diagnosed with T-cell lymphoma when he was four years old. We had noticed a black lump on his anus which grew to the size of a small grape.

We took him to the vet within the first few days of seeing the lump and, after a test, he was diagnosed with the dreaded T-cell lymphoma. This is a particularly nasty and aggressive form of cancer which can spread to the lymph system and is often fatal for dogs.

As soon as the diagnosis was confirmed, our vet Graham operated and removed the lump. He also had to remove one of his anal glands, but as dogs have two this was not a serious worry. Afterwards, we were on tenterhooks, not knowing if another lump would grow or if the cancer had already spread to his lymph system.

After a few months, Max had another blood test and was finally given the all-clear. Max is now happy, healthy and nine years old. We were very lucky. I would strongly advise anyone who suspects that their dog has cancer to get him or her to your local vet as soon as possible.

10. Bulldog Skin and Allergies

Skin conditions are one of the more common ailments in Bulldogs. A whole book could be written on this subject alone. As with the human population, skin conditions, allergies and intolerances appear to be on the increase.

The skin is the single largest organ and acts as the protective barrier between the dog's internal organs and the outside word. Skin can be affected from the inside by things that the dog eats or drinks, triggering an allergic reaction.

Skin can also be affected from the outside by fleas, parasites, inhaled or contact allergies triggered by grass, pollen, man-made chemicals, dust, mold etc. Allergies are especially common in certain Terriers as well as the Pug, Miniature Schnauzer and Bulldog. There are also ailments that can be passed on genetically, such as a predisposition to interdigital cysts (between the toes) in the Bulldog. Some Bulldogs may also get a yeast infection, which can occur if the skin folds (wrinkles) on the face are not cleaned and dried regularly.

While many Bulldogs have no problems at all, some suffer from sensitive skin, allergies, yeast infections or skin disorders, causing them to scratch, bite or lick themselves excessively on the paws and/or other areas. Symptoms may vary from mild itchiness to a chronic reaction.

Canine skin disorders are a complex topic. Some dogs can spend hours running through fields, digging holes and rolling around in the grass with no after-effects at all. Others may spend most of their time indoors and have an excellent diet, but still experience severe itching.

Skin problems may be the result of one or more of a wide range of causes - and the list of potential remedies and treatments is even longer. It's by no means possible to cover all of them in this chapter. The aim is to give a broad outline of some of the ailments most likely to affect Bulldogs and how to deal with them. We have also included remedies tried with some success by ourselves (our dog has skin issues) and other owners of dogs with skin problems.

This information is not intended to take the place of professional help. We are not animal health experts and you should always contact your veterinarian when your dog appears physically unwell or uncomfortable. This is particularly true with skin conditions. **If a vet can find the source of the problem early on, there is more chance of successfully treating it before it has chance to develop into a more serious condition.**

One of the difficulties with this type of ailment is that the exact cause is often difficult to diagnose, as the symptoms may be common to other ailments as well. If allergies are involved, some specific tests are available costing hundreds of dollars or pounds. You will have to take your vet's advice on this, as the tests are not always conclusive and if the answer is pollen or dust, it's often difficult to keep your dog away from the triggers while still having a normal life. It is often a question of managing a skin condition, rather than curing it.

Skin issues and allergies often develop in adolescence or early adulthood, which in a Bulldog may be anything from a few months to three years old. Our dog Max was perfectly normal until he reached two years old when he began scratching, caused by environmental allergies, most likely pollen. He's now nine and over the years he's been on various different remedies which have all worked for a time. As his allergies are seasonal, he normally does not have any medication between October and March. But come spring and as sure as daffodils are daffodils, he starts scratching again. Luckily, they are manageable and Max lives a happy, normal life.

Another issue reported by some Bulldog owners is food allergy or intolerance (there is a difference). Whatever the cause, before a vet can diagnose the problem, you have to be prepared to tell him or her all about your dog's diet, exercise regime, habits, medical history and local environment. The vet will then carry out a thorough physical examination, possibly followed by further tests, before a course of treatment can be prescribed.

We'll start with one of the skin issues known to affect Bulldogs more than many other breeds.

Interdigital Cysts

Have you ever noticed a fleshy red bump between your dog's toes that looks a bit like an ulcerated sore or a hairless bump? If so, then your Bulldog probably has an interdigital cyst (or "interdigital furuncle" to give the condition its correct medical term).

These can be very difficult to get rid of, since they are not the primary issue, but a secondary manifestation of some other condition. Actually they are not cysts, but the result of **furunculosis**, a condition of the skin which clogs hair follicles and creates chronic infection. They can be caused by a number of factors, including allergies, obesity, poor foot conformation, mites, yeast infections, ingrown hairs or other foreign bodies. Sadly the Bulldog and the Labrador Retriever are the two breeds most likely to suffer from them, along with overweight dogs of all breeds.

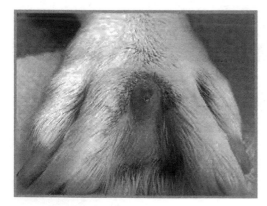

These nasty-looking bumps are painful for your dog and will probably cause him to limp. Veterinarians might recommend a whole range of treatments to get to the root cause of the problem. It can be extremely expensive if your dog is having a barrage of tests or biopsies and even then you are not guaranteed to find the underlying cause.

The first thing he or she will probably do is put your dog in an E-collar to stop him licking the affected area, which will never recover properly as long as he's constantly licking it. This again is stressful for your dog.

Here are some remedies your vet may suggest:

- ❖ Antibiotics and/or steroids and/or mite killers
- ❖ Soaking his feet in Epsom salts twice daily to unclog the hair follicles
- ❖ Testing him for allergies or thyroid problems
- ❖ Starting a food trial if food allergies are suspected
- ❖ Shampooing his feet
- ❖ Cleaning between his toes with medicated (benzoyl peroxide) wipes
- ❖ A referral to a veterinary dermatologist
- ❖ Surgery

If you suspect your Bulldog has an interdigital cyst, take him to the vet for a correct diagnosis and then discuss the various options. A course of antibiotics may be suggested initially, along with switching to a hypoallergenic diet if a food allergy is suspected. If the condition persists, many owners get discouraged, especially when treatment may go on for many weeks. Before you resort to any drastic action, first try soaking your Bulldog's affected paw in Epsom salts for five or 10 minutes twice a day. After the soaking, clean the area with medicated wipes, which are antiseptic and control inflammation. They are sold under the brand name Stridex pads in the skin care section of any grocery, or at the pharmacy.

If you think the cause may be an environmental allergy, wash your dog's paws and under his belly when you return from a walk, this will help to remove pollen and other allergens from his body.

Surgery is a drastic option and although it might solve the immediate problem, it will not deal with whatever is triggering the interdigital cysts in the first place. Not only is healing after this surgery a lengthy and difficult process, it also means your dog will never have the same foot as before - future orthopedic issues and a predisposition to more interdigital cysts are a couple of problems which can occur afterwards.

All that said, your veterinarian does understand that interdigital cysts aren't so simple to deal with, but they are always treatable. Get the right diagnosis as soon as possible, limit all offending factors and give medical treatment a good solid try before embarking on more drastic cures.

Acute Moist Dermatitis (Hot Spots)

Acute moist dermatitis or "hot spots" are not uncommon in Bulldogs. A hot spot can appear suddenly and is a raw, inflamed and often bleeding area of skin. The area becomes moist and painful and begins spreading due to continual licking and chewing. They can become large, red, irritated lesions in a short pace of time.

The cause is often a local reaction to an insect bite; fleas, ticks, biting flies and even mosquitoes have been known to cause acute moist dermatitis. Other causes of hot spots include:

- ❖ Allergies - inhalant allergies and food allergies
- ❖ Mites
- ❖ Ear infections
- ❖ Poor grooming
- ❖ Burs or plant awns
- ❖ Anal gland disease
- ❖ Hip dysplasia or other types of arthritis and degenerative joint disease

Diagnosis and Treatment

The good news is that, once diagnosed and with the right treatment, hot spots disappear as soon as they appeared. The underlying cause should be identified and treated, if possible. You should treat your Bulldog for fleas and ticks at the same time as any medical treatment, which might include anti-inflammatory medications and antibiotics. These might come in the form of injections, tablets or creams – or your Bully might need a combination of them. Your vet will probably clip and clean the affected area to help the effectiveness of any spray or ointment he or she may have prescribed. Your poor Bully might also have to wear an E-collar until the condition subsides, but usually this does not take long.

Seborrhea

Seborrhea (or seborrheic dermatitis) is a skin disorder in which sebaceous glands produce an excessive amount of sebum. Sebaceous glands are microscopic glands found below the skin which secrete an oily substance (sebum) to lubricate the dog's skin and hair. The diagram shows a healthy gland.

There are two types: **seborrhea sicca** (dry seborrhea) and **seborrhea oleosa** (oily seborrhea).

Most affected dogs have a combination of dry and oily seborrhea. They may have dry flaky skin, greasy scaly skin, or both. The flakes of dry seborrhea are easy to lift off the skin, whereas the scales of oily seborrhea stick to the fur. In oily seborrhea the hair follicles can become plugged and infected, resulting in the development of folliculitis, which is treated the same as acne or with antibiotics, depending on its severity.

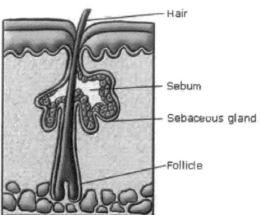

Some breeds have a genetic predisposition to the condition, but the Bulldog is not one of these. If a Bulldog does get seborrhea, it is most likely caused by one of the following:

* Hormonal imbalances, such as thyroid disease, Cushing's disease, etc.
* Allergies
* Parasites (internal and external) - fleas, ticks, mange, mites
* Fungal infections - especially yeast skin infections (*Malassezia*)
* Dietary abnormalities - poor diets containing low levels of omega-3 fatty acids
* Environmental factors (temperature, humidity changes)
* Obesity
* Musculoskeletal disease or pain - the dog is unable to groom itself properly.

(In some cases, the exact cause cannot be determined, this is called **idiopathic seborrhea).**

Seborrhea usually affects skin areas rich in sebaceous glands, especially the skin along the back. In the affected areas, skin often flakes off in whitish scales (dandruff) that can be seen on the dog's bedding and other places where the dog lies. Some skin areas may be red and inflamed, with either a dry or an oily feel. The dermatitis may be worse in areas with skin folds such as the wrinkles, feet, neck, lips, armpits, thighs and belly.

Many dogs with seborrhea give off an unpleasant odor, which is worse if the dog also has a secondary bacterial or yeast skin infection.

Diagnosis and Treatment

Tests that can help your veterinarian to diagnose seborrhea include:

- ❖ Complete blood cell count (CBC), serum chemistries and electrolytes - looking for underlying conditions or imbalances
- ❖ Skin cytology and/or skin scrapings
- ❖ Skin culture - for bacterial and fungal infections, including ringworm
- ❖ Skin biopsy
- ❖ Hormone tests - including thyroid disease and Cushing's disease testing

The condition cannot be cured, but it can be managed and treatment is aimed at addressing the underlying cause. If no underlying cause can be found, then a diagnosis of primary or idiopathic seborrhea is made. Unfortunately, there is no specific treatment for primary seborrhea.

In general, treatments that help manage seborrhea include:

- ❖ Omega-3 fatty acid supplements
- ❖ Antiseborrheic shampoos
- ❖ Moisturizers
- ❖ Retinoids (treatments which act similar to Vitamin A)
- ❖ The drug cyclosporine (Atopica) taken orally
- ❖ Antibiotics - to treat secondary bacterial infections

Prognosis (Outlook)

This depends on your dog's specific condition and severity. The prognosis is better if an underlying cause has been identified and treated. Once diagnosed, your vet will discuss a treatment plan for your dog to help you manage this common and often frustrating condition.

Types of Allergies

'Canine dermatitis' means inflammation of a dog's skin and it can be triggered by numerous things, but the most common by far is allergies. Vets estimate that one in four dogs in their clinics is there because of some kind of allergy.

Symptoms

- Chewing on feet
- Rubbing the face on the carpet
- Scratching the body
- Recurrent ear infections
- Hair loss
- Mutilated skin

A Bulldog who is allergic to something will show it through skin problems and itching, your vet may call this 'pruritus'. It may seem logical that if a dog is allergic to something he inhales, like certain pollen grains, his nose will run; if he's allergic to something he eats, he may vomit, or if allergic to an insect bite, he may develop a swelling. But in practice this is seldom the case. The skin is an organ and with dogs it is this organ which is often affected by allergies. So instead, he will have a mild to severe itching sensation over his body and maybe a chronic ear infection.

Dogs with allergies often chew their feet until they are sore and red. You may see your Bully rubbing his face on the carpet or couch or scratching his belly and flanks. Because the ear glands produce too much wax in response to the allergy, ear infections can occur, with bacteria and yeast often thriving in the excessive wax and debris.

An allergic dog may cause skin lesions or hot spots by his constant chewing and scratching. Sometimes he will lose hair, which can be patchy or inconsistent over the body, leaving a mottled appearance. The skin itself may be dry and crusty, reddened or oily, depending on the dog. It is very common to get secondary bacterial skin infections due to these self-inflicted wounds. An allergic dog's body is reacting to certain molecules called 'allergens.' These may come from:

- ❖ Trees
- ❖ Grass
- ❖ Pollens
- ❖ Foods and food additives, such as specific meats, grains or colorings
- ❖ Milk products
- ❖ Fabrics such as wool or nylon
- ❖ Rubber and plastics
- ❖ House dust and dust mites
- ❖ Mold
- ❖ Flea bites

These allergens may be **inhaled** as the dog breathes, **ingested** as the dog eats or caused by **contact** with the dog's body when he walks or rolls. However they arrive, they all cause the

immune system to produce a protein (IgE), which causes various irritating chemicals, such as histamine, to be released. In dogs these chemical reactions and cell types occur in sizeable amounts only within the skin, hence the scratching.

Inhalant Allergies (Atopy)

The most common allergies in dogs are inhalant and seasonal (at least at first, some allergies may develop and worsen). Substances which can cause an allergic reaction in dogs are similar to those causing problems for humans.

A clue to diagnosing these allergies is to look at the timing of the reaction. Does it happen all year round? If so, this may be mold or dust. If the reaction is seasonal, then pollens may well be the culprit.

A diagnosis can be made by allergy testing - either a blood or skin test where a small amount of antigen is injected into the dog's skin to test for a reaction. The blood test can give false positives, so the skin test is many veterinarians' preferred method. Whether or not you take this route will be your decision; allergy testing is not cheap, it takes time and may require your dog to be sedated, which is always a risk with Bulldogs. There's also no point doing it if you are not going to go along with the recommended method of treatment afterwards, which is immunotherapy, or **'hyposensitization'**, and this can also be an expensive and lengthy process.

It consists of a series of injections made specifically for your dog and administered over weeks or months to make him more tolerant of allergens. It may have to be done by a veterinary dermatologist if your vet is not familiar with the treatment. Veterinarians in the USA claim that success rates can be as high as 75% of cases. Both these tests work best when carried out during the season when the allergies are at their worst.

But before you get to this stage, your vet will have had to rule out other potential causes, such as fleas or mites, fungal, yeast or bacterial infections and hypothyroidism. Due to the time and cost involved in skin testing, most mild cases of allergies are treated with a combination of avoidance, fatty acids and antihistamines.

Environmental or Contact Irritations

These are a direct reaction to something the dog physically comes into contact with. It could be as simple as grass, specific plants, dust or other animals. If the trigger is grass or other outdoor materials, the allergies are often seasonal. The dog may require treatment (often tablets, shampoo or localized cortisone spray) for spring and summer, but be perfectly fine with no medication for the other half of the year. This is the case with our dog.

If you suspect your Bully may have outdoor contact allergies, get him to stand in a tray or large bowl of water on your return from a walk. Washing his feet and under his belly will get rid of some of the pollen and other allergens, which in turn will reduce his scratching and biting. Other possible triggers include dry carpet shampoos, caustic irritants, new carpets, cement dust, washing powders or fabric conditioners. If you wash your dog's bedding or if he sleeps on your bed, use a fragrance-free laundry detergent and fabric conditioner.

The irritation may be restricted to the part of the dog - such as the underneath of the paws or belly - which has touched the offending object. Symptoms are skin irritation - either a general problem or specific hotspots - itching (**pruritis**) and sometimes hair loss. Readers sometimes report to us that their dog will incessantly lick one part of the body, often the paws, bottom, belly or back.

Flea Bite Allergies

These are a very common canine allergy and affect dogs of all breeds. To compound the problem, many dogs with flea allergies also have inhalant allergies. Flea bite allergy is typically seasonal, worse during summer and fall – peak time for fleas - and is worse in warmer climates where fleas are prevalent.

This type of allergy is not to the flea itself, but to proteins in flea saliva, which are deposited under the dog's skin when the insect feeds. Just one bite to an allergic Bulldog will cause intense and long-lasting itching. If affected, the dog will try to bite at the base of his tail (impossible for a Bulldog) and scratch a lot. Most of the damage is done by the dog's scratching, rather than the flea bite, and can result in his fur falling out or skin abrasions.

Some Bulldogs will develop hot spots. These can occur anywhere, but are often along the back and base of the tail. Flea bite allergies can only be totally prevented by keeping all fleas away from the dog. Various flea prevention treatments are available – see our next section on Parasites. If you suspect your dog may be allergic to fleas, consult your veterinarian for the proper diagnosis and medication.

Diet and Food Allergies

Food is the third most common cause of allergies in dogs, and there is some anecdotal evidence that food allergies are on the increase within the Bulldog population.

Cheap dog foods bulked up with grains and other ingredients can cause problems. Some Bulldog owners have reported their dogs having problems with wheat and other grains. If you feed your dog a dry commercial dog food, make sure that it's a high quality, preferably hypoallergenic, one and that the first ingredient listed on the sack is meat or poultry and not grain.

Without the correct food a dog's whole body - not just his skin and coat - will continuously be under stress and this manifests itself in a number of ways. The symptoms of food allergies are similar to those of most allergies:

- ❖ itchy skin affecting primarily the face, feet, ears, forelegs, armpits and anus
- ❖ excessive scratching
- ❖ chronic or recurring ear infections
- ❖ hair loss
- ❖ hot spots
- ❖ skin infections that clear up with antibiotics but return after the antibiotics have finished
- ❖ possible increased bowel movements, maybe twice as many as normal

The bodily process which occurs when an animal has a reaction to a particular food agent is not very well understood, but the veterinary profession does know how to diagnose and treat food allergies. As many other problems can cause similar symptoms to food allergies (and also the fact that many sufferers also have other allergies), it is important that any other problems are identified and treated before food allergies are diagnosed.

Atopy, flea bite allergies, intestinal parasite hypersensitivities, sarcoptic mange and yeast or bacterial infections can all cause similar symptoms. This can be an anxious time for owners as vets try one thing after another to get to the bottom of the allergy.

The normal method for diagnosing a food allergy is elimination. Once all other causes have been ruled out or treated, then a food trial is the next step – and that's no picnic for owners either. See **Chapter 5. Feeding** for more information. As with other allergies, dogs may have short-term relief by taking fatty acids, antihistamines, and steroids, but removing the offending items from the diet is the only permanent solution.

Some Allergy Treatments

Treatments and success rates vary tremendously from dog to dog and from one allergy to another, which is why it is so important to consult a vet at the outset. Earlier diagnosis is more likely to lead to a successful treatment. Some owners whose Bulldogs have recurring skin issues find that a course of antibiotics or steroids works wonders for their dog's sore skin and itching. However, the scratching starts all over again when the treatment stops.

Food allergies require patience, a change of diet and maybe even a food trial, and the specific trigger is notoriously difficult to isolate – unless you are lucky and hit on the culprit straight away. With inhalant and contact allergies, blood and skin tests are available, followed by hypersensitization treatment.

However, these are expensive and often the specific trigger for many dogs remains unknown. So the reality for many owners of Bulldogs with allergies is that they manage the ailment with various medications and practices, rather than curing it completely.

Our Personal Experience

After corresponding with numerous other dog owners and speaking to our vet, it seems that our experiences with allergies are not uncommon. Our dog was perfectly fine until he was about two years old when he began to scratch a lot (he's nine now). He seemed to scratch more in spring and summer, which meant that his allergies were almost certainly inhalant or contact-based and related to pollens, grasses or other outdoor triggers.

One option was to have a barrage of tests on the dog to discover exactly what he was allergic to. We decided not to do this, not because of the cost, but because our vet said it was highly likely that he was allergic to pollens. If we had confirmed an allergy to pollens, we were not going to stop taking him outside for walks, so the vet treated him on the basis of seasonal inhalant or contact allergies, probably related to pollen.

One recommendation he makes to reduce the itching is to rinse the dog's paws and underneath his belly after a walk in the countryside. This is something he does with his own dogs and has found that the scratching reduces as a result. Regarding medications, Max was at first put on to a tiny dose of Piriton, an antihistamine for hay fever sufferers (human and canine) and for the first few springs and summers, this worked well.

One of the problems with allergies is that they often change and the dog can also build up a tolerance to a treatment – this has been the case over the years with our dog. The symptoms change from season to season, although the main symptoms remain and they are: general scratching, paw biting and ear infections. One year he bit the skin under his tail a lot and this was treated fairly effectively with a cortisone spray. This type of spray is useful if the area of itching is localized, but no good for spraying all over a dog's body.

A couple of years ago he started biting his paws for the first time - a habit he persists with - although not to the extent that they become red and raw. Over the years we have tried a number of treatments, all of which have worked for a while, before he comes off the medication in fall for five or six months when plants and grasses stop growing outdoors. He manages perfectly fine the rest of the year without any medication.

According to the vet, every spring there are more and more dogs appearing in his waiting room with various types of allergies. Whether this is connected to how we breed our dogs remains to be seen. One season he put Max on a short course of steroids. These worked very well for five months, but steroids are not a long-term solution, as prolonged use can cause organ damage.

Another spring Max was prescribed a non-steroid daily tablet called Atopica, sold in the UK only through vets. (The active ingredient is cyclosporine, which suppresses the immune system. Some dogs can get side effects, although Max didn't, and holistic practitioners believe that it is harmful to the dog.) This treatment was expensive, but initially extremely effective – so much so that we thought we had cured the problem completely. However, after a couple of seasons on cyclosporine he developed a tolerance to the drug and started scratching again.

Last year he went back on the antihistamine, a higher dose than when he was two years old, and this worked very well again. One advantage of this drug is that is it manufactured by the million for dogs and is therefore very inexpensive. We also feed him a high quality hypoallergenic dry food.

In May 2013 the FDA approved Apoquel (oclacitinib) to control itching and inflammation in allergic dogs, and in 2014 we tried it – with good results. Max still scratches, but not so much.

Many vets recommend adding fish oils (which contain Omega-3 fatty acids) to a daily feed to keep your dog's skin and coat healthy all year round – whether or not he has problems. We also add a liquid supplement called Yumega Plus, which contains Omega-3 and 6, to one of his two daily feeds all year round and this definitely seems to help his skin. When the scratching gets particularly bad, we bathe Max in an antiseborrheic shampoo called Malaseb twice a week, which also seems to help.

The main point is that most allergies are manageable. They may change throughout the life of the dog and you may have to alter the treatment. Our Max still scratches, but not as much as when he was younger. He may have allergies, but he wouldn't miss his walks for anything and, all in all, he is one contented canine.

We've compiled some anecdotal evidence from our website from owners of dogs with various allergies, here are some of their suggestions for alleviating the problems:

Bathing - Regularly bathing your dog – anything from twice a week to once every two weeks - using shampoos that break down the oils which plug the hair follicles. These shampoos contain antiseborrheic ingredients such as benzoyl peroxide, salicylic acid, sulfur or tar. One example is Sulfoxydex shampoo, which can be followed by a cream rinse such as Episoothe Rinse afterwards to prevent the skin from drying out.

Dabbing – Using an astringent such as witch hazel or alcohop on affected areas. We have heard of zinc oxide cream being used to some effect. In the human world, this is rubbed on to mild skin abrasions and acts as a protective coating. It can help the healing of chapped skin and nappy rash in babies. Zinc oxide works as a mild astringent and has some antiseptic properties and is safe to use on dogs, *as long as you do not allow the dog to lick it off*.

Daily supplements - Vitamin E, vitamin A, zinc and omega oils all help to make a dog's skin healthy. Feed a daily supplement which contains some of these, such as fish oil, which provides omega.

Holistic – there are a number of products made from natural ingredients available as ointments or as supplements for your dog.

Here are some specific remedies from owners. We are not endorsing them, we're just passing on the information. *Check with your vet before trying any new remedies:*

A medicated shampoo with natural tea tree oil has been suggested by one owner. Some have reported that switching to a fish-based diet has helped lessen scratching. Ann G. said: "Try Natural Balance Sweet Potato and Fish formula. My dog Charlie has skin issues and this food has helped him tremendously! Plus he LOVES it!" Others have suggested home-cooked food is best, if you have the time to prepare the food.

This is what another reader had to say: "My 8-month-old dog also had a contact dermatitis around his neck and chest. I was surprised how extensive it was when I clipped his hair. The vet recommended twice-a-week baths with an oatmeal shampoo. I also applied organic coconut oil daily for a few weeks. This completely cured the dermatitis. I also put a capsule of fish oil with his food once a day and continue to give him twice-weekly baths. His skin is great now."

Several owners have tried coconut oil with some success. Here are a couple of links for articles on the benefits of coconut oils and fish oils, and why it might be worth considering alternating them. Check with your vet first: www.cocotherapy.com/fishoilsvsvirginoil_coconutoil.htm and http://redwhiteandbulldogs.com/coconut-oil-for-bulldogs/

And from another reader: "I have been putting a teaspoon of Canola Oil in my dog's food every other day and it has helped with the itching. I have shampooed the new carpet in hopes of removing any of the chemicals that could be irritating her. And I have changed laundry detergent. After several loads of laundry everything has been washed."

Another reader wrote that her dog is being treated for seasonal allergies with half a pill of Claritin a day. Reader Cindi says that local health food stores may be able to offer advice on suitable ingredients for a diet - for dogs as well as humans!

Parasites

Fleas - When you see your dog scratching and biting, your first thought is probably: "He's got fleas!" and you may well be right. Fleas don't fly, but they do have very strong back legs and they will take any opportunity to jump from the ground or another animal into your Bulldog's lovely warm coat. You can sometimes see the fleas if you part your dog's fur.

And for every flea that you see on your pet, there is the awful prospect of hundreds of eggs and larvae in your house or apartment. So if your Bulldog is unlucky enough to catch fleas, you'll have to treat your environment as well as your dog in order to completely get rid of them.

The best form of cure is prevention. Vets recommend giving dogs a preventative flea treatment every four to eight weeks. This may vary depending on your climate, the season (fleas do not breed as quickly in the cold) and how much time your dog spends outdoors. Once-a-month topical (applied to the skin) insecticides - like Frontline and Advantix - are the most commonly used flea prevention products on the market. You part the skin and apply drops of the liquid on to a small area on your dog's back, usually near the neck. Some kill fleas and ticks, and others just kill fleas - check the details.

It is worth spending the money on a quality treatment, as cheaper brands may not rid your Bulldog completely of fleas, ticks and other parasites. Sprays, dips, shampoos and collars are other options, as are tablets and injections in certain cases, such as before your dog goes into boarding kennels or has surgery. Incidentally, a flea bite is different from a flea bite allergy.

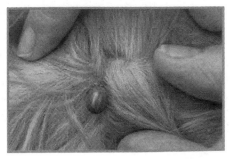

NOTE: There is considerable anecdotal evidence from dog owners of various breeds that the flea and worm tablet **Trifexis,** available in the USA, may cause severe side effects in some dogs. You may wish to read some owners' experiences at: www.max-the-schnauzer.com/trifexis-side-effects-in-schnauzers.html

Ticks – A tick is not an insect, but a member of the arachnid family, like the spider. There are over 850 types of them, divided into two types: hard shelled and soft shelled. Ticks (right) don't have wings - they can't fly, they crawl. They have a sensor called 'Haller's organ' which detects smell, heat and humidity to help them locate food, which in some cases is a Bulldog. A tick's diet consists of one thing and one thing only – blood! They climb up onto tall grass and when they sense an animal is close, crawl on him.

Ticks can pass on a number of diseases to animals and humans, the most well-known of which is Lyme Disease, a serious condition which causes lameness and other problems. Dogs which spend a lot of time outdoors in high risk areas such as woods can have a vaccination against Lime Disease. If you do find a tick on your Bulldog's coat but are not sure how to get it out, have it removed by a vet or other expert. Pulling it out yourself and leaving a bit of the tick behind can be detrimental to your dog's health. Prevention treatment is similar to that for fleas. If your Bulldog has particularly sensitive skin, he might do better with a natural flea or tick remedy.

Ringworm -This is not actually a worm, but a fungus and is most commonly seen in puppies and young dogs. It is highly infectious and often found on the face, ears, paws or tail. The ringworm fungus is most prevalent in hot, humid climates, but surprisingly, most cases occur in the fall and winter. Ringworm infections in dogs are not that common, in one study of dogs with active skin problems, less than 3% had ringworm.

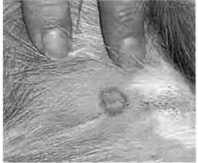

Ringworm is transmitted by spores in the soil and by contact with the infected hair of dogs and cats, which can be typically found on carpets, brushes, combs, toys and furniture. Spores from infected animals can be shed into the environment and live for over 18 months, but fortunately most healthy adult dogs have some resistance and never develop symptoms.

The fungi live in dead skin, hairs and nails - and the head and legs are the most common areas affected. Tell-tale signs are bald patches with a roughly circular shape (see photo) Ringworm is usually treated with fungicidal shampoos or antibiotics from a vet.

Humans can catch ringworm from pets, and vice versa. Children are especially susceptible, as are adults with suppressed immune systems and those undergoing chemotherapy. Hygiene is extremely important, if you have a dog with ringworm, wear gloves when handling him and wash your hands well afterwards. And if a member of your family catches ringworm, make sure they use separate towels from everyone else or the fungus may spread.

Heartworm - Heartworm is a serious and potentially fatal disease in pets in the United States and many other parts of the world. It is caused by foot-long worms (heartworms) that live in the heart, lungs and associated blood vessels of affected pets, causing severe lung disease, heart failure and damage to other organs in the body.

The dog is a natural host for heartworms, which means that heartworms that live inside the dog mature into adults, mate and produce offspring. If untreated, their numbers can increase, and dogs have been known to harbor several hundred worms in their bodies. Heartworm disease causes lasting damage to the heart, lungs and arteries, and can affect the dog's health and quality of life long after the parasites are gone. For this reason, prevention is by far the best option, and treatment—when needed—should be administered as early as possible.

The mosquito plays an essential role in the heartworm life cycle. When a mosquito bites and takes a blood meal from an infected animal, it picks up baby worms which develop and mature into "infective stage" larvae over a period of 10 to 14 days. Then, when the infected mosquito bites another dog, cat, or susceptible wild animal, the infective larvae are deposited onto the surface of the animal's skin and enter the new host through the mosquito's bite wound. Once inside a new host, it takes approximately six months for the larvae to mature into adult heartworms. Once mature, heartworms can live for five to seven years in a dog.

In the early stages of the disease, many dogs show few or no symptoms. The longer the infection persists, the more likely symptoms will develop. Symptoms may include:

- ❖ A mild persistent cough
- ❖ Reluctance to exercise
- ❖ Tiredness after moderate activity
- ❖ Decreased appetite
- ❖ Weight loss

As the disease progresses, dogs may develop heart failure and a swollen belly due to excess fluid in the abdomen. Dogs with large numbers of heartworms can develop sudden blockages of blood flow within the heart leading to the life-threatening caval syndrome. This is marked by a sudden onset of labored breathing, pale gums, and dark bloody or coffee-colored urine. Without prompt surgical removal of the heartworm blockage, few dogs survive.

Although more common in the south east of the US, heartworm disease has been diagnosed in all 50 states. And because infected mosquitoes can fly inside, even Bulldogs which spend most of their time indoors are at risk. For that reason, the American Heartworm Society recommends that you get your dog tested every year and give your dog heartworm preventive treatment for 12 months of the year. (**Source: American Heartworm Society**).

Sarcoptic Mange

Also known as canine scabies, this is caused by the parasite *Sarcoptes scabiei*. This microscopic mite can cause a range of skin problems, the most common of which is hair loss and severe itching. The mites can infect other animals such as foxes, cats and even humans, but prefer to live their short lives on dogs. Fortunately, there are several good treatments for this mange and the disease can be easily controlled.

In cool, moist environments, they live for up to 22 days. At normal room temperature they live from two to six days, preferring to live on parts of the dog with less hair. These are the areas you may see him scratching, although it can spread throughout the body in severe cases.

Diagnosing canine scabies can be somewhat difficult, and it is often mistaken for inhalant allergies. Once diagnosed, there are a number of effective treatments, including selamectin (Revolution), a topical solution applied once a month which also provides heartworm prevention, flea control and some tick protection. Various Frontline products are also effective – check with your vet for the correct ones.

Because your dog does not have to come into direct contact with an infected dog to catch scabies, it is difficult to completely protect him. Foxes and their environment can also transmit the mite, so keep your dog away from areas where you know foxes are present.

(Demodetic mange occurs when a dog's immune system is compromised and in elderly dogs where mite numbers get out of control. It is not contagious. Demodetic mange is generally treated with Ivermectin until the infestation is eliminated.)

Bacterial infection (Pyoderma)

Pyoderma literally means 'pus in the skin' (yuk!) and fortunately this condition is not contagious. Early signs of this bacterial infection are itchy red spots filled with yellow pus, similar to pimples or spots in humans. They can sometimes develop into red, ulcerated skin with dry and crusty patches.

Pyoderma is caused by several things: a broken skin surface, a skin wound due to chronic exposure to moisture, altered skin bacteria, or impaired blood flow to the skin. Dogs have a higher risk of developing an infection when they have a fungal infection or an endocrine (hormone gland) disease such as hyperthyroidism, or have allergies to fleas, a food or parasites.

Pyoderma is often secondary to allergic dermatitis and develops in the lesions on the skin which happen as a result of scratching. Puppies often develop 'puppy pyoderma' in thinly-haired areas such as the groin and underarms. Fleas, ticks, yeast or fungal skin infections, thyroid disease, hormonal imbalances, heredity and some medications can increase the risk.

If you notice symptoms, get your dog to the vet quickly before the condition develops from **superficial pyoderma** into **severe pyoderma**, which is much more unpleasant and takes a lot longer to treat.

Bacterial infection, no matter how bad it may look, usually responds well to medical treatment, which is generally done on an outpatient basis. Superficial pyoderma will usually be treated with a two to six-week course of antibiotic tablets or ointment. Severe or recurring pyoderma looks awful, causes your dog some distress and can take two or three months' of treatment to completely cure. Medicated shampoos and regular bathing, as instructed by your vet, are also part of the treatment. It's also important to ensure your dog has clean, dry, padded bedding.

Ear Infections

Infection of the external ear canal (outer ear infection) is called otitis externa and is one of the most common types of infections seen in Bulldogs.

The fact that your Bulldog has recurring ear infections does not necessarily mean that his ears are the source of the problem.

One reason may be moisture in the ear canal, allowing bacteria to flourish there. However, many Bulldogs with chronic or recurring ear infections have inhalant or food allergies or low thyroid function (hypothyroidism). Sometimes the ears are the first

sign of allergy. The underlying problem must be treated or the dog will continue to have chronic ear problems. Tell-tale signs include your dog shaking his head, scratching or rubbing his ears a lot, or an unpleasant odor coming from the ears.

If you look under his ear flap, you may notice it is red and inflamed with a lot of wax or discharge. Your dog may also appear depressed or irritable; this is because ear infections are painful. In chronic cases, the inside of his ears may become crusty or thickened. Dogs can have ear problems for many different reasons, including:

- ❖ Allergies such as atopy or food allergies
- ❖ Ear mites or other parasites
- ❖ Bacteria or yeast infections
- ❖ Injury, often due to excessive scratching
- ❖ Hormonal abnormalities, e.g. hypothyroidism
- ❖ The ear anatomy and environment, e.g. excess moisture
- ❖ Hereditary or immune conditions and tumors

Treatment depends on the cause of the ear problem and what other conditions your dog may have. Antibiotics are used for bacterial infections and antifungals for yeast infections. Glucocorticoids, such as dexamethasone, are often included in these medications to reduce the inflammation in the ear. Your vet may also flush out and clean the ear with special drops, something you may have to do daily at home until the infection clears.

A dog's ear canal is L-shaped, which means it can be difficult to get medication into the lower (horizontal) part of the ear. The best method is to hold the dog's ear flap with one hand and put the ointment or drops in with the other, if possible tilting the dog's head away from you so the liquid flows downwards with gravity. Make sure you then hold the ear flap down and massage the medication into the horizontal canal before letting go of your dog, as the first thing he will do is shake his head – and if the ointment or drops aren't massaged in, they will fly out.

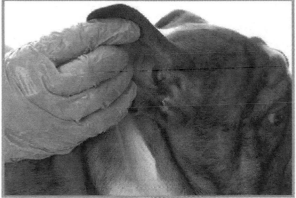

Nearly all ear infections can be successfully managed if properly diagnosed and treated. But if an underlying problem remains undiscovered, the outcome will be less favorable. Deep ear infections can damage or rupture the eardrum, causing an internal ear infection and even permanent hearing loss. Closing of the ear canal (*hyperplasia* or *stenosis*) is another sign of severe infection. Most extreme cases of hyperplasia will eventually require surgery as a last resort; the most common procedure is called a *lateral ear resection*.

To avoid or alleviate recurring ear infections, check your dog's ears and clean them regularly, especially if your Bully is one of the few which enjoys swimming, or after a bath. Be careful not to put anything too far down into your dog's ears. Visit YouTube to see videos of how to correctly clean inside your Bully's ears without damaging them.

If your dog appears to be in pain, has smelly ears, or if his ear canals look inflamed, contact your vet straight away. If he has a ruptured or weakened eardrum, ear cleansers and medications could do more harm than good. Early treatment is the best way of preventing a recurrence.

Yeast Infections

Brachycephalic breeds of dogs with skin folds, such as Bulldogs and Pugs are at increased risk of getting yeast infections. The nose-rope, deep facial wrinkles and folds around his body are what help to make the Bulldog unique. The wrinkles are an attractive feature, but they can also pose a significant health problem if they aren't kept clean.

If you notice an awful smell from your Bulldog's face, ears or tail, he may well have a yeast infection – and it's up to you to get rid of it. You should clean underneath the folds and tail pocket of your Bully's skin at least two or three times a week with a medicated wipe or pad to keep the areas free of debris, bacterial and fungal growth. If you bathe your Bulldog, make sure you clean between the folds, flush the medicated shampoo out with running water and dry thoroughly.

When a Bulldog's facial folds, ears and tail aren't cleaned on a regular basis, the warm, moist pockets underneath are ideal breeding grounds for infection. Yeast infections are usually easy to diagnose, due to the terrible stench! Wrinkles that have been continuously neglected will become swollen and red, sometimes you might find a yellow pus between the folds. You may also notice your Bully rubbing his face on the floor in an effort to alleviate the irritation.

Your vet may recommend bathing your dog in a medicated shampoo and applying cream to the affected areas. It is important that once your Bulldog returns to health, you regularly clean his wrinkles and tail pocket (if he has one).

Hormonal Imbalances

These occur in dogs of all breeds. They are often difficult to diagnose and occur when a dog is producing either too much (hyper) or too little (hypo) of a particular hormone. One visual sign is often hair loss on both sides of the dog's body. The condition is not usually itchy. Hormone imbalances can be serious as they are often indicators that glands which affect the dog internally are not working properly. However, some types can be diagnosed by special blood tests and treated effectively.

This chapter has only just touched on the complex subject of skin disorders. As you can see, the causes and treatments are many and varied. One thing is true, whatever the condition, if your Bulldog has a skin issue, seek a professional diagnosis from a veterinarian as soon as possible before attempting to treat it yourself. Early diagnosis and treatment can often nip the problem in the bud before it develops into anything more serious. Some skin conditions cannot be cured, but they can be successfully managed, allowing your Bulldog to live a happy, pain-free life.

Remember: good quality diet and attention to cleanliness and grooming go a long way in preventing and managing canine skin problems.

11. Grooming Your Bulldog

Grooming doesn't just entail giving your Bulldog a quick brush a couple of times a month. It is an essential part of Bulldog maintenance. Good grooming and care help your Bully look and feel his best, they keep him clean, keep skin-related health problems at bay and help you and your dog to bond.

Routine grooming sessions allow you to examine his coat, skin, teeth, eyes, ears, paws and nails for signs of problems. Bulldogs require fairly minimal brushing but more regular personal attention from their owners than many other breeds in order to maintain their health.

The Bulldog Coat

There are several different coat colors. These are the official colors accepted by the Kennel Clubs in order of preference (any Bulldog of a different color is not acceptable to the Kennel Clubs and could not be entered for a show run under KC rules, but you could still enter him for other, less formal shows):

❖ Red brindle (pictured right)
❖ All other brindles. Brindle is a coloring pattern sometimes described as "tiger striped", although the brindle pattern is more subtle than that of a tiger. The color streaks are irregular and usually darker than the coat's base color, although very dark markings can still be seen on a coat that is only slightly lighter. Brindles should have a fine and even distribution of colors to be considered perfect.
❖ Solid white
❖ Solid red
❖ Fawn or yellow
❖ Piebald (irregular patches of two colors, such as brown and white)

A Bulldog has a short, smooth coat with a fine texture and if yours is in good health, it should be glossy. Although the hairs are short, the Bulldog sheds 365 days a year - unlike many other breeds which shed seasonally – which means that your dog needs regular brushing throughout the year. Fortunately Bulldogs are low-maintenance on the brushing front and you don't need a lot of expensive equipment.

Other benefits of regular brushing are that it removes dead hair and skin, stimulates blood circulation and spreads natural oils throughout the coat, helping to keep it in good condition. If you brush your Bulldog regularly you don't need to bathe him very often. If you do notice an unpleasant smell coming from him (in addition to the normal gassy emissions from your Bully!) and he hasn't been rolling in some form of animal excrement, then he may have a yeast infection which needs checking out by the vet.

You should begin at the dog's head and brush backwards towards the tail; brush strokes should always be in the direction that the hair grows, not against the fur. It's easier to do it when your

Bully is standing, it's OK if he prefers to sit or lie down, just make sure you cover all areas including his legs and under his belly.

If you gently squirt the coat with a fine spray of water beforehand it prevents the hairs from breaking. Then use a rubber curry comb to remove loose and dead hair, and finally use a bristle brush to remove all the remaining loose hair. Bristle brushes are expensive, but they last forever.

Regular grooming isn't just about brushing. Bulldogs are physically very inflexible due to their short necks and broad bodies; they also generally don't get a huge amount of outdoor exercise, so you need to perform a few extra regular health and hygiene tasks for your dog.

If you don't think you have time for this extra care several times a week, don't get a Bulldog.

Wrinkle and tail cleaning

Your Bulldog would not be a Bulldog without his distinctive wrinkles. The nose-rope, deep facial wrinkles and body skin folds are part of what makes the breed so unique. However, the Bulldog's beauty is more than just skin deep, there are health issues that can arise if the wrinkles are not properly and routinely cleansed. Prevention is better than cure and it's definitely better to keep the skin folds clean than have your Bulldog develop painful problems which later require expensive and time-consuming medical attention.

Some Bulldogs only need their wrinkles cleaning a couple of times a week, while others will need a check or a clean every day. Air cannot circulate in these hidden pockets and they can become a

breeding ground for yeast or bacteria. The skin in the fold can become red and infected, and sometimes yellow pus can be seen if not kept clean and - most important – dry.

Wipe between the folds of your Bulldog's skin using a medicated pad or baby wipe with lanolin or aloe to keep the crevices free of debris and bacteria – or you can use a drop of medicated dog shampoo from your vet in a cup of warm water.

Whatever you choose for the task, it is essential that you thoroughly dry the area after cleaning – damp areas are breeding grounds for the aforementioned nasty bugs. Dry with a towel or cloth, don't use talc or cornstarch which can clump. If the skin is irritated, a dab of petroleum jelly (Vaseline) in the fold after cleaning will soothe the skin and prevent moisture getting in.

Overweight dogs are at greater risk of developing a skin infection because the excess fat makes the wrinkles more pronounced.

It's impossible to say exactly how often to clean the wrinkles on any individual Bulldog, but the short answer is: more often than you think. And if a nose-wrinkling smell is coming off your Bully, you're probably not doing it often enough.

Bulldogs cannot clean the area around their own tails – so that job it up to you. It might not be very pleasant, but you owe it to your furrowed friend to do it for him. Some Bulldog tails, particularly corkscrew ones, actually fold back into the body, leaving a hidden "tail pocket" underneath. This area is also attractive to bacteria and yeast (which is a fungus) and if your Bulldog has one, it needs regular cleaning. You might not know whether he has a tail pocket or not; if you're unsure ask your vet on your next routine visit.

If yours does have a tail pocket, it will need regular cleaning and drying in a similar way to the other skin folds. If the tail area becomes red and itchy, your poor Bulldog will not be able to reach it and it will be very uncomfortable for him, so get him to the vet for an anti-fungal treatment ASAP.

If your Bully gets little red pimples on his face and chin, it means he has got acne (right). He can get acne at any age, not just as a teenager. Plastic bowls can also trigger the condition, which Is why stainless steel ones are better. Often a daily washing followed by an application of an antibiotic cream is enough to get rid of the problem, if it persists it will mean a visit to your veterinarian.

A Bulldog's skin can dry out, especially with artificial heat in the winter months. If you spot any dry patches, for example on the inner thighs, armpits or a cracked nose, massage a little petroleum jelly or baby oil on to the dry patch.

Nail Trimming

Bulldogs seldom get enough exercise outdoors on hard surfaces to wear their nails down, so they have to be clipped or filed regularly. Nails must be kept short for the paws to remain healthy. Long nails interfere with the dog's gait, making walking awkward or painful. They can also break easily. This usually happens at the base of the nail, where blood vessels and nerves are located, and will require a trip to the vet's.

Get your dog used to having his paws inspected from puppyhood. It is also a good opportunity to check for other problems such as cracked pads, thorns and splinters and the Bulldog's nemesis - interdigital cysts.

To trim your dog's nails, use a specially designed clipper. Most have safety guards to prevent you from cutting the nails too short. Do it before they get too long, if you can hear the nails clicking on the floor, they're too long. You want to trim only the ends, before "the quick," which is a blood vessel inside the nail. You can see where the quick ends on a white nail, but not on a dark nail.

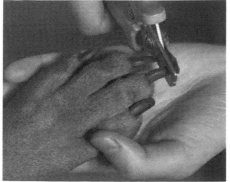

Clip only the hook-like part of the nail that turns down. Start trimming gently, a nail or two at a time, and your dog will learn that you're not going to hurt him. If you accidentally cut the quick, stop the bleeding with some styptic powder. Many Bulldogs dislike having their nails trimmed.

Another option is to file your dog's nails with a nail grinder tool. Some dogs may have tough nails which are hard to trim and this may be less stressful for your dog, with less chance of pain or bleeding. The grinder is like an electric nail file and only removes a small amount of nail at a time. Some owners would rather use one as it is harder to cut the quick, and many dogs prefer them to a clipper.

You have to introduce your Bully gradually to the grinder, first let him get used to the noise and then gradually the vibration before you actually begin to grind his nails. If you find it impossible to clip your dog's nails, or you are at all worried about doing it, take him to a vet or a groomer.

Ear Cleaning

This should be part of your normal at-home grooming schedule. Ear canals are generally warm and moist, making them a haven for bacteria. This can lead to repetitive ear infections and, in severe cases, the dog going deaf or requiring an operation to change the shape of his ear canal. In Bulldogs recurring ear infection can also be a sign of other issues such as food or environmental allergies.

Checking the inside of the ear is clean and not foul-smelling should be a regular part of grooming. Some owners also regularly bathe the ear flap and inner ear with cotton wool and warm water or a veterinary ear cleaner. If your Bully's ears have an unpleasant smell, if he scratches them a lot or they look red, consult your vet as simple routine cleaning won't clear up an infection - and ear infections are notoriously difficult to get rid of once the dog has got one. Keeping your Bulldog's ears clean is the best way to avoid infections starting in the first place. NEVER put anything sharp or narrow inside your dog's ear.

Eye Care

Like all dogs, a Bulldog's eyes should be clean and clear. Cloudy eyes, particularly in an older dog, could be early signs of cataracts. Red or swollen tissue in the corner of the eye could be a symptom of cherry eye. If your Bully gets dust or dirt in his eyes, gently clean them with warm water and cotton wool – NEVER put anything sharp anywhere near your Bully's eyes.

Many Bulldogs do, however, suffer from tear staining (below), often reddish-brown, and most obvious on white or light-colored dogs and those with more pronounced wrinkles. There are many reasons for tear stains, sometimes it can be perfectly natural, other times it may be a sign of an underlying problem, such as an over-active tear duct, diet, or a genetic predisposition caused by the physical structure of the eye.

Excessive tearing results in damp facial hair, which becomes a breeding ground for bacteria and yeast, the most common of which is "red yeast." This often makes the tear stains a stronger red-brown color and may emit a moderate to strong odor. Vets can prescribe medication to treat bacterial and yeast infections. If the tear staining is related to diet, it may take some time to get to the root cause of the problem, see **Chapter 5. Feeding.**

There are various manufactured products freely available to reduce tear staining, as well as a number of home remedies. One is to add a teaspoon of white cider vinegar to your dog's drinking water to alter his internal pH and control new tear stains. It may take him a while to get used to the new flavor of his water, so start with a tiny bit at a time.

Another is to use an equal volume of plain white milk of magnesia and peroxide, and to mix them into a paste with corn starch. Work this into the stained area and let it dry. Then wash and condition the skin, repeat for several days, preferably every other day, until tear staining is gone. Always be extremely careful with peroxide or bleach near your dog's eyes and check with your vet before trying any home remedy.

Bathing your Bulldog

If you regularly groom your Bulldog and clean his skin folds, you shouldn't need to bath your dog very often – unless he's been rolling is something horrible. If a Bulldog's coat and skin get too dirty it can cause irritation, leading to scratching and excessive shedding. It's all a question of getting the balance right, and this will to some extent depend on how much outdoor exercise your Bully gets and what sort of areas he's running in. A Bulldog regularly exercising in dirt or mud will need more bathing than one living in an apartment and getting little outdoor exercise.

If you bath your dog too often you may wash off the dog's natural protective oils, leading to his skin drying out. Never use human shampoos on your Bulldog as you will irritate the skin. Instead use a shampoo specially medicated for dogs, such as Malaseb or similar. It is expensive but lasts a long time.

Teeth cleaning

Veterinary studies show that by the age of three, 80% of dogs exhibit signs of gum disease. Symptoms include yellow and brown build up of tartar along the gum line, red inflamed gums and persistent bad breath. You can give your dog a daily dental treat such as Dentastix or Nylabone to help keep his mouth and teeth clean, but you should also brush your Bully's teeth every now and again. Take things slowly in the beginning, give him lots of praise and many Bulldogs will start looking forward to teeth brushing sessions, especially if they like the flavor of the toothpaste!

Use a pet toothpaste as the human variety can upset a canine's stomach. The real benefit comes from the actual action of the brush on the teeth, and various brushes, sponges and pads are available - the choice depends on factors such as the health of your dog's gums, the size of his mouth and how good you are at teeth cleaning.

Get your dog used to the toothpaste by letting him lick some off your finger when he is young. If he doesn't like the flavor, try a different one. Continue this until he looks forward to licking the paste – it might be instant or take days. Put a small amount on your finger and gently rub it on one of the big canine teeth at the front of his mouth. Then get him used to the toothbrush or dental sponge - praise him when he licks it –for several days. The next step is to actually start brushing.

Lift his upper lip gently and place the brush at a 45º angle to the gum line. Gently move the brush backwards and forwards. Start just with his front teeth and then gradually do a few more. You don't need to brush the inside of his teeth as his tongue keeps them relatively free of plaque. With a bit of encouragement and patience, it can become a pleasant task for both of you.

---

12. The Birds and the Bees

Judging by the number of questions our website receives from owners who ask about the canine reproductive cycle and breeding from their dogs, there is a lot of confusion about the doggie facts of life out there.

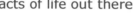

Some owners want to know whether they should breed from their dog, while others ask at what age they should have their dog spayed (females) or neutered (males).

Owners of females often ask when she will come on heat, how long this will last and how often it will occur. Sometimes they want to know how you can tell if a female is pregnant or how long a pregnancy lasts. So here, in a nutshell, is a short chapter on the facts of life as far as Bulldogs are concerned.

Should I Breed From My Bulldog?

The short and very simple answer is: **NO!**

More than with any other type of dog, the Bulldog is a breed where specialized knowledge is an absolute must. The pitfalls and risk to life with Bulldog breeding are enormous if you don't know what you are doing. Not to mention the fact that breeding is a very expensive, time-consuming and complicated procedure with Bulldogs, which is perhaps the most difficult breed of all to whelp (give birth).

Contrary to what you might think, breeding dogs is a complex issue – if you want a healthy mother and pups, that is. The pedigree breed societies discourage regular dog owners from breeding from their pets, as doing so properly requires a great deal of knowledge and experience.

Bulldogs are on a "watch list" in the UK of dogs which have had traits bred into them which have inadvertently led to health problems. Today's responsible breeders are continually looking at ways of improving the health of the Bulldog through selective breeding.

When it comes to reproduction, the Bulldog has very specific requirements. You can't just put a male and a female together, let them get on with it and then sit back and wait for a litter of gorgeous wrinkly pups to arrive two months later.

For a start, most Bulldogs do not mate naturally; instead many females are artificially inseminated with specially stored semen from a syringe. With their deep, heavy chests, short legs and tendency to overheat quickly, most male Bulldogs cannot successfully mate without human assistance. This may also lead to frustration which can in turn lead to aggression, overheating or even injury. And when the patience of a Bulldog bitch (female) runs out, she may attack her stud.

In Britain, some breeders use a breeding board or table which keeps the female in place and takes some of the male's weight off her body. Stud dogs are trained in the art of mounting and mating – with human assistance where necessary! Another option is for a third person to hold the female while the stud mates with her - similar to what goes on in the horse world.

A further reason for artificial insemination is that venereal disease and herpes in dogs is as real as it is in humans. Herpes can kill a litter and render the mother unable to breed in future, and artificial insemination removes this risk as all the semen is screened.

Another fact peculiar to Bulldogs is that more than four out of five pregnant female Bulldogs do not give birth naturally, but by Caesarian section (known as C-section in the USA). Whether the female can give birth naturally largely depends on her bone structure. Generally, Bulldogs have narrow hips, while the puppies have relatively massive heads and very wide shoulders, which make passing through the pelvis and birth canal extremely painful – if not downright impossible in some cases. Typical veterinary fees for a C-section are around $800-$1,200 in the USA (£500-£750 in the UK).

The breeding of Bulldogs is a demanding and expensive practice. Purebred Bulldog puppies in the

USA may fetch $2,000-$3,000 or more, while you can expect to pay over £1,500 for a pedigree dog with Kennel Club papers in the UK. Despite this high cost, many dedicated and caring Bulldog breeders make little or no money from the practice, due to the high costs of veterinary fees, health screening, stud fees and expensive special diets for the female and her pups.

Responsible breeding is backed up by genetic information and screening as well as a thorough knowledge of the desired traits of the Bulldog. It is definitely not an occupation for the amateur hobbyist. Breeding is not just about the look of the dogs; health and temperament are important factors too. Many dog lovers do not realize that the single most important factor governing health and certain temperament traits is genetics.

Top breeders have years of experience in selecting the right pair for mating after they have considered the lineage (ancestry), health, temperament, size and physical characteristics of the two dogs involved. They may travel hundreds of miles to find the right breeding partner for their dog. Anyone breeding from their Bulldog must first consider these questions:

❖ Are you 100% sure that your dog has no health or temperament problems which may be inherited by his or her puppies?

- ❖ Have you researched his or her lineage to make sure there are no problems lurking in the background? Puppies inherit traits from their grandparents and great-grandparents as well as from the dam (female) and sire (male).
- ❖ Are you positive that the same can be said for the dog you are planning on breeding yours with?
- ❖ Have your dog, the mate and their parents all been screened for health issues which can be bred into Bulldogs? Has your dog got OFA (Orthopedic Foundation for Animals) certificates for inherited diseases such as hip dysplasia, deafness and eye disease? In the UK the Bulldog Breed Council has led the way in introducing a Bulldog Health Assessment scheme supported nationally by a network of 60 veterinarians. Similar schemes have now been adopted by other breeds and in April 2014, the Bulldog Assessment Scheme was updated to Bronze and Silver with pass and fail.
- ❖ Do you have expert knowledge of Bulldog genetics and health, as well as the know-how and finances to successfully deal with keeping the mother healthy through pregnancy, birthing and C-sections, and care of the puppies and mother after birth?

Having said that, experts are not born, they learn their trade over many years. Anyone who is seriously considering getting into the specialized art of breeding Bulldogs should first spend time researching the breed and its genetics. Make sure you are going into Bulldog breeding for the right reasons and not just to make a quick buck - ask yourself how you intend to improve the breed.

Visit dog shows and make contact with established breeders. If possible, find yourself a mentor, someone who is already very familiar with the breed, and make sure you have a vet who is familiar with Bulldogs and able to perform a C-section at whatever time of day or night it may be required. Committed Bulldog breeders aren't in it for the money. They use their skills and knowledge to produce healthy pups with good temperaments which conform to breed standards and ultimately improve the breed. Our strong advice is: when it comes to Bulldogs, leave it to the experts.

Females and Heat

Just like all other animal and human females, a female Bulldog has a menstrual cycle - or to be more accurate, an estrus cycle. This is the period when she is ready (and willing!) for mating and is more commonly called **heat** or being **on heat**, **in heat** or **in season**.

A female Bulldog has her first cycle from about six to nine months old. However, there are some bloodlines with longer spans between heat cycles and the female will not have her first heat until she is anywhere from 10 months to one year old.

She will generally come on heat every six to eight months, though the timescale becomes more erratic with old age and can also be irregular with young dogs when cycles first begin.

Heat will last on average from 12 to 21 days, although it can be anything from just a few days up to four weeks. Within that time there will be several days which will be the optimum time for her to get pregnant. This middle phase of the cycle is called the *estrus.*

The third phase, called *diestrus*, then begins. During this time, her body will produce hormones whether or not she is pregnant. Her body thinks and acts like she is pregnant. All the hormones are present; only the puppies are missing. This can sometimes lead to what is known as a false pregnancy.

Bulldog breeders normally wait until a female has been in heat at least three times before breeding from her. Some believe that two years old is the right age for a first litter, while others think that as Bulldogs do not reach full maturity until three years of age, it is prudent to wait until she is a little older, especially as a pregnancy will draw on her calcium reserves which she needs for her own growing bones.

There is no right or wrong, but some breeders err on the side of caution, as if the female breeds too early she may break down structurally and have more health issues in later life.

While a female dog is on heat, she produces hormones which attract male dogs. Because dogs have a sense of smell hundreds of times stronger than ours, your girl on heat is a magnet for all the males in the neighborhood. They may congregate around your house or follow you around the park, waiting for their chance to prove their manhood – or mutthood in their case.

Don't expect your precious Bulldog princess to be fussy. Her hormones are raging when she is on heat and during her most fertile days, she is ready, able and ... very willing!

As she approaches the optimum time for mating, you may notice her tail bending slightly to one side. She will also start to urinate more frequently. This is her signal to all those virile male dogs out there that she is ready for mating.

The first visual sign you may notice is when she tries to lick her rear end – or vulva to be more precise. She will then bleed, this is sometimes called spotting. It will be a light red or brown at the beginning of the heat cycle, then some bitches bleed a lot after the first week. Some female Bulldogs can bleed quite heavily, this is normal. But if you have any concerns about her bleeding, contact your vet to be on the safe side.

Bulldog breeding requires a lot of specialized knowledge on the part of the owner, but this does not stop a female on heat from being extremely interested in attention from any old male. To avoid an unwanted pregnancy - which could lead to complications and in extreme cases the death of the mother and puppies- you must keep a close eye on your female and not allow her to freely wander where she may come into contact with other dogs when she is on heat.

Unlike women, female dogs do not go through the menopause and can have puppies even when they are quite old. However, a first litter for an elderly female Bulldog can also result in complications.

If you don't want your female Bulldog to get pregnant, you should have her spayed. In the United States and Europe, humane societies, animal shelters and rescue groups urge dog owners to have their pets spayed or neutered to prevent unwanted litters which contribute to too many animals in the rescue system or, even worse, having to be destroyed. Normally all dogs from rescue centers and shelters will have been spayed or neutered. Many responsible breeders also encourage early spaying and neutering.

Spaying

Spaying is the term used to describe the removal of the ovaries and uterus (womb) of a female dog so that she cannot become pregnant. Although this is a routine operation, it is major abdominal surgery and she has to be anesthetized.

A popular myth is that a female dog should have her first heat cycle before she is spayed, but this is not the case. Even puppies can be spayed. You should consult your vet for the optimum time, should you decide to have your dog done.

If spayed before her first heat cycle, one of the advantages is that your dog will have an almost zero risk of mammary cancer (the equivalent of breast cancer in women). Even after the first heat, spaying reduces the risk of this cancer by 92%.

Some vets claim that the risk of mammary cancer in unspayed female dogs can be as high as one in four. Some females may put weight on easier after spaying and will require slightly less food afterwards. As with any major procedure, there are pros and cons.

Spaying is a much more serious operation for a female than neutering is for a male. This is because it involves an internal abdominal operation, whereas the neutering procedure is carried out on the male's testicles, which are outside his abdomen.

Ad from an animal shelter

For:

- Spaying prevents infections, cancer and other diseases of the uterus and ovaries.

- Your dog will have a greatly reduced risk of mammary cancer.

- It reduces hormonal changes which can interfere with the treatment of diseases like diabetes or epilepsy.

- Spaying can reduce behavior problems, such as roaming, aggression to other dogs, anxiety or fear.

- It eliminates the risk of the potentially fatal disease pyometra, which affects unspayed middle-aged females.

- A spayed dog does not contribute to the pet overpopulation problem.

Against:

- Complications can occur, including an abnormal reaction to the anesthetic, bleeding, stitches breaking and infections. This is not common.

- Occasionally there can be long-term effects connected to hormonal changes. These may include weight gain, urinary incontinence or less stamina and these problems can occur years after a female has been spayed.

- Older females may suffer some urinary incontinence, but it only affects a few spayed females. Discuss it with your vet.

- Cost. This can range from £100 to £300 in the UK ($160 - $480 in the USA).

- Bulldogs are sensitive to anesthesia – select a vet who is familiar with the breed.

If you talk to a vet or a volunteer at a rescue shelter, they will say that the advantages of spaying far outweigh any disadvantages. If you have a female puppy, you can discuss with your vet whether, and at what age, spaying would be a good idea for your Bulldog when you take her in for her vaccinations.

Neutering

Neutering male dogs involves castration; the removal of the testicles. This can be a difficult decision for some owners, as it causes a drop in the pet's testosterone levels, which some humans – males in particular! - feel affects the quality of their dog's life.

Fortunately, dogs do not think like people and male dogs do not miss their testicles or the loss of sex! Our own experience is that our dog Max is much happier having been neutered. We decided to have him neutered after he went missing three times on walks – he ran off on the scent of a female on heat. Fortunately, he is micro-chipped and has our phone number on a tag on his collar and we were lucky that he was returned to us on all three occasions.

Unless you specifically want to breed from or show your dog, or he has a special job, neutering is recommended by animal rescue organizations and vets. Guide Dogs for the Blind, Hearing Dogs for Deaf People and Dogs for the Disabled are routinely neutered and this does not impair their ability to perform their duties.

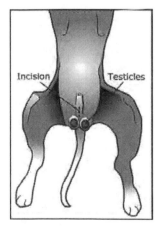

There are countless unwanted puppies, especially in the USA, many of which are destroyed. There is also the problem of a lack of knowledge from the owners of some breeding dogs, resulting in the production of puppies with congenital health or temperament problems.

Neutering is usually performed around puberty, i.e. about six months old. It can, however, be done at any age over eight weeks, provided both testicles have descended. The operation is a relatively straightforward procedure. Dogs neutered before puberty tend to grow a little larger than dogs done later. This is because testosterone is involved in the process which stops growth, so the bones grow for longer without testosterone.

The neutering operation for a male is much less of a major operation than spaying for a female. Complications are less common and less severe than with spaying a female. Although he will feel tender afterwards, your dog should return to his normal self within a couple of days.

When he comes out of surgery, his scrotum (the sacs which held the testicles) will be swollen and it may look like nothing has been done. But it is normal for these to slowly shrink in the days following surgery. Here are the main pros and cons:

For:

- Behavior problems such as roaming and aggression are usually reduced.

- Unwanted sexual behavior, such as mounting people or objects, is usually reduced or eliminated.

- Testicular problems such as infections, cancer and torsion (painful rotation of the testicle) are eradicated.

- Prostate disease, common in older male dogs, is less likely to occur.

- A submissive entire (uncastrated) male dog may be targeted by other dogs. After he has been neutered, he will no longer produce testosterone and so will not be regarded as much of a threat by the other males, so he is less likely to be bullied.

- A neutered dog is not fathering unwanted puppies.

Against:

- As with any surgery, there can be bleeding afterwards, you should keep an eye on him for any blood loss after the operation. Infections can also occur, generally caused by the dog licking the wound, so try and prevent him doing this. If he persists, use an E collar. In the **vast majority** of cases, these problems do not occur.

- Some dogs' coats may be affected, but supplementing their diet with fish oil can compensate for this.

- Cost. This starts at around £80 in the UK ($130 in the USA).

- Bulldogs are sensitive to anesthesia – select a vet who is familiar with the breed.

Myths

Here are some common myths about neutering and spaying:

Neutering or spaying will spoil the dog's character - There is no evidence that any of the positive characteristics of your dog will be altered. He or she will be just as loving, playful and loyal. Neutering may reduce aggression or roaming, especially in male dogs, because they are no longer competing to mate with a female.

A female needs to have at least one litter - There is no proven physical or mental benefit to a female having a litter. Pregnancy and whelping (giving birth to puppies) can be stressful and can have complications. In a false pregnancy, a female is simply responding to the hormones in her body.

Mating is natural and necessary - Dogs are not humans, they do not think emotionally about sex or having and raising a family. Because Bulldogs like the company of humans so much, we tend to ascribe human emotions to them. Unlike humans, their desire to mate or breed is entirely physical, triggered by the chemicals called hormones within their body. Without these hormones – i.e. after neutering or spaying – the desire disappears or is greatly reduced.

Male dogs will behave better if they can mate - This is simply not true; sex does not make a dog behave better. In fact it can have the opposite effect. Having mated once, a male may show an increased interest in females. He may also consider his status elevated, which may make him harder to control or call back.

Pregnancy

A canine pregnancy will normally last for 61 to 65 days - typically 63 days – regardless of the size or breed of the dog. Sometimes pregnancy is referred to as the "***gestation period.***"

There is now a blood test available which measures levels of a hormone called ***relaxin***. This is produced by the developing placenta and pregnancy can be detected as early as 22 to 27 days after mating. The level of relaxin remains high throughout pregnancy and declines rapidly following whelping (giving birth). After 45 days, X-rays can confirm the pregnancy. X-rays also give the breeder an idea of the number of puppies, can help if the bitch has had previous whelping problems, and give the vet more information if a C-section is to be performed.

Here are some of the signs of pregnancy:

-   After mating, many females become more affectionate. (However, some will become uncharacteristically irritable and maybe even a little aggressive)

-   The female may produce a slight clear discharge from her vagina about one month after mating

-   Her appetite will increase in the second month of pregnancy

-   She may seem slightly depressed and/or show a drop in appetite. These signs can also mean there are other problems, so you should consult your vet

-   Her teats (nipples) will become more prominent, pink and erect 25 to 30 days into the pregnancy. Later on, you may notice a fluid coming from them

-   After about 35 days, or seven weeks, her body weight will noticeably increase

-   Her abdomen will become noticeably larger from around day 40, although first-time mums and females carrying few puppies may not show as much

-   Many pregnant females' appetite will increase in the second half of pregnancy

Ever since I've started showing, my husband has affectionately called me "Three Humps"...

- Her nesting instincts will kick in as the delivery date approaches. She may seem restless or scratch her bed or the floor

- During the last week of pregnancy, females often start to look for a safe place for whelping. Some seem to become confused, wanting to be with their owners and at the same time wanting to prepare their nest.

Even if the female is having a C-section, she should still be allowed to nest in a whelping box with layers of newspaper, which she will scratch and dig as the time approaches. However, natural birthing – or free whelping - still presents many problems for Bulldogs and should only be attempted by very experienced breeders with a Bulldog-savvy vet on call. And even then they will not leave the pregnant female unattended when she is near her time.

The Bulldog is a unique breed in many ways and this is especially true when producing puppies. If your female becomes pregnant – either by design or accident - your first step should be to consult a veterinarian familiar with Bullies straight away. Pregnant Bulldogs simply cannot be left to get on with it like many other breeds.

How Many Puppies?

The size of the litter can vary greatly, with a Bulldog bitch producing anything from one to 10 puppies, although a litter of four or five would be more common. Large litters are seen less often due to the large size of the puppies. Very young and elderly dogs usually have smaller litters.

False Pregnancies

As many as 50% or more of intact (unspayed) female dogs may display signs of a false pregnancy. In the wild it was common for female dogs to have false pregnancies and to lactate (produce milk). This female would then nourish puppies if their own mother died.

False pregnancies occur 60 to 80 days after the female was in heat - about the time she would have given birth – and are generally nothing to worry about for an owner. The exact cause is unknown. However, hormonal imbalances are thought to play an important role. Some dogs have shown symptoms within three to four days of spaying. Typical symptoms include:

❖ Mothering or adopting toys and other objects
❖ Making a nest
❖ Producing milk (lactating)

❖ Appetite fluctuations
❖ Barking or whining a lot
❖ Restlessness, depression or anxiety
❖ Swollen abdomen
❖ She might even appear to go into labor

Try not to touch your dog's nipples, as touch will stimulate further milk production. If she is licking herself repeatedly, she may need an Elizabethan collar (a large plastic collar from the vet) to minimize stimulation.

Under no circumstances should you restrict your Bulldog's water supply to try and prevent her from producing milk. This is dangerous as she can become dehydrated.

Some unspayed bitches may have a false pregnancy with each heat cycle. Spaying during a false pregnancy may actually prolong the condition, so better to wait until the false pregnancy is over and then have her spayed to prevent it happening again. False pregnancy is not a disease, but an exaggerated response to normal hormonal changes. Owners should be reassured that even if left untreated, the condition almost always resolves itself.

However, if your Bulldog appears physically ill or the behavioral changes are severe enough to worry you, visit your vet. He or she may prescribe tranquilizers to relieve anxiety, or diuretics to reduce milk production and relieve fluid retention. In rare cases, hormone treatment may be necessary. Generally, dogs experiencing false pregnancies do not have serious long-term problems, as the behavior disappears when the hormones return to their normal levels - usually in two to three weeks.

One exception is pyometra, a disease mainly affecting unspayed middle-aged females, caused by a hormonal abnormality. Pyometra follows a heat cycle in which fertilization did not occur and the dog typically starts showing symptoms within two to four months. These are excessive drinking and urination, with the female trying to lick a white discharge from her vagina. She may also have a slight temperature. If the condition becomes severe, her back legs will become weak, possibly to the point where she can no longer get up without help.

Pyometra is serious if bacteria take a hold and in extreme cases it can be fatal. It is also relatively common and needs to be dealt with promptly by a vet, who will give the dog intravenous fluids and antibiotics for several days. In most cases this is followed by spaying.

With thanks to Kathy Jacobsen for her invaluable assistance with this chapter.

14.Bulldog Rescue

Making the Commitment

Are you thinking of adopting a Bulldog from a rescue organization? What could be kinder and more rewarding than giving a poor, abandoned Bully a happy and loving home for the rest of his or her life?

Not much really, adoption saves lives. The problem of homeless dogs is truly depressing, particularly in the USA. The sheer numbers in kill shelters is hard to comprehend. Randy Grim states in "Don't Dump The Dog" that 1,000 dogs are being put to sleep every hour in the US.

Many Bulldogs which need rehoming may have health or behavioral issues and if you decide to offer a home to one of these poor souls, you need to do it with your eyes wide open. Offering a home to a rescue Bulldog is not recommended if you are a first-time dog owner. The Bulldog – even a healthy, well behaved one - is a breed which requires specialist knowledge and care.

Some Bulldogs may have issues with dogs, other animals or children and will require a great deal of time and patience from their new owners. Many Bulldogs available for adoption are older and although you can teach an old dog new tricks and good manners – it is not easy with an older Bulldog.

This is what the Bulldog Club of America Rescue Network (BCARN) has to say: "A Bulldog may not be the right choice for every family. Living with a Bulldog can be very rewarding, but you must be committed to meeting the Bulldog's particular needs.

"**Some Things to Consider** - Bulldogs are perpetual children: they never grow up. A Bulldog does best in a loving environment, free from fear and neglect. They are happiest when with people and require lots of attention from people. When left alone, Bulldogs can be very destructive. They may chew throughout their lifetimes. They may need to be crated when they are not being supervised. A Bulldog should never be left unattended in your backyard. Not only is it dangerous to your Bulldog's wellbeing, but Bulldogs are often targeted for theft.

"**Possible Health Problems -** Bulldogs have numerous known genetic defects and are subject to various illnesses that affect many breeds. Common Bulldog health problems you may encounter include: elongated soft palate, small trachea, allergies, dermatitis, demodetic mange, eye lid anomalies, hip dysplasia and heart problems. Some of them have a tendency toward self-mutilation (especially if they have itchy skin), so owners should watch carefully for signs of skin irritation and scratching. If you are adopting an older dog, many of these conditions will already have been identified.

"Twenty-four hour care by a qualified veterinarian must be available. Since not all veterinarians are knowledgeable about the health problems Bulldogs may have, you should consult experienced Bulldog owners or the rescue center to find a capable veterinarian. Any veterinarian who will be doing surgery on your Bulldog should have previous experience with putting Bulldogs under anesthesia.

"Danger of Overheating - Bulldogs are extremely intolerant of heat. They must be kept in an air-conditioned area with limited trips outside when the outside temperature is over 80 degrees or the humidity is high.

"Close supervision is required during outside activity, especially in spring and summer to prevent over-exertion leading to over-heating. They also are not usually capable of prolonged physical activity whether the temperature is very warm or cold: a Bulldog is not for someone who enjoys taking a dog for long walks through the countryside.

"After Adoption - Although all Bulldogs that we place are subjected to a thorough veterinary examination and are evaluated for soundness of temperament, we do not guarantee that they will not have any problems in their new homes. In fact, a period of adjustment is expected during which the Bulldog and the new owner will be getting acquainted with each other, and the Bulldog will be "settling in" to a new routine.

"If we have any doubts about a Bulldog's ability to deal with certain situations, we put restrictions on the type of home in which it will be placed (for example, by requiring no young children and/or no other pets.) We also provide guidelines for the new owners to ensure that they are aware of any special treatment the Bulldog may require. With the application of a little common sense in following the guidelines, new owners will find the transition into owning a rescue Bulldog to be relatively simple."

With thanks to BCARN for the above article.

BCARN also reproduce the AKC Gazette December 1999 article entitled **_The Importance of Temperament_** (below) which gives a great insight into the Bulldog and the demands on an owner:

"The Importance of Temperament - When selecting a pet, the most important breed characteristic to consider by far is its temperament or disposition. Failure to thoroughly investigate temperament is the biggest mistake anyone can make in selecting a pet, especially a Bulldog.

"In my experience, far too many people select a dog based solely on its physical appearance, and those who do so usually live to regret it. People who shop for a pet the same way they shop for a new car, a piece of furniture or designer jeans should never own one.

"If it is a status symbol you want, please do not even consider buying a Bulldog! You and the dog are sure to be disappointed in each other. For one thing, the modern Bulldog cannot tolerate isolation. Some breeds are able to thrive on only occasional human contact, but Bulldogs simply cannot stand to be ignored. They crave attention, and they will do almost anything to get it.

"To the dismay of their owners, many Bulldogs prefer to pursue the role of a lapdog. They fail to comprehend that some humans find their typical weight of 50 to 60 pounds less than comfortable on their laps.

"It is nearly impossible to lavish too much love and attention on a Bulldog - and only he decides when he has had enough of it. When he has had enough loving, he will finally wander off somewhere to find peace and quiet. If you're not a hands-on type of dog lover who enjoys close and frequent contact and a few wet kisses, a less affectionate pet may better satisfy your needs. The Bulldog's constant craving for attention and the need to entertain humans and be entertained by them is not for everyone.

"There is a limit, however, to how much strenuous physical activity a typical Bulldog can safely tolerate. Their short muzzles and narrow windpipes, relative to the size of their bodies, limits their oxygen intake and causes them to become easily winded. This can result in acute respiratory distress and sometimes death. Like it or not, most Bulldogs do not have great physical endurance. They are more like short-distance sprinters than long-distance runners. Bulldogs don't realize this; your own common sense must prevail.

"Neither do Bulldogs respond obediently to heavy-handed physical discipline. Despite 1,000 years of selective breeding, most Bulldogs I am familiar with, both male and female, instinctively detest and resist violence or the threat of it. This is especially evident with regard to children. A screaming child immediately causes grave concern and routinely triggers a decidedly protective response. They seem to sense trouble, and they are likely to intervene in their own special way to end the disturbance.

"Nonetheless, Bulldogs are not easily provoked by other dogs unless they are seriously threatened or attacked. A Bulldog that has been carefully bred for temperament and lovingly cared for and properly socialized from birth likes to meet other dogs and strangers. Visitors to the household are always welcomed, often enthusiastically. It never occurs to a Bulldog that other dogs and other people might be less than friendly. An intruder might even be a welcome guest, but it is difficult to say what might happen when you are away.

"Modern Bulldogs are not by nature good guard dogs or attack dogs. However they are fairly reliable watchdogs. They will normally alert you to any unusual activity in the home or yard.

"A common misconception is that Bulldogs are "one-man" dogs. It may sometimes seem apparent that one family member is preferred over another, but Bulldogs regard each family member as their own personal property. Bulldogs can be possessive to a fault. You don't own

them, they own you, and don't ever forget it! If you can't appreciate their possessive nature, you certainly will not appreciate their inherent stubbornness and determination. Training takes lots of patience, but they can be successfully trained for obedience and agility competition.

"Unless they choose to behave otherwise, I don't believe there is a more obstinate creature alive. And while a Bulldog might appear to be lazy or stupid, that's only a facade."

According to Jo-Anne Cousins, a leading figure in canine rescue, the situations leading to a dog ending up in rescue can be summed up in one phrase: ***unrealistic expectations.***

She said: "In many situations, dog ownership was something that the family went into without fully understanding the time, money and commitment that it takes to raise a dog. While they may have spent hours on the internet pouring over cute puppy photos, they probably didn't read any puppy training books or look into actual costs of regular vet care, training and boarding."

Some of the most common reasons for giving up a Bulldog for rehoming are:

❖ Finances –the owners can no longer afford to keep the dog
❖ Bulldog health issues – the owner has not got the money and/or time needed to deal with them
❖ Lifestyle changes, such as new partner, new job, or moving home
❖ Poor behavior, such as chewing, biting, not being housetrained, being too rough
❖ Lack of time, what may have seemed like a great gift becomes too much of a burden when owners realize how much time and care a dog, especially a Bulldog, requires.

There is, however, a ray of sunshine for some of these dogs. Every year many thousands of people in North America, the UK and countries all around the world adopt a rescue dog and the story often has a happy ending.

The Dog's Point of View...

But if you are serious about adopting a Bulldog, then you should do so with the right motives and prepared for a ride which may not always be smooth – especially in the beginning when you are both getting to know each other and fit in with each others' lives. If you're expecting a perfect dog, you could be in for a shock. Rescue Bulldogs can and do become wonderful companions, but much of it depends on you.

Bulldogs are outstanding companion dogs, however, many of them in rescue centers are traumatized. They don't understand why they have been abandoned by their beloved owners and in the beginning may arrive with problems of their own until they adjust to being part of a loving family home again.

What could be worse for a Bulldog which has been traumatized by the loss of his or her family to lose another home if things don't work out with you? Do not consider adopting a Bully - or any other dog - unless you are 100% committed to making it work and you are prepared to be there for the long haul.

Ask yourself a few questions before you take the plunge:

❖ Are you prepared to accept and deal with any problems - such as bad behavior, shyness, aggression or making a mess in the house - which the dog may display when he initially arrives in your home?

❖ How much time are you willing to spend with your new pet to help him integrate back into normal family life?

❖ Can you take time off work to be at home and help your Bulldog settle in at the beginning?

❖ Are you prepared to take on a new addition to your family that may live for many years? Think about the implications before taking on a rescue dog - try and look at it from the dog's point of view. What could be worse for the unlucky Bulldog than to be abandoned again if things don't work out between you?

Other Considerations

Adopting a rescue dog is a big commitment for all involved. It is not a cheap way of getting a Bulldog and shouldn't be viewed as such. It could cost you several hundred dollars - or pounds. You'll have adoption fees to pay and often vaccination and veterinary bills as well as worm and flea medication and spaying or neutering. Make sure you're aware of the full cost before committing.

Many rescue Bulldogs have had difficult lives. You need plenty of time to help them rehabilitate. Some may have initial problems with housebreaking. Others may need socialization with people as well as other dogs.

If you are serious about adopting, you may have to wait a while until a suitable dog comes up. One way of finding out if you, your family and home are suitable is to volunteer to become a foster home for one of the rescue centers. Fosters offer temporary homes until a forever home becomes available It's a shorter term arrangement, but still requires commitment and patience. Or you could help by becoming a fundraiser to generate cash to keep these very worthy rescue groups providing such a wonderful service.

And it's is not just the dogs that are screened - you'll probably have to undergo a screening by the rescue organization to ensure you are suitable. You might even have to provide references.

If you haven't been put you off with all of the above …. Congratulations, you may be just the family or person that poor homeless Bulldog is looking for.

Good Luck!

Saving one dog will not change the world
But it will change the world for one dog

There are many dedicated people out there who give up their time free of charge to help find loving and permanent homes for Bulldogs which would often otherwise be put down (euthanized). There are networks of these worthy people who have set up excellent rescue services for Bulldogs. Here are some of the main ones:

Bulldog Rescue Organizations

This is by no means an exhaustive list, but it does cover some of the main organizations involved. Other online resources are the Pet Finder website at www.petfinder.com and Adopt a

Pet site at www.adoptapet.com. Many of the dogs listed with the Bulldog-specific rescue organizations are also advertised on these websites. If you do visit these websites, you cannot presume that the descriptions are 100% accurate, even when they have been given in good faith.

NEVER buy a puppy or an adult dog from eBay, Craig's List, Preloved, Gumtree or any of the other advertising websites which sell old cars, washing machines, golf clubs etc. You might think you are getting a cheap dog, but in the long run you will pay the price.

If the dog had been well bred and properly cared for, he or she would not be advertised on a website such as this. If you buy or get a free one, you may be storing up a whole load of trouble for yourselves in terms of behavioral, temperament and/or health issues due to poor breeding and/or training.

NEVER buy a Bulldog from a pet shop. Good Bulldog breeders never sell their puppies to pet shops.

USA Rescue Groups

The Bulldog Club of America Rescue Network (BCARN) is the largest umbrella Bulldog rescue organization in North America, with volunteers working throughout the US as well as some in Canada. It only rescues purebred Bulldogs, which are also sometimes referred to as "English" or "British" Bulldogs.

Anyone interested in adopting one will require screening and has to complete the detailed online adoption form before contacting a local BCA Rescue Network representative. This contains a number of questions to help decide if you would be a suitable person or family to adopt a Bulldog. The questions include:

❖ Why do you want to adopt a bulldog?

❖ What age bulldog are you willing to accept – puppy/up to age three/up to age six/any age? (BCARN does not often get puppies offered for adoption)

❖ Must the bulldog be good with children?

❖ Must the bulldog get along with other dogs in your household and/or with visiting dogs?

❖ Are you willing to accept a bulldog needing additional care? (If yes, which level of care are you comfortable providing – Accept (Daily medications, special food, etc), Accept (Frequent medications, house training issues, difficulty walking, behavior issues, etc) Accept (blindness, deafness, incontinence, spina bifida, seizure disorder, etc) Please Note: ALL Bulldogs require some daily care.

❖ Employment information

❖ Details of household members

❖ Who will be responsible for caring for the Bulldog?

- ❖ Is anyone in the household allergic to dogs?

- ❖ Are all members of the household in favor of adopting a Bulldog?

- ❖ Type of home and whether you have a fenced yard

- ❖ How will the dog be exercised, how often, and who will supervise the dog while outdoors?

- ❖ Does your home have stairs that the Bulldog will have to go up and down?

- ❖ Do you have a swimming pool, pond or other body of water near your home?

- ❖ Are your home and car air-conditioned?

- ❖ Where will the Bulldog be kept during the day - and night?

- ❖ Are any family members at home during the day time?

- ❖ Do you expect any changes in your family in the next few years?

- ❖ Do you own any other cats or dogs?

- ❖ Do all your pets receive regular veterinary care and are they up-to-date on vaccinations?

BCARN also needs responsible rescue volunteers. If you think you are up to the challenge, contact the BCA Rescue network representative nearest you or the co-coordinator for your area of the country. Details of these and local Bulldog rescue organizations can be found online here:

www.rescuebulldogs.org/rescueroster/rescueroster.pl

Other Bulldog-specific organizations with their own websites include:

California – San Diego Bulldog Rescue **www.sdbr.org**

Southern California Bulldog Rescue **www.socalbulldogrescue.org**

Northern California Bulldog Rescue **www.norcalbulldogrescue.org**

Chicago English Bulldog Rescue (covers the Midwest) **www.ebullymatch.com**

Detroit Bulldog Rescue **www.detroitbulldogrescue.org**

Florida: **www.floridaenglishbulldogrescue.com**

Illinois, southeastern Wisconsin and northwestern Indiana **www.adoptabull.org**

Illinois English Bulldog Rescue **www.ilenglishbulldogrescue.org**

Indiana **www.indianabulldogrescue.com**

Mid Atlantic **http://midatlanticbulldogrescue.com**

Mideastern States – On the Rebound Bulldog Rescue **www.otrbulldogrescue.org**

New York and New England **http://longislandbulldogrescue.org**

NJ, PA, DE and MD **www.heavensentbulldogrescue.com**

Ohio - **http://www.rescueohioenglishbulldogs.org**

Pacific North West **www.cascadebulldogrescue.org**

Tennessee Smoky Mountains Bulldog Club Rescue **http://smbcarn.org**

Canada - In Alberta and British Columbia contact Kodie Burgess by email: bulldogwrangler@yahoo.com or phone 971-267-0744.

In Ontario and Quebec contact Laurette Richin at 631-689-6245.

UK Rescue Groups

Bulldog Rescue and Rehoming Trust (Registered Charity number 1115009)

 The Trust rehomes around 120 Bulldogs in the UK every year as well as giving free advice, memorials and operating a list for lost and stolen Bulldogs. The service is made up of a network of around 70 volunteers, who between them travel over 10,000 miles a year checking out new homes and collecting Bulldogs for rehoming and fostering.

The Trust may have up to 50 bulldogs in the system at any given time, but sadly many are older or sick and are not so easy to find new homes for. The total annual veterinary bill can be anything from £20,000 to £30,000.

The most common reasons for a Bulldog needing a new home in the UK is divorce or separation, then a new baby, followed by house moves and emigration abroad. This is what the Trust has to say:

"We are a mainly voluntary organisation, offering a Rescue and Rehoming service for pure bred bulldogs across the UK, who, for whatever reason cannot stay where they are. We are not a dog's home or a shelter and aim to always do our best for every bulldog we are asked to help. We will subsequently stand by him for the rest of his life, offering support, education and advice to his new owners whenever it is required.

"Only a few bulldogs end up in rescue because they have been abused, mis-treated or abandoned, the majority of bulldogs looking for a second chance are simply victims of circumstance – i.e. divorce, new baby or a change in the family situation. All the owner wants is a good pet home and by using our rehoming service they are going some way to ensure the new home is the right home first time. Homes are selected on a system of area and suitability from our extensive waiting list of people across the country, in most cases we are able to work within the dog's own area and find a home that matches his criteria.

"Adoption fees, fund raising and donations are our only means of funding – every bulldog that simply needs a good home will help us to pay for those that require veterinary treatment, transportation or fostering. Our adoption fees are nominal – regardless of how much we had to spend on the dog before we could rehome it.

"Everything is coordinated from one central point and thanks to our dedicated team of volunteers across the UK we can act quickly if necessary, home check potential new homes and supply short stay foster care where required.

"Please feel free to contact us if you would like to know more about Bulldog Rescue and what we do or visit our website at www.bulldogrescue.org.uk "

The Trust's Aims:

❖ To promote responsible dog ownership amongst those that own a pure bred bulldog

❖ To ensure that all those who can no longer keep their bulldog, for whatever reason, have the option of safely placing their dog in a vetted pet home

❖ To ensure a place of safety is available to all bulldogs whose owners can no longer cope or look after their dog properly

❖ To be available to offer unbiased breed advice to all those that own a pure bred bulldog

❖ To educate bulldog owners in the hope that bulldogs in the future can be free from cruelty, abuse and neglect.

In its annual report for the year ended March 31, 2013, the Trust stated: "The most significant change from the previous year is the increase in the number of dogs which could not be re-homed because of behavioural issues, and had to be put to sleep. The charity does its best to ensure that the temperament of every dog in its care is tested thoroughly, and that all those that are re-homed are safe for the adopting family."

It added: "Finding homes is proving to be more difficult as people applying for bulldogs don't want dogs with problems and although we rarely see a bad breather, skin problems continue to be an issue in the breed as do problems with ears and eyes.

"The numbers of dogs needing new homes is going to rise as the numbers being bred continues to increase. We calculate that between 2.5% and 4.00% of bulldogs that are bred in this country will need re-homing at some stage in their lives."

Visit **www.bulldogrescue.org.uk** or **www.bulldogrescue.co.uk** and click on the **Donate** button to help this dedicated band with their tremendous work in giving so many Bulldogs a second chance.

Bulldog Stories

Handsome Dan

In the late 1880s, Princeton and Harvard already had football mascots. Princeton had a tiger and Harvard had the "Orange Man" as a stand-in for Puritan John Harvard.

In 1889, Andrew B. Graves saw a bulldog sitting in front of a New Haven blacksmith shop. Graves was an Englishman in the Yale class of 1892 and a member of the crew team as well as a football tackle. He offered $50 for the dog and the blacksmith countered with $75. He eventually purchased the dog for $65.

Graves cleaned up the dog and named him "Handsome Dan." Soon the dog followed Graves everywhere around campus, including to sporting events. The students quickly adopted Dan as the Yale mascot. After Graves graduated and returned to England, Dan stayed on campus with his master's brother.

Before football and baseball games would begin, Handsome Dan founded a tradition and a dynasty by being led across the field. One newspaper reported: "He was a big white bulldog, with one of the greatest faces a dog of that breed (English) ever carried".

This was not an exaggeration, as Handsome Dan was one of the finest specimens of his breed in America, and went on to win first prize at the Westminster Dog Show, and at least 30 other first prize ribbons in the United States and Canada.

According to the Hartford Courant: "In personal appearance, he seemed like a cross between an alligator and a horned frog, and he was called handsome by the metaphysicians under the law of compensation. The title came to him, he never sought it. He was always taken to games on a leash, and the Harvard football team for years owed its continued existence to the fact that the rope held."

The Philadelphia Press reported that "a favorite trick was to tell him to 'Speak to Harvard.' He would bark ferociously and work himself into physical contortions of rage never before dreamed of by a dog. Dan was peculiar to himself in one thing - he would never associate with anyone but students. Dan implanted himself more firmly in the hearts of Yale students than any mascot had ever done before."

Handsome Dan crossed the Atlantic to join his old master in 1897 and died in 1898. Graves had Dan stuffed and returned him to be displayed at Yale in the old gymnasium. When it was torn down, Dan was sent to the Peabody Museum for reconstruction. Handsome Dan is now in a sealed glass case in one of the trophy rooms of Yale's Payne Whitney Gymnasium where, according to Stanton Ford, "he is the perpetual guardian of the treasures which attest to generations of Yale athletic glory."

Handsome Dan was the first live college mascot in America, and therefore he is also believed to be the first live mascot in the entire world. Since the tradition started in 1889, a total of 17 Bulldogs have held the position.

Today Handsome Dan is selected based on his ability to tolerate bands and children, as well as negative reaction to the color crimson and to tigers (the symbols of rival schools Harvard and Princeton) and cleanliness.

Igor's Home from Home

A family from Lillestrom in Norway were very excited about their holiday to Thailand. There was just one drawback, they had to leave Igor, their beloved Bulldog, in kennels for the first time.

Igor's Dad, Kai, wanted to make sure Igor would feel at home, so he set about making some elaborate arrangements. He couldn't leave his Bulldog at home, so he did the next best thing - he brought his home to Igor! The family pulled out all the stops and completely recreated their living room at the kennels – and Igor loved it!

Tazzie's Safe Return

Here's a story from First Coast News in July 2014: South Carolina man Michael Buckley was reunited with the beloved bulldog he feared he'd never see again, after Tazzie was in his car which was stolen in Atlanta the previous week.

Buckley was headed from Charleston, S.C. to Colorado last week when he had car trouble. After asking three teens for directions near the intersection of Martin Luther King, Jr. Drive and Joseph Lowery Boulevard, he went to the back of his Ford Explorer to check on Tazzie. Two of the teens jumped his vehicle and drove off.

Police found his vehicle the next day, but Tazzie was nowhere to be found.

Buckley stayed in Atlanta to search for his best friend of five years. After the story aired on 11Alive, more than 10,000 people shared the story about the search for Tazzie on Facebook. On Tuesday, Tazzie was found about two blocks from where Buckley's car had been stolen.

Melissa Robinson, who lives on Westmoor Drive, said that she found Tazzie roaming the streets on Friday. Robinson, who said she owns an American bulldog, said she fed Tazzie, bathed her and took care of her. When she came home from work on Tuesday, she saw a flyer about Tazzie and called Buckley. "He was like, 'Oh my God, it's her,'" Robinson said. "Yeah he just kept hugging me."

Michael and Tazzie are back together again and can continue their journey to Colorado, where Michael was moving to when he ran into trouble in Atlanta. But before he goes, he wants everyone to know that the incident should not give the city a black eye.

He said: "Yeah, there was the negativity of the fact that this happened in Atlanta, but you know, it just goes to show you how many people around here and in this community came...to my aid and tried to help me find this dog and it was just great."

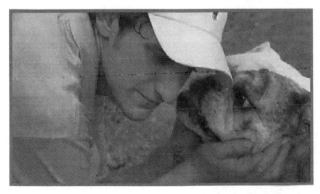

Buckley said he's grateful for everyone who helped - from the volunteers who helped him post flyers, to the hotel staff where he stayed, to the complete stranger who drove him around the city the past few days helping him get his car back and looking for Tazzie.

"I'm so grateful that everything ended up like this and I'm actually back with her because I'm going to be honest with you, I didn't think that I was gonna have her back," Buckley said.

The next story is a wonderful success tale from Chigaco English Bulldog Rescue, which does fantastic work in giving Bulldogs a second chance at a happy life, many of whom have been living a nightmare.

The Bella of the Ball

There's not much that Bella likes more than a tennis ball. Well, except for just about everything - people, kids, cats, dogs, you name it. But this very special girl came very close to not having a life at all. Bella's story and her never wavering spirit and the impact she has made on anyone fortunate enough to have made her acquaintance is at the very heart of why we do what we do.

Bella came to us at 1.5 years old almost completely paralyzed in her back legs. You see, Bella was purchased from a pet store. And as we all know, pet stores get their dogs from puppy mill breeders who don't really care about the health of their breeding lines. So Bella was born with a congenital defect that was affecting her spine and her ability to walk.

Her condition was rapidly deteriorating - she was incontinent and dragging her back legs behind her 100% of the time. Her family was facing two options; expensive spinal surgery or euthanasia.

Thankfully her family loved her enough to contact us for help. They knew they couldn't give her what she needed to recover; and they couldn't bear the thought of this sweet and silly girl who loved everyone being put down. When we saw the puppyish gleam in her eye there was no question that we would try to help her. In September of 2009 after Bella underwent spinal surgery, a loving foster home opened up their hearts to this partially paralyzed and incontinent bulldog.

Bella came through the surgery with flying colors, but would need extensive physical therapy to walk again and would need a home that would be willing to give her lifelong care. Bella could have a normal and happy life, she just would need to avoid roughhousing and jumping. After eight weeks of recovery (through which Bella remained a happy and silly bully) she began her rehab. After contacting Carol Jurca at the Animal Rehabilitation Clinic (ARC) in North Aurora, we knew we had found just the right person to get Bella over the final hurdle.

Carol quickly got Bella on the right track with hydrotherapy, physical therapy exercises, Alpha Stimm electrical treatments and lots and lots of homework for us. Bella grew to love her therapy sessions and that's when we discovered a key personality trait that would come to define Bella. Unlike most bulldogs, treats are not a big motivator, but what she will do just about anything for is - a tennis ball! The girl is obsessed with them. At her therapy sessions we'd sit in front of the hydro-tank as if it was a widescreen TV watching Bella walk and walk with a ball in her mouth.

After 12 weeks of therapy we knew that we finally had Bella where she needed to be and she was ready to move on to her final forever home. Although Bella had found a special place in each of our hearts we knew that when the right home came along, she deserved to find her own happiness and then we could move on to help other bulldogs in need.

Lo and behold, Bella's rescue angels found her. Lynsey H. and Erica S. had read Bella's story online and watched her videos and knew that this was the girl for them. They applied to adopt and were everything that we could hope for Bella and more. As we had, they immediately fell in love with her and were willing to continue to work with her and provide her with a safe and loving home for the rest of her life.

Bella with friends Buddha and Molly

And boy does Bella love her new life with Lynsey and Erica and her new doggy siblings! She continues to improve and to get stronger every day and even went on vacation to Kentucky Lake this summer. Lynsey and Erica really get what rescue is about. They have never seen Bella's limitations, just her potential and her huge capacity for love.

We knew that saving Bella was well worth the expense of surgery and the hours of rehab when Lynsey and Erica came to take her home. We reiterated that Bella would never be 100% perfect and Erica simply responded, "What do you mean, she's perfect already".

Roxanne to the Rescue!

Bulldogs are not known for their barking - so when they do, you'd better pay attention.

That's exactly what the Herlihy family did in Long Island when their 5-year-old Bulldog Roxanne started barking in the middle of the night in August 2014.

Here's the report from Newsday:

> A sleeping family was saved from a fire raging in their Huntington house early Monday after they were awakened by the family dog, fire officials said.
>
> Homeowner Michael Herlihy said Roxanne, a 5-year-old English bulldog, kept barking in his adult son's bedroom until his son woke up and alerted his parents.
>
> The three fled their Dumbarton Drive home, where flames were consuming the first and second floors when firefighters arrived shortly after 1:40 a.m., said Huntington Fire Chief Robert Berry.
>
> "Upon arrival, we had fire through the roof," he said. Berry said the son was shaken when he told him he was saved by man's best friend."I thought that was great," said the chief, noting that it isn't uncommon for pets to alert their families to fires.
>
> About 50 firefighters from Huntington, Halesite, Cold Spring Harbor, Huntington Manor and Greenlawn helped battle the blaze, which took about 90 minutes to bring under control. Firefighters were on the scene until 4 a.m., sifting through the damage and dousing hot spots, officials said.

The fire made the house uninhabitable, but no one was injured, authorities said. Suffolk police arson detectives said it was an electrical fire.

Monday afternoon, Herlihy had little time to digest what had happened as he checked into a hotel and met with insurance adjusters. He said he had been awake for 24 hours.

"I lost my home, I'm trying to find a place to stay," Herlihy said. He said it will be at least nine months before the house is rebuilt and the family moves back in.

The house Monday was boarded up and a blue tarp covered the dormer windows and a hole in the roof, said Michael Marcinik, who lives across the street and had watched firefighters shoot water into the house from a ladder and truck.

Marcinik got a kick out of the dog's role as the "star" of the story, saying she is a "super affectionate" dog who gets daily morning walks and often lies in the front window, looking out. Marcinik thinks the white and brown bulldog has even figured out how to unlatch the back gate.

Whenever he's working in the front yard, she gets out and runs across the street to him, he said. "It's too much of a coincidence," the neighbor said. "She'll run right to me and jump up on me."

Herlihy said Roxanne is staying with a neighbor for now because the hotel doesn't allow pets, even hero dogs. The family canine has been a "spoiled dog," Herlihy said: "I love her to death."

Quiz – How Well Do You Know Bulldogs?

20 Questions

So, you think you know your Bulldogs? Well, here are 20 brainteasers to test the old grey matter. Answers are at the end.

1. Who was the only American President ever to own a Bulldog while in office?

A) George Washington

B) Ulysses S. Grant

C) Warren G. Harding

D) Dwight D. Eisenhower

E) Jimmy Carter

2. What is the world's most popular name for a male Bulldog in English-speaking countries? Is it:

A) Harley

B) Sammy

C) Buster

D) Tank

E) Max

3. **Which of these breeds has webbed feet? Is it:**

A) Newfoundland

B) Bulldog

C) Cocker Spaniel

D) Duckhound

E) Chihuahua

4. **According to the American Kennel Club, how much should an adult male Bulldog weigh?**

A) 35lb

B) 40lb

C) 45lb

D) 50lb

E) It varies, the color is more important

5. **Humans have about 9,000 taste buds. How many do Bulldogs have?**

A) 1,700

B) 7,700

C) 770,700

D) 700,000

E) 7 million

6. **What is the gestation period for Bulldogs? In other words, how long does a Bulldog pregnancy last?**

A) One month

B) Two months

C) Three months

D) Four months

E) Five months

7. **What country did Bulldogs originate in? Was it:**

A) USA

B) Canada

C) South Africa

D) Spain

E) England

8. Which of these celebrities own Bulldogs?

A) Leonardo DiCaprio

B) Reese Witherspoon

C) David Beckham

D) Hugh Jackman

E) Martha Stewart

9. For what purpose were the first Bulldogs bred?

A) To hunt rabbits and other small animals

B) To herd bulls

C) As therapy dogs in hospitals

D) To fight bulls

E) To make humans laugh

10. Some Bulldogs are prone to hyperthermia. What does this mean?

A)   They overheat easily

B)   They cannot tolerate cold and easily freeze

C)   They love to sunbathe

D)   They are overactive

E)   They love to exaggerate

11. In England in 1891 the two top bulldogs competed in a 10-mile race. The modern Bulldog is based on the dog that lost, what was his name?

A) Sneezewort

B) Thistle

C) Dandelion

D) Bilberry or   E) Dockleaf

12. What is a piebald Bulldog?

A) One which loves to eat pies

B) One which is white and another color

C) An unruly Bulldog

D) One which ignores you when you give a command

E) One which suffers from bald spots on his or her skin

13. What is the Bulldog's nickname?

A) Uglymug

B) Mugwump

C) Sourmug

D) Muggins

E) Muggles

14. What percentage of Bulldog puppies are born by Caesarian section (C-section)?

A) More than 20%

B) More than 40%

C) More than half

D) More than 80%

E) 100%

15. From which of these breeds is the modern Bulldog descended?

A) Chihuahua

B) Great Dane

C) Poodle

D) Mastiff

E) German Shepherd

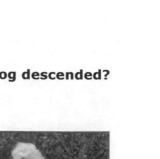

16. What was the name of the first Bulldog listed in the newly-formed Kennel Club register of 1874?

A) Adam

B) Bully

C) Charles

D) Digger

E) Ethelred

17. Which of these foods is poisonous to dogs?

A) Grapes

B) Chocolate

C) Onions

D) Macadamia nuts

E) Alcohol

18. According to the American Kennel Club, which category are Bulldogs grouped in?

A) Sporting

B) Non-Sporting

C) Hound

D) Working

E) Herding

19. The Bulldog Handsome Dan dates back to 1889 and was the first live college mascot in the world. Which college does he belong to?

A) Duke University

B) University of Virginia

C) Stanford University

D) University of Georgia or E) Yale University

20. 'English Bulldog' and 'British Bulldog' are both exactly the same breed as the 'Bulldog' listed by the AKC and Kennel Club. True or False?

Answers

1. C – Warren G. Harding, the 29th President of the USA. His pet bulldog, Oh Boy, died early during his term as President and was replaced as First Dog by Laddie Boy, an Airedale Terrier.

2. D – Tank. Other favorite Bulldog names are Diesel, Winston, Dozer - and Max, which is the most popular name for all male dogs of whatever breed. Bella is the top name for a female Bulldog, followed by Lola, Daisy, Lucy and Stella.

3. A – Newfoundland. Hunters bred dogs with webbed feet to swim and retrieve ducks and other waterfowl. Other webbed feet breeds include the Akita, Chesapeake Bay Retriever, Chinook, Field Spaniel, Irish Water Spaniel, Labrador Retriever, Nova Scotia Duck Tolling Retriever, Otterhound, Portuguese Water Dog, Spanish Water Dog and Weimaraner. There is no such dog as a Duckhound and most Bulldogs cannot swim.

4. D – 50lb. Ideal weight for a female is 40lb according to the AKC. The Kennel Club (UK) states that a fully grown male should weigh 25kg (55lb) and females 23kg (50lb).

5. A - 1,700, which is the same as all other dogs. Cats only have about 470. However, if you often wondered why your Bulldog enjoys drinking from muddy puddles instead of his metal bowl, it is because he enjoys the flavor. He has taste buds for water, something we do not have.

6. B - Two months or 61 to 65 days. It is the same for all breeds of dog, regardless of size.

7. E - England. The Bulldog is one of England's oldest indigenous breeds and known as the national dog of Great Britain. It is associated throughout the world with British determination and the legendary John Bull, a fictitious character who personified the great British spirit.

8. All of them.

9. D – To fight bulls. Original English bulldogs were bred for the sport of bull-baiting, where they would launch themselves at a tethered bull and hang on to the animal's head with great tenacity. Bull-baiting was banned in England in 1835 and since then the aggressive nature of the Bulldog has been bred out of the breed.

10. A – They overheat easily. Bulldogs also love to sunbathe but can become overheated before they realize it, so owners need to monitor them outdoors. **Hypo**thermia means having a dangerously low body temperature.

11. E - Dockleaf. King Orry and Dockleaf took part in a challenge to see which dog could walk the farthest. King Orry was reminiscent of the original fighting Bulldogs — lighter boned and very athletic. Dockleaf was smaller and heavier set and only managed two miles before being withdrawn, while King Orry completed the 10 miles. Despite that, Dockleaf was chosen as the prototype for the modern Bulldog.

12. B – One which is white and another color. The AKC says: "The various colors found in the breed are to be preferred in the following order: (1) red brindle, (2) all other brindles, (3) solid white, (4) solid red, fawn or fallow, (5) piebald, (6) inferior qualities of all the foregoing."

13. C – Sourmug.

14. D – More than 80%. The puppies' large heads and the mother's relatively narrow hips rules out natural birth in most cases.

15. D - Mastiff.

16. A – Adam

17. All of them

18. B – Non-Sporting, along with other breeds such as the Boston Terrier, Chow Chow, Dalmatian, French Bulldog, Finnish Spitz, Lhasa Apso, Poodle, Shiba Inu, Tibetan Terrier.

19. E – Yale University. Since the start of the tradition, 17 dogs have held the position. Georgia University's Uga is the mascot of its Bulldogs athletic teams and arrived much later.

20. True – English Bulldog and British Bulldog are just different names for the same breed, described as the 'Bulldog' by the AKC and Kennel Club. The American Bulldog, Olde English Bulldogge, Dorset Olde Tyme Bulldogge, Victorian Bulldog, Olde Boston Bulldogge, French Bulldog, Banter Bulldog, Aussie Bulldog, Valley Bulldog, Buldogue Campeiro, Catahoula Bulldog, Ca de Bou, and the rare Alapaha Blue Blood Bulldog are all different breeds, and none of them except the French Bulldog is recognized by the Kennel Clubs.

Useful Contacts

www.bulldogclubofamerica.org The Bulldog Club of America

www.bulldogclubofamerica.org/bca.aspx?id=188 List of BCA registered breeders state by state

www.rescuebulldogs.org The Bulldog Club of America Rescue Network

www.bulldogbreedcouncil.co.uk It promotes the health and wellbeing of the breed in the UK

www.bulldogbreedcouncil.co.uk/contact.html List of affiliated UK Bulldog clubs

www.bulldogbreedcouncil.co.uk/health.html List of UK vets recommended for Bulldogs

www.bulldogrescue.co.uk UK rescue organisation also helps to find lost or stolen Bulldogs

www.akc.org American Kennel Club

www.akc.org/classified/search/landing_puppy.cfm?breed_code=302 AKC classified ads for Bulldog breeders

www.akcreunite.org Helps find lost or stolen dogs in USA, register your Bulldog's microchip

www.ukcdogs.com United Kennel Club (North America)

www.ckc.ca Canadian Kennel Club

www.thekennelclub.org.uk The Kennel Club UK

www.thekennelclub.org.uk/services/public/acbr/Default.aspx?breed=Bulldog List of Kennel Club assured Bulldog breeders

www.thekennelclub.org.uk/services/public/findapuppy/display.aspx?breed=4084&area=0 KC list of breeders with Bulldog puppies available

www.bulldoginformation.com Bulldog information website

www.englishbulldognews.com – Bulldog owners' forum

www.bulldogsworld.com Information website and owners' forum

www.apdt.com Association of Pet Dog Trainers USA

www.cappdt.ca Canadian Association of Professional Pet Dog Trainers

www.apdt.co.uk Association of Pet Dog Trainers UK

www.dogfoodadvisor.com Useful information on grain-free and hypoallergenic dogs foods

There are also several Bulldog groups on Facebook.

Disclaimer

This book has been written to provide helpful information on Bulldogs. It is not meant to be used, nor should it be used, to diagnose or treat any medical condition. For diagnosis or treatment of any animal medical problem, consult a qualified veterinarian. The author is not responsible for any specific health or allergy conditions that may require medical supervision and is not liable for any damages or negative consequences from any treatment, action, application or preparation, to any person reading or following the information in this book. References are provided for informational purposes only and do not constitute endorsement of any websites or other sources.

Help Save a Bulldog

Leave a review of The Bulldog Handbook on Amazon, send an email with the link to your review to thehandbooks@btinternet.com and we promise to donate US$3, £2 or equivalent to Bulldog rescue.

Made in the USA
San Bernardino, CA
31 January 2016